jovis

Smart City in Practice

Converting Innovative Ideas into Reality

Evaluation of the T-City Friedrichshafen

Lena Hatzelhoffer
Kathrin Humboldt
Michael Lobeck
Claus-C. Wiegandt

[A]   [B]

Contributing authors

[C] [D]

01

Enter

011

Enter Smart Cities

JEI 재능교육
JEI
PRESIDENT
WAIT

Enter Smart Cities

*"I can't understand why people are frightened of new ideas.
I'm frightened of the old ones."*
John Cage, composer

Smart City, Smart Spaces, Smart World—the concept of "smart" has become an integral part of the current debate about the future of our cities. However, what does the term "Smart City," which is used so frequently, actually mean? Is it a marketing label? An academic concept? Or just an empty word? Can this so-called Smart City be an answer to the current and future challenges and problems faced by our cities? And what does all this have to do with a small city near Lake Constance?

Our book deals with these questions and attempts to provide some answers. Despite all the vagueness and lack of precision surrounding the term "Smart City," all approaches agree that the new information and communication technologies (ICT) play a key role in the area of future urban development. Nowadays, the new media have pervaded most areas of everyday life almost all over the world, influencing communal life in our cities. The ways in which we communicate with each other and how we deal with the vast array of ubiquitously accessible information have changed significantly. It is not just owing to the "hardware"—in other words the new devices, PCs and notebooks, simple cell phones and high-performance smartphones, or the high-speed landline and mobile connections—the use of which most of us now take for granted and which have spread and advanced so rapidly in recent years.

The use of new information and communication technology (ICT) in Smart Cities is more about the multitude of applications and solutions that apply these new technologies and make use of the Internet in many different ways. There are various fields in which the new applications are meant to improve everyday life in the cities. These areas are often denoted with a combination of the letter "E" for "electronic" followed by the English word for the respective area in which improvements are sought. Therefore, the area of E-government is about the streamlining and reorganization of administrative processes, E-health is concerned with the possibilities of telemedicine and telemonitoring, E-mobility deals with measures that optimize traffic systems, E-learning is about using digital media for teaching and learning, and E-energy deals with the digital networking and optimization of the energy supply system—to name just five areas where modern information and communication technology is being implemented.

The layout of this book is based on the use of the new ICT, which has accompanied us since the mass spread of computers at the end of the nineteen-eighties. Still today, the computer programs and software that are developed have to be installed before they can be opened and used. Even on the newest smartphones, apps still have to be installed and the risk of the device crashing remains.

Smart Cities and the new information and communication technologies go hand in hand.

All aspects of social life are affected.

The layout of the book

Furthermore, regular updates are required in order to stay up-to-date. Develop—install—open—avoid crash—update. This sequence in the world of new media is the template for the layout principle of this book.

The numerous applications that have been developed, based on the new technologies, are reflected in the concepts and visions of Smart Cities. In the second chapter "Develop," the various Smart City approaches—with their often strikingly colorful visions and sensational plans for a city of the future—are presented, to show what is being developed where under the motto of "Smart City." 02 Develop

There are various examples from all over the world of new solutions in areas such as mobility, energy, or healthcare being developed and trialed. A shared feature of all these schemes is that they apply to many different—sometimes even only selected—areas of life of entire cities and attempt to make the most of synergies. The first chapter presents what lies behind these concepts and ideas.

There are only a few examples of the idea of a Smart City already being concretely put into practice. In 2006, Deutsche Telekom embarked on the search for a partnering city, holding a national T-City contest. The city of Friedrichshafen at Lake Constance won this contest and was awarded the highest level of state-of-the-art broadband technology. Over the course of five years, many ideas and plans have been implemented there to make the entire city "smart" in practice.

The third chapter, "Install," shows how Deutsche Telekom and the city of Friedrichshafen set up their Smart City project together on the basis of broadband technology. Over five years, more than forty individual projects were set up and tested in T-City. New information and communication technologies are a prerequisite for the applications they provide in various spheres of life. This chapter presents how this project was integrated into the city of Friedrichshafen and the large corporation of Deutsche Telekom and which applications were put into practice in the Smart City. The nature of the cooperation between the global corporation and the sedate city at Lake Constance is clarified. 03 Install

The residents of the city of Friedrichshafen play a special role. In "Open," the fourth chapter, we show how they cope with the new information and communication technologies and what new opportunities these technologies open up, as well as what their limitations are. The residents and partner enterprises were the addressees of the T-City project, whose aim was to improve their quality of life and the attractiveness of the location. "Open" shows concretely how the residents perceive the T-City project and how they deal with Smart City. The chapter is based on direct experiences. 04 Open

As is generally the case in the day-to-day use of new information and communication technologies, T-City is also concerned with avoiding crashes. The fifth chapter presents the measures that had to be taken to ensure the Public-Private Partnership's (PPP) long-term viability. At the same time, the new technologies were not met with universal enthusiasm by the local population. A telecommunications enterprise and a city that seek to become "smart" therefore have to deal with people's concerns surrounding the use of new media. Only then can a viable Smart City for all be created.

The final chapter "Update" provides a summary. It outlines again how Deutsche Telekom, the city of Friedrichshafen and their unusual Public-Private Partnership managed to develop a thriving Smart City over the last five years. It gives advice on how future Smart City projects could be managed and how the support of residents for such forward-looking urban development concepts can be secured.

This book would not have come into being without the T-City project in Friedrichshafen. At the beginning of 2006, Deutsche Telekom—one of the largest telecommunications enterprises—had the ambitious idea to put a Smart City into practice in Germany. It advertised Smart City concepts through a nationwide city contest. Finally, Deutsche Telekom entered into a special PPP with the city of Friedrichshafen, which forms the basis for some extensive debates in this book. Deutsche Telekom had the project assessed from the outset through scientific research by the Geographical Institute at the University of Bonn, granting it a high degree of independence. Thus, the result is not a public relations exercise but a study that summarizes the outcome of the project evaluation over five years.

Two perspectives are represented in this book. On the one hand, it is about the presentation of a Smart City concept that was actually put into practice, rather than just a consideration of idealized visions. On the other hand, it is about the concrete cooperation between a private-sector business and an entire city, from which a great deal can be learned. More than twenty partners, who were involved in the Smart City project as decision-makers or who assessed the project objectively as social scientists, make small contributions as guest authors to present the various possible perspectives on such a vast project. Furthermore, they show how the topic of Smart Cities relates to recent social trends.

To conclude this introduction, here is a small note on how to approach reading the book. A book is not a homepage: the clicks and quick use of links that we are accustomed to can hardly be reproduced by this traditional medium. Instead, internal references and indexes are designed to help with cross-referencing within the book. However, references to external sources can be made as a rule only by means of referrals to publications or websites. Following these links demands effort on the part of the reader: visiting a library or typing a URL into the browser. The numerous QR Codes in our book provide some help with this, containing references to information on the Internet that offer additional reading material.

Enter Smart Cities—we invite you, our readers, to share our thoughts about the future of our cities while reading the book. The T-City project in Friedrichshafen might be unique so far in Germany, but smart applications are already part of many areas of our daily life. You can participate: Develop—Install—Open—Avoid crash—Update—these aspects are universal notions for shaping communal life in our cities, which we all play a role in on a daily basis.

cityandict.de

As a service, we provide the QR Codes on the webpage "cityandict.de" to keep the references up-to-date.

02
Develop

Smart Cities are currently widely talked about, mostly
without a clear notion of what the concept means.
Therefore, this chapter first defines the terminology
and then presents examples from around the world, in
which cities are attempting to master the current social
challenges using new information and communication technologies. Various points of view, approaches,
and models regarding Smart Cities are presented. It
becomes clear that many of these are still just visions.
The chapter ends with the presentation of a city
contest, in which Deutsche Telekom had invited more
than 400 cities and municipalities to take part. The
city of Friedrichshafen emerged as the winner, thereby
becoming the T-City. To gain a perspective on this contest, other city contests are portrayed in this chapter,
in which equally large private sector enterprises took
on the idea of a Smart City.

現代
203
현대
홈타운
202
現代
201
sky
SAMSUNG

Global challenges— cities get smarter

*"The nineteenth century was a century of empires.
The twentieth century was a century of nation states.
The twenty-first century will be a century of cities."*
Wellington E. Webb, former mayor of the city of Denver

Population growth, urbanization, climate change—cities around the world are faced with complex social and ecological challenges. On October 31, 2011, the world population reached seven billion people for the first time and 2.6 people are added to that figure every second (World Population Foundation 2012).

However, it is not only the number of people living in the world that is rising, the number of cities is also rapidly increasing. It is expected that in the next forty years the number of people living in cities will increase by 2.9 billion and that by the year 2050 as much as 69 percent of the world's population will live in cities. This means that existing cities will continue to expand and that, especially in developing and emerging countries, hundreds of new cities have to be built and enlarged in order to accommodate the growth and migration trends of the world's population (United Nations 2010, UNFPA 2011).

As can be observed all over the world, the long-term urbanization trends lead to changes that present new challenges for cities. In Bangkok, for example, the overburdened transport systems costs as much as 6 percent of the gross domestic product, and in the Rhine-Ruhr area in Germany, commuters have to face daily traffic jams of up to 100 or 200 kilometers. In 2011, the number of new vehicle registrations permitted in Beijing was restricted to 240,000 to prevent a complete traffic collapse in the city. In Tokyo, the subway system has reached the limits of its capacity with nearly three billion passengers per year. Transport infrastructure problems are thus a feature of cities right around the globe. Other municipal infrastructure systems are also affected by the enormous strain and are often overburdened. In Spain, for example, waste generation increased by 39 percent per capita over ten years. In London, a third of the drinking water is lost because of old and leaking water pipes (Vaggione 2011; Acatech 2011; Just/Thater 2008).

Therefore, cities urgently need more efficient infrastructure systems to reduce traffic congestion and noise, air, and water pollution. However, it is not only the various infrastructure systems that are in need of new solutions. The growing concern about the consequences of global climate change has also made aspects of energy consumption and CO2 emissions important fields of action. Furthermore, the consequences of demographic development, such as an ageing population, present an additional challenge for cities.

Demands on cities in the twenty-first century

In 1900, just 10 percent of the world's population lived in cities.

Further insights into twenty-first century cities, their problems, and challenges: Burdett / Sudjic (2011), UN (2011) amd Sieman (2007)

Infrastructure

The need to take action in order to prepare cities for current and future challenges is, however, restricted by the limited financial resources of public budgets. Cities are therefore increasingly entering into open competition against each other to secure private investments. In light of this, an attractive working and living environment is a prerequisite for keeping the people and businesses that are key to economic success in the area and for attracting new ones. This leads to cities pushing the limits of economic, social, and ecological sustainability (Hodgkinson 2011).

In view of this, cities are increasingly concerned with providing a reliable network of public services and infrastructures, so as to maintain their quality of life and to increase the attractiveness of the location. In connection with this, the implementation and usage of new information and communication technologies (ICT) are gaining more and more significance. The technologies are not only meant to support cities in establishing more efficient structures, but should also help to make municipal policies more transparent for the residents (Green 2011). The implementation of measures and practices designed to achieve these ambitious and challenging goals are integrated all over the world today into schemes and initiatives that are often labeled "smart."

Increase of attractiveness through ICT

Unclear concept—
smart what?

The use of the term "Smart Cities" has sharply increased in recent years. While in the beginning the term was used primarily in a scientific context, nowadays governments use this label for their national strategies for the future and cities apply it to their development schemes, as do the large global technology companies to their visions for the future (Abdoullaev 2011).

If one takes a closer look at the Smart City phenomenon, one soon comes across further thematically similar concepts such as Digital City, Intelligent City, Ubiquitous City, Connected City, Sustainable City, or Green City. This list could be extended further. Even if the various labels suggest specific emphases in terms of content, it is difficult to make clear distinctions between them. Generally though, one can conclude that the term Smart City covers the most comprehensive range of themes. Whilst it emphasizes the use of ICT, an integral role is also played by the networking and integration of various aspects of a city, as shown in the following sections.

Gibson et al. (1992) and Mahizhnam (1999) provide further information on Smart Cities.

In order to consider the concept and the model of a Smart City further, it makes sense to come up with some definitions first. The dictionary tells us that the word "smart" means clever or intelligent. Considering the term from an Anglo-American perspective, "smart" can have a whole array of meanings. It can be used in the sense of brisk, elegant, competent, or fashionable, as well as meaning clever or intelligent. This short digression into the multiple meanings of the word "smart" is an indication of the many ways it can be interpreted and implemented.

The exact origin of the "Smart City" concept, in other words the combination of "smart" and "city," is not altogether clear.

The term was already in frequent use in the nineteen-nineties. At that time, the focus of the debate was especially on the significance of new ICT with regard to a modern infrastructure within cities. The California Institute for Smarter Communities was among the first to focus on how communities could become smart. John M. Eger, chairman of the institute, thinks that a city or municipality can be designated as smart if it consciously and consistently makes an effort to implement information technologies, in order to achieve a fundamental improvement of the living and working conditions within the region.

smartcommunities.cityandict.de

"Smart communities [are] communities using information technology as a catalyst for transforming life and work to meet the challenge of the new millennium."

John M. Eger

Amanda Coe and her colleagues (2001) from the Center on Governance at the University of Ottawa criticize the idea of Smart Communities as being too technically oriented. It shouldn't be just about the availability and quality of ICT. In their understanding, the achievement potential of a city doesn't depend only on the availability of a concrete infrastructure and the implementation of technical solutions. They suggest a more strongly governance-oriented approach and emphasize the role of social capital and relations in urban development. In this sense, a city is "smart" if the urban society has learned to be adaptable and innovative. The residents have to be capable of using technologies in a way that benefits them.

However, current definitions are still underpinned by an emphasis on technology. This was apparent at the Smart City Forum 2011 in the Ukraine, as well as at Forrester Research, a US technology and market research institute, which defines a Smart City a follows: *"The use of Smart Computing technologies to make the critical infrastructure components and services of a city—which include city administration, education, healthcare, public safety, real estate, transportation, and utilities—more intelligent, interconnected, and efficient"* (Washburn/ Sindhu 2010).

The international scientific team led by Andrea Caragliu (2009), on the other hand, drew up six important criteria for a Smart City:

1. the use of a network infrastructure to increase economic and cultural efficiency and enable social, cultural, and urban development
2. emphasis on economic competitiveness
3. support of social inclusion
4. emphasis on the role of the high-tech and creative industries with regard to long-term growth
5. taking social inequality into account
6. social and ecological sustainability as an important strategic component

On the basis of these criteria they have formulated the following definition of a Smart City: *"We believe a city to be smart when investments in human and social capital and traditional (transport) and modern (ICT) communication infrastructure fuel sustainable economic growth and a high quality of life, with a wise management of natural resources, through participatory governance."*

The practical execution of this theoretical definition of a Smart City is reflected in the vision formulated by the city of Vienna together with the Viennese public utilities. Their understanding of a Smart City appears to be based on the criteria formulated by Andrea Caragliu et al., as it reflects many aspects of the definition above:

"Smart City describes a city in which information and communication technologies as well as resource-efficient technologies are systematically implemented, in order to pave the way for a society beyond fossil fuels, to become more resource-efficient, to lastingly improve the quality of life for citizens and the competitiveness of the local economy, thereby strengthening the future viability of the city. At the very least the areas of energy, mobility, urban planning and govern-

ance have to be taken into account. A basic indicator of a Smart City is the integra-tion and interconnection of these areas, in order to realize the ecological and social improvement potential. A comprehensive integration of social aspects of the urban population and a participatory approach are essential to this" (Wiener Stadtwerke Holding AG 2011).

This holistic understanding of a Smart City, which integrates and intercon-nects all aspects of urban life, shall also underpin this book.

smartvienna.cityandict.de

U-Life in U-South Korea

The concept of U-Cities frequently comes up in the debate about Smart Cities and is often equated with it. If one assumes, as in this book, a holistic understanding of a Smart City, parallels can be found between some U-City initiatives and the characteristics of a Smart City. However, the emphasis of these U-City initiatives is primarily on the installation of technology, particularly of the so-called ubiquitous technology (Hatzelhoffer 2011a). The concept of a U-City mainly pursues the aim of technologically interconnecting nearly all aspects of the urban space. The prerequisite is the implementation of ubiquitous technology and of ubiquitous computing. This means that sensors—built into buildings, the infrastructure and everyday objects—gather information and transmit it via wireless networks.

The U(biquitous)-City approach has been widely adopted, especially in South Korea. The largest, and no doubt, most well-known U-City initiative is New Songdo City, sixty-five kilometers from the South Korean capital. The city is to be built from the ground up by 2015 on an artificial island in the Yellow Sea, to house 75,000 inhabitants within in a total area of six square kilometers. This is approximately the equivalent in size to downtown Boston. The project was started in 2001 and is therefore not only one of the first, but also one of the most ambitious and expensive urban mega projects of this kind, assuming a certain pioneering role in the development of new towns in the Smart City context.

The first section of the city became "operational" in 2009. An urban space is to be created with the help of ubiquitous technology, with which every resident can access or transmit information at any time from any place, using various devices. The plan also includes installing a tele-presence unit in every apartment, as a standard, integral part of the facilities. The city will have a centrally integrated control headquarters, a "brain," where all data streams come together.

New Songdo was planned—like all other U-City projects in South Korea—on a drawing board and is a key part of the U-Korea initiative. The Korean government launched this initiative in 2006, reflecting the long-term national strategy of increasing their competitiveness. Despite all the ambitious objectives, architecture and urban planning play a minor role in New Songdo. Greg Lindsay is of the opinion that Songdo was also commissioned to entice direct foreign investment especially from China.

At present, there are thirteen U-City projects in progress in South Korea. The first U-City was Hwaseong-Dongtan, with the first sections completed in 2007 (Lindsay 2010 and 2011; Alusi et al. 2008; Hodgkinson 2011; Kim 2009).

Technology focus within U-Cities

New Songdo—example of a U-City in South Korea

songdo.cityandict.de

Various fields of action— a cross-section of smart spheres

The New Songdo project in South Korea and the vision of the city of Vienna already touched on various topic areas that are handled in the context of Smart Cities. Energy, transport, and participation are just a few of the key words. The following passage takes a closer look at the various fields of action of a Smart City.

Rudolf Giffinger and his team from the Technical University of Vienna, who in 2007 developed an evaluation tool for mid-sized European towns, defined six principle fields of action of a Smart City, covering many aspects of urban life and its economy. The topic area "Smart Economy" covers innovation and entrepreneurship and also, for example, the economic competitiveness of a city and a flexible and productive labor market. The area "Smart People" denotes the social and human capital with its various facets, including educational attainment, lifelong learning, openness towards what is "new," and integration into public life. "Smart Governance" comprises aspects of political participation, accessible city governance and a functioning administration, as well as the provision of public services for residents. Local and international accessibility, sustainable and innovative transport systems, and the availability of ICT infrastructures fall under the category of "Smart Mobility." "Smart Environment" includes aspects of environmental protection, sustainable resource management, and the preservation of the natural environment (green space, etc.). Finally, the area "Smart Living" covers various location factors that affect the quality of life within the city, such as cultural and healthcare institutions, security aspects, and social cohesion (Giffinger et al. 2007).

The management consultancy Arthur D. Little identified five dimensions of a Smart City on behalf of the city of Vienna: Smart Business, Smart Municipal Services, Smart Living, Smart Mobility, and Smart Energy (Wiener Stadtwerke Holding AG 2011). The Smart City model in Sant Cugat in Spain is built on the five pillars of Smart Environment, Smart People & Governance, Smart Living, Smart Mobility, and Smart Street (City Administration of Sant Cugat 2011).

Regardless of how many topic areas are defined, the fundamental point is that a Smart City should deal with all aspects of urban life and its economy. Contrary to Giffinger et al., who determined the ranking of the cities according to a series of indicators from these fields of action, our understanding of the topic areas and how they relate to each other has led to our adopting an integrated and holistic approach, in which information and communication technologies are not merely a partial aspect of a field of action. Instead, ICT plays a part in all of the aforementioned topic areas; it is the "door opener" that enables the various aspects of a city to become smarter. Furthermore, from our point of view, quality of life doesn't represent a separate field of action. All the actions and measures taken in the various sub-areas should have the objective of raising the quality of life within a city. Thus, quality of life represents an overriding dimension, which is always a matter of subjective perception.

However, in the debate about Smart Cities it is not always the city and its various spheres of life that form the center of attention. For example, the two German language studies SMART2020 Addendum Deutschland: Die IKT-Industrie als treibende Kraft auf dem Weg zu nachhaltigem Klimaschutz (SMART2020 Addendum Germany: the ICT industry as the driving force behind sustainable climate protection) and Smart Cities—Grüne IKT zur Zukunftssicherung unserer Städte (Smart Cities—Green ICT to safeguard the future of our cities) adopt a rather different point of view. While both studies also discuss how to structure the cities of the future more efficiently, the focus is on climate protection. The first study, published by Boston Consulting Group, shows which technologies can be used to reduce emissions and the focus is on the companies that provide these technologies. A range of business models—e.g., in the areas of Smart Logistics and Smart Buildings—are identified and evaluated. The latter study, published by Bitkom, is dedicated to the possibilities that are opened up through the use of ICT in relation to climate protection and resource efficiency. The various possible uses are summarized under the heading "SMART Life" (BCG 2009; Bitkom 2011).

smart2020.cityandict.de

greenict.cityandict.de

The various definitions and the subdivision of fields of action delineate topic areas, but do not fully explain the concepts. Even after deciding on a concrete definition, the concept of Smart City remains superficial and elusive among the wider public and can cause friction. Therefore, one must always probe further as to what associations are being made with the concept of Smart City.

Practical approaches—
projects and rankings

It is a fact that an increasing number of Smart Cities are sprouting up all over the world. However, their visions and the corresponding objectives vary widely. In Kochi, India, for example, a newly built IT Park is labeled as a Smart City, and Smart Village Cairo is a business park and technology cluster in the suburbs of Cairo. In Santander, Spain, the term Smart City denotes a project for researching the urban network using sensors. The aim of the Portuguese project PlanIT Valley is to build an intelligent research city. The Amsterdam Smart City initiative, on the other hand, emphasizes the significance of cooperation between residents, authorities, and enterprises, with its projects focusing primarily on aspects of energy efficiency and climate protection. In Edinburgh and Southampton the focus is especially on activities in the area of E-government.

This is just a small selection of the self-proclaimed Smart Cities in the world, but it shows the wide range of interpretations and enables a differentiated perspective on the project content. These examples use the term primarily in conjunction with notions of economic prosperity and employment potential, with visions of a city that benefits from "intelligent" industry—i.e., especially from companies in the ICT sector. In practice, it is often about commercial zones or business parks. The project in Santander, Spain is a rather different type of technology park, as a whole city has been made into a research laboratory. As with the U-Cities in South Korea, the focus is on sensors and interconnection. However, the sensors are intended not only to research the urban network, but also to improve the quality of life in the process.

Examples:
India
Egypt
Spain
Portugal
Netherlands
Great Britain

smartsantander.cityandict.de

About city rankings and
league tables

Cities do not only proclaim themselves as Smart Cities though, they can also be declared as such by external sources. A number of indicators and rankings are used to determine this and the findings are published in the form of league tables.

One of these ranking systems on a European level is based on the already mentioned evaluation tool developed by the Technical University of Vienna, for cities with between 100,000 and 500,000 inhabitants. The six defined topic areas were analyzed more closely according to thirty-one factors and specified further on the basis of seventy-four indicators. Seventy so-called mid-sized cities were analyzed, of which the city of Luxembourg came out on top. The six German cities included in the analysis were ranked between 22nd and 34th (Giffinger et al. 2007).

In the United States, there is a national ranking system set up by the Natural Resources Defense Council (NRDC), an international non-profit organization for environmental protection. The NRDC Smarter Cities Ranking is based on an online questionnaire. The focus is on the environmental sustainability of cities. In order to enable a more accurate comparison between the cities, it is divided into three size categories. In 2010, a total of twenty-two cities were awarded the title of "Smarter Cities." The winners include Austin and Boston in the category of over 250,000 inhabitants, Berkeley and Fort Collins in the mid-size category of 100,000 to 249,999 inhabitants, and Beaverton and Denton for cities with less than 100,000 inhabitants (Gordon, 2010).

The Top 10 list "World's Smartest Cities," published by Forbes in 2009, is a worldwide ranking system. The list was created by the American scientist Joel Kotkin. He views "smartness" as a quality that should not only be applied in relation to the sustainability agenda, but should also be expressed in the form of a fundamental commitment to economic progress and upward mobility. According to Kotkin, cities can be considered smart if they are compact and efficient and provide favorable economic conditions. Singapore emerged as the winner. In the study, the city is described as an economic hub with a visionary government, which has not only increased income levels within the city and improved the educational opportunities, but has also made strategic investments in the ICT infrastructure (Clark/Moonen 2011).

Owing to the unclear use of terminology, however, it is difficult to identify worldwide Smart City projects. IBM alone, according to their own statements, is involved in more than 2,000 projects (Banavar 2011). The New York market research company ABI Research estimates a much lower number of Smart Cities so far. In their market research report published in 2011, they identified 102 Smart Cities worldwide. The majority of the projects are located in Europe (thirty-eight) and North America (thirty-five). In the Asia-Pacific area, a total of twenty-one Smart Cities were identified. The development in Latin America (two) and Africa/Middle East (six) is less pronounced thus far. German cities do not feature in the ABI Research listings.

giffinger.cityandict.de

nrdc.cityandict.de

Greg Clark and Tim Moonen provide further details about rankings.

Which cities are smart?

Motivations— makeover or necessity

The motivations that drive cities to become smart are very varied. London and Rio de Janeiro, for example, have reasons to restructure because of the Olympic Games and the Soccer World Cup respectively. Also in previous decades, such mega events have often been the catalyst for giving a city a new, modern "face-lift" (e.g., the Olympic Games in Munich in 1972 or in Barcelona in 1992). A new aspect of this, however, is the role ICT plays in these transformations. The cities that have to reinvent themselves because of economic changes in recent decades (e.g., Detroit and Sheffield) have different starting situations, but the same objective in undergoing a makeover.

Mega events as catalysts

Some cities, on the other hand, take action because of the strain of poor conditions. The smog or traffic burden is so acute in some cities that they are "forced" to take measures. In Chinese cities, it is especially about dealing with a lack of resources. On the other hand, the ambitions of Amsterdam and Vienna are based, among others, on reaching the high standards of climate protection objectives (Pulakkat 2011).

Last but not least, the increase of international competitiveness between locations is a motive for using the label of "smart"—not only on a municipal level, as shown in the examples regarding South Korea and Singapore. The South Korean U-City initiative is intended to help the domestic industrial enterprises gain better access to other markets. The city-state of Singapore seeks to gain a top position among the global cities by implementing its masterplan iN2015.

Competitiveness

Singapore on the way to the international top

"In this intensely competitive world, infocomm is key to providing a seamless and virtual connection of the physical, financial and information flows…" (Chong Chiet Ping, Chairman iN2015 Manufacturing & Logistics Sub-Committee)

This quote can be found in the IDA report (2006).

The city-state of Singapore, a center for international trade and a global hub for shipping and finance, is considered a global city, owing to its economic, political, and cultural significance. The city is equipped with the latest ICT solutions and is therefore optimally networked worldwide (Ng 2010). In the international competition between cities for multinational businesses and a highly qualified workforce, the former center of western colonial power in Southeast Asia has once again become the focus of attention in Asia, with a high concentration of international company and bank headquarters, a large expatriate community, and outstanding research and development structures (Yeoh and Huang 2004). In view of this, large-scale state strategies regarding development initiatives and the availability of new high-performance ICT infrastructures and solutions play an important role for Singapore (Ng 2010).

Yeoh and Chang (2001) deal with the subject of Singapore as a global city.

"Many cities, such as Singapore […], are reinventing themselves. They are redefining their role as orchestrators of net¬worked information and knowledge-based services, organized around the needs of their citizens and their role in a global and inclusive information society."

Hanna 2010

Through targeted and state-controlled promotion of developments in the area of ICT, Singapore is seeking to maintain and improve its position in the international competition between cities. Since the nineteen-eighties, state schemes and initiatives have been carried out with the aim of increasing the distribution and range of uses of ICT. In 2006, the government of Singapore launched its Master Plan Intelligent Nation (iN2015), led by Infocomm Development Authority Singapore (IDA) (Tan 2007; IDA 2006; IDA Singapore 2012a).

The multiagency approach of the Master Plan, funded by both public and private means and implemented by both state and private partners in various constellations, goes beyond the mere development of the infrastructure. The vision of the ten-year scheme is to strengthen the ICT sector and to develop a highly interconnected society. The implementation of innovative and ubiquitous technologies is intended to contribute to the competitiveness and quality of life of Singapore.

In order to achieve these objectives, the Master Plan sets out
four strategies:
developing state-of-the-art, non-wireless and wireless infrastructure
fostering an internationally competitive ICT industry
training and sponsoring an internationally competitive workforce
in the area of ICT
transforming specific sectors (digital media and entertainment,
education and learning, financial services, healthcare
and biomedical sciences, manufacturing and logistics, tourism,
hospitality, and retail) of the government and of society
through the development and use of advanced and innovative
ICT solutions.

Thus Singapore is following its Master Plan, in order to become the *"world's digital hub using ubiquitous and digital technologies"* (Tan 2007), and to a certain extent has already put these visions into practice. The first projects have been implemented, fiber optic cables have been installed throughout the city, and the program Wireless@SG provides residents with free mobile Internet access anywhere in the city (IDA Singapore 2012b).

in2015.cityandict.de

It remains to be seen whether the island state will achieve all its objectives by 2015. Following Master Plan iN2015, it is most likely that there will be a new scheme stipulating even higher goals, so as to remain at the forefront of international competition.

wirelesssg.cityandict.de

032

Spatial context—
integration and new building

It seems almost impossible to compare different international Smart City projects, as their concepts vary so widely with regard to approach, objectives, size of investment, forms of cooperation, etc. Smart City approaches can be broadly divided into two categories:

1. "Greenfield" projects (new cities)
2. "Retrofitting" of existing cities

The former category comprises Smart City projects where cities are newly conceived on the drawing board and mostly seek to convert a complete vision of a Smart City into reality. These sorts of concepts have some common features. First of all, they emphasize ecological sustainability through the installation of intelligently networked infrastructure systems, the use of renewable energy sources, and energy-efficient architectures. Secondly, they primarily occupy a strategically convenient location near existing airports or metropolises. This can be noted especially in developing and emerging countries, and the building of more cities of this kind can be expected in the future. Arabian and Asian countries are the pioneers here: prominent examples are Masdar City in the United Arab Emirates and New Songdo City in South Korea. However, PlanIT Valley in Portugal is the first project in Europe that involves the building of a completely new intelligent city (Green 2011; Acatech 2011).

The PlanIT Valley project in Paredes, Portugal shows that it is not only Asians and Arabs who aspire to realize large-scale Greenfield projects. An *"intelligent research city"* is to be built near Porto on an area of 1,700 hectares. The city of the future, in which 100 million sensors are to be installed, is intended for up to 225,000 inhabitants and has an investment capacity of ten billion euros. Completion is planned for 2015 and the first residents will move into this vast testing ground in mid-2012. It remains to be seen whether this schedule is still realistic, as building is not due to start until the beginning of 2012. The aims of this project are the creation of a real-life and large-scale research environment for IT companies, as well as the reduction of energy consumption and improving the quality of life through ICT (Living PlanIT 2012; Osorio 2011; Rooney 2011).

planitvalley.cityandict.de

A grand vision is also being pursued with the Arabian Masdar City. It is one of the large-scale Greenfield projects in the vicinity of Abu Dhabi. The city in the desert is conceived for around 40,000 residents and 50,000 commuters, who will be provided with the use of environmentally friendly technologies in a carbon-neutral and car-free environment. The city is being built over six square kilometers. In contrast to PlanIT Valley, construction began in February 2008. The cost of this ambitious project is estimated at around 22 billion dollars.

masdarcity.cityandict.de

Masdar City was and still is advertised as one of the most sustainable urban development projects in the world, as it sets out to be a car-free, carbon-neutral, and waste-free city, supported entirely by renewable energy sources. The expectations regarding this newly created Smart City have since been significantly lowered Now the aim is, for example, to reduce the total energy consumption by 50 percent compared to the "normal" consumption in Abu Dhabi, whereby one has to take into consideration that Abu Dhabi's per capita emissions are amongst the highest in the world.

Some of the visionary ideas that were supposed to be implemented in Masdar City have been abandoned or will only be put into practice later because of the weakening world economy. The completion date has also been postponed to 2025. Originally, the eco-city was supposed to be completed as early as 2016 (Heumann 2008; Hoornweg 2011, Alusi et al. 2008).

These examples show that cities planned on drawing boards open up many possibilities, but their successful realization is far from easy. While the establishment of smart technologies in Greenfield projects might be spectacular, making existing cities "more intelligent" poses the real challenge in the Smart City debate. Existing infrastructures have to be transformed and upgraded through the use of sustainable technologies, so that our cities become smarter and more efficient, providing and maintaining a better quality of life. However, the establishment of innovative solutions within existing infrastructures involves complex adaptation processes. These projects are not only faced with the challenge of whether and how the infrastructure systems can be retrofitted. It also always depends on to what extent there is political willingness to make significant investments, considering the often overstretched public budgets and difficult global economic circumstances. Furthermore, one has to consider the wishes of the people who live in the existing cities and who also have to support the changes.

Projects for "retrofitting" existing cities are to be found especially in Europe and (North) America (Green 2011; Acatech 2011). The T-City project in Friedrichshafen belongs to this category, as do the projects in Amsterdam, Vienna, and Luxembourg.

HotCity Luxembourg—a city on its way to becoming a Smart City

Luxembourg is the smartest city in Europe in the size category of 100,000 to 500,000 inhabitants. At least this was the outcome of the ranking carried out in 2007 by Rudolf Giffinger and his team. The city itself doesn't flaunt this title in the way that many other projects do. Luxembourg's initial approach as a "HotCity" was to pursue the idea of setting up a comprehensive WLAN network throughout the city. In 2006, the HotCity stated that its objective was the improvement of urban life. This includes the quality of life of the residents, the locational advantages, and the efficiency of public services. A strategy was drawn up with ideas and concepts designed to improve the quality of urban life.

In 2010, there were 330 hotspots covering 75 percent of the urban area of Luxembourg. Complete coverage with 450 hotspots was targeted for 2011.

hotcity.cityandict.de

Apart from setting up an urban WLAN infrastructure, the HotCity tasked itself with providing a public and independent Internet platform. The city aims to provide each resident with access to the Internet and to municipal services.

The development of the WLAN network is very advanced and, owing to the platform, the various target groups (residents, tourists, etc.) have access to intelligent and integrated applications that are intended to contribute to improving the urban quality of life. One of these applications is for example the "HotCityWalker" App, which supplies information about bus timetables, airplane departure and arrival times, and the availability of car parking spaces. In addition, the information portal was linked to the public bicycle rental system "vel'oh!," so that through the App, which is offered free of charge in the iTunes store, one can find out about the availability of bicycles at the various stations.

veloh.cityandict.de

For the participating partners in Luxembourg, this represents an important step towards the future viability of the city. The infrastructural framework has been set up and mobile services have been developed and made available. Further aspects of a Smart City are to be worked on as part of this holistic approach, as the organizers in charge would call it. This includes primarily the areas of Smart Metering, Smart Energy, and electromobility.

Similar to the T-City Friedrichshafen, two partners have joined forces in the form of a Public Private Partnership (PPP), namely the city of Luxembourg and the telecommunications enterprise P&T Luxembourg. The telecommunications enterprise in this case is a public sector company, therefore the PPP has a very special constellation. The hitherto loose cooperation between the two partners has now developed into an independent enterprise, set up as a limited company. Clearly defined structures are one of the components of the project's success. However, the project was faced with the challenge of harmonizing the various interests of the two parties, i.e., ecological objectives and improving public welfare, and of formulating external communications, as they didn't want the project to be associated just with open and free Internet availability (Spaus 2010; Helminger 2010).

Harmonization of interests as a success factor

036

*Participants—the state,
cities, and businesses*

Complex projects such as Smart Cities demand the integration of a wide range of participants, in different constellations and related to each other in different ways. On the one hand, the projects are integrated into national or municipal development schemes; on the other hand, they are initiated by companies and executed in the form of Public-Private Partnerships. One can often see the emergence of hybrids and of overlapping. It is noticeable that in Asian countries, the state has so far played a greater role in the development of ICT and the driving of Smart City initiatives than in the Western world. Particularly in Europe and in America, one is under the impression that projects are initiated more often by the private sector. However, in Portugal this is now changing: the PlanIT Valley project was declared a "project of national interest" and receives strong support from the local administration in Paredes as well as from the national government (Rooney 2011).

In connection with this, the activities of the EU are gaining in significance. "EU 2020" designates the growth strategy of the European Union and stipulates an intelligent, sustainable, and integrative European economy. The use of ICT forms part of the agenda, as do the development of new, environmentally friendly technologies and of efficient and intelligent power grids (European Commission 2012a).

To drive their endeavors forward with regard to this, the European Commission launched the "European Initiative on Smart Cities" to sponsor cities and regions seeking to reduce their greenhouse gas emissions through the sustainable generation and use of power. Furthermore, the sponsorship scheme "Smart Cities and Communities" was introduced in 2011: 80 million euros were made available for funding integrated, innovative, and energy-efficient solutions that contribute to the reduction of CO_2 emissions. The sponsorship scheme is part of the Strategic Energy Technology Plan (SET) of the EU (European Commission 2012b; Energy Agency NRW 2011).

The politically initiated schemes are limited to a few specific fields of action, as are the various municipal projects. The environment and energy are among the fields receiving the most attention.

*It can only function if
we work together*

The various Smart City projects show that they can't be managed by a single party. Smart Cities are very complex because they always involve several fields of action, and as a result demand a range of skills in terms of planning and execution. The solutions also require differing types of regulatory measures. Furthermore, the investment risks are often very high, so that it makes sense for several economic sectors to cooperate. Hence, the successful creation of a Smart City seems virtually impossible without a Public-Private Partnership, in whatever organizational form.

024
New Songdo, presented in this chapter, is an example of a state-run project

setis.cityandict.de

A Public-Private Partnership is the result of a cooperation between public and private sector partners, in some cases agreeing to a common organizational platform and setting out a timescale for the attainment of concrete objectives. The more the partners involved cooperate on an equal footing, the more it can be considered a true partnership. Especially in complex projects, whose development is not clearly foreseeable, a close cooperation of this kind can prove essential. In addition, it is helpful if the various parties can work towards complementary results. This can apply, for example, to investment capital on the one hand, and the ability to regulate on the other. It is an advantage if the parties complement each other within their cooperation and do not compete against each other.

However, in projects involving Smart Cities, there are frequently different parameters than in classical PPPs. The roles of the partners are defined differently from those in construction projects. Instead of hierarchical solutions, network-orientated moderation processes are required. The task of developing a new "operating system" for an urban community is naturally more complex than planning, building, and managing a road or a new building. When it involves the whole urban society, it is not so much about the planning and funding of individual products that are clearly defined from the outset. Instead, it has more to do with the creation of an open and innovation-friendly atmosphere during the course of the development and "building" of the Smart City, which is conducive to generating ideas for dealing with information differently and enabling a different level of interaction between the partners.

Smart advertising and big money

The private sector plays an important role in Smart City projects. It is not only a partner in Public-Private Partnerships, it is also one of the essential driving forces behind projects, alongside the cities and public sector initiators. The private sector is very interested in realizing such projects and their motives are fairly mundane. Apart from widening their business interests, companies are also keen to boost their image by being publicly concerned about the future of the cities.

There is a wide range of companies involved in this. A common feature, however, is that each has their very own vision of a Smart City. This is hardly surprising, as their primary objective is to sell products and solutions to their potential customers. The titles of their visions sound impressive: Smarter Planet (IBM), Smart + Connected Communities (Cisco), Sustainable Cities (Siemens), Smart Cities (Orange und Oracle), City 2.0 (Hewlett Packard), Next-Generation Smart Cities (Hitachi). The list goes on. Apart from the aforementioned technology enterprises, companies representing other sectors are also involved, such as architecture and management consultancy (e.g., Accenture, Buro Happold, Arup).

In 2011, the market research company Greenbang studied eighteen different companies that supply solutions and services for Smart Cities and evaluated them according to their level of innovation and the evidence of providing solutions. According to the researchers, this is almost as important as the solutions themselves in such a dynamically developing market as that of Smart Cities. This means that the companies not only have to develop intelligent products and solutions, but also have to communicate their idea and their message effectively (Greenbang 2011).

One outcome of this study is the so-called Greenbang Smart Matrix — Smart Cities. Upon taking a closer look at this Matrix, IBM emerges as the best performer among technology companies. Alongside Siemens and Cisco, IBM is one of the three most important representatives of this sector.

The objective of all these companies is to make our cities more efficient, more effective, more sustainable, and more livable through the development of intelligent infrastructures. Nevertheless, there are some clear differences in their approaches. IBM acts primarily from a software perspective and focuses especially on the transformation of business processes through data analysis, concentrating on already existing cities. Siemens applies its expertise to various branches of technology and focuses on the integration of different infrastructure systems on the premise of sustainability. The company is represented in new Greenfield cities as well as in existing cities. Cisco's approach focuses especially on the network and the corresponding services. The company operates mostly on Greenfield projects (S+CC 2012).

The telecommunications companies were apparently not considered in the Greenbang study. They also play an important role in the debate about more intelligent and sustainable cities. Whether it is P&T in Luxembourg, BT in Great Britain, or Deutsche Telekom in Germany.

Compared to Cisco, Siemens, and others, Deutsche Telekom doesn't explicitly adopt a holistic vision of the city of the future, and the company's Internet presence provides little information to those interested in Smart Cities. Nevertheless, Deutsche Telekom is actively involved in various spheres of urban life, offering their solutions. Furthermore—and in this Deutsche Telekom is far more advanced than many other companies and their pompous visions — the company has already put an integrated Smart City project into practice. Namely the T-City project, the reason behind this book.

greenbang.cityandict.de

smartconnected.cityandict.de

A *new start*—
Germany goes smart

Apart from Deutsche Telekom, there are many organizations, research institutes, networks, initiatives, and political parties in Germany involved with the topic of Smart Cities. Apart from the Bitkom study and the SMART2020 study, the National Academy of Science and Engineering (Acatech) in Germany also published a position paper in 2011, illuminating the topic of Smart Cities from the point of view of Germany as a business location, as a lead market and as a leading provider of new technologies and expertise. Among other things, this study covers various topic areas ranging from demography, education, and healthcare to mobility, security, communication, energy, and the environment. However, in order to be worthy of the title Smart City, these individual areas have to be interconnected and brought together as an overall concept and master plan (Acatech 2011).

The subjects of the sixth National IT Summit, a conference held annually by the Federal Ministry of Economics and Technology since 2006, were the future application fields and usage scenarios of ICT, according to the motto "networked—smart—mobile." The central topic of the previous summit was smart information and communication technologies that fundamentally transform not only the economy and working life, but also our private lives (BMWi 2011).

Furthermore, the German Federal Government initiated schemes highlighting specific aspects of a Smart City. One of these, launched in 2007, is the technology scheme "E-energy—Smart Grids made in Germany," with new technologies and business models being developed and tested as pilot projects until 2012. The aim is to digitally network and optimize the energy supply system. The government program "electromobility" steps up the research further, applying advances in the area of ICT to electromobility and adding Smart Car to the Smart Grid and Smart Traffic initiatives (BMWi; 2012a, BMWi; 2012b).

Finally, in some cities there are Smart City pilot projects—either as a result of sponsorship schemes, contests or based on a PPP between a municipality and a business. Most of the municipal projects deal explicitly with a single specific field of action, while projects with an integrated and comprehensive Smart City approach are rare. The "Wireless City Project" in Berlin and "SmartCity Cologne" will be outlined briefly below as examples, since they explicitly use the term "Smart City" and adopt a more comprehensive approach. However, to our knowledge T-City Friedrichshafen is the only project in Germany in which many-faceted solutions were implemented concurrently within a single city.

The project "Wireless City Berlin" was launched in 2009, based on the idea of sponsoring innovations and establishing Berlin as a leading city for Smart City solutions. Numerous regional and transregional business partners, as well as various research groups, were involved in the project. The objective of the project, set out over three years and supported by the European Regional Development Fund (ERDF), apart from the promotion of innovation and strengthening the position of

026
Further details about the Bitkom study and the SMART2020 study can be found at the beginning of the chapter.

"networked—smart—mobile"

e-energy.cityandict.de

German sponsorchip schemes

electricmobility.cityandict.de

bewitec.cityandict.de

Berlin, is to bring together a range of partners from business and research and to support the transfer of knowledge. The initiative expects to achieve the long-term influence of mobile network technologies in the urban area and the improvement of efficiency and effectiveness in various fields of application (e.g., Smart Metering, E-health, waste management). The pilot schemes are to be introduced in stages into the urban context (Winkler et al. 2009). As part of the project, the Wireless Transfer and Development Center in Berlin was founded in 2011 with the task of advising companies and establishments with regard to the performance and usage of wireless information systems and providing demonstrations. In addition, the center has a showroom, where the technologies and their various applications can be tested (Bewitec 2012).

In autumn 2011, a Smart City project was launched in Cologne. The city and the energy provider Rheinenergie have formed a strategic partnership with the aim of creating an exemplary green city. All existing and future individual projects focusing on climate protection are to be brought together under the umbrella brand of "SmartCity Cologne." For 2012, the city of Cologne has set a budget of around 900,000 euros for staff and the first new projects. The first step for the energy supplier is to install 30,000 Smart Meters, providing data not only about electricity but also about gas, heating, and water consumption. Another project is in the area of energy conservation, involves the installation of a package of different technologies and solutions (e.g., a charging station for electric vehicles, dimmable street lamps, houses conforming to climate protection guidelines) (Jendrischik 2012; City of Cologne 2012).

SmartCity Cologne

Smart City in practice— T-City Friedrichshafen

The format of a city contest has been increasingly used in recent years. Very differing objectives are pursued on the part of the organizers of city contests as well as on the part of the participants. Contests should serve the purpose of generating ideas for solving problems and of publicly profiling the participants. It is expected that greater attention will be drawn to the organizers and the winner(s) by allocating awards, determining the locations of big events and festivals, and as a result of the corresponding investments and subsidies. Therefore, the setup of such city contests clearly differs from the general market competition that all cities and municipalities are constantly faced with. City contests are often held as a unique event, which cities and municipalities participate in voluntarily (Lobeck et al. 2009d; Hennemann/Wiegandt 2010).

A brief retrospective evaluation of the contest

On May 31, 2006, Deutsche Telekom launched such a nationwide city contest in cooperation with the German Association of Towns and Municipalities (DStGB), inviting all German cities and municipalities with 25,000 to 100,000 inhabitants to take part. The T-City contest set out to demonstrate the social added value provided already by innovative information and communication technologies and what potential and opportunities these technologies still hold—for example, through improved communications, technical simplification, saving time and money, and the conservation of resources. The contest was to show how people's quality of life can be raised and the locational advantages of businesses increased using innovative, user-friendly ICT applications. Furthermore, it was to demonstrate how all participants within the urban society can achieve a better level of interconnection and how new solutions for public fields of action can be developed.

The eligible cities were requested in their application to: *"… put forward concepts about how you could manage your particular tasks and challenges better using modern information and communication technology, while creating a closely networked community"* (Deutsche Telekom 2006).

The chosen city with the most innovative and viable overall concept was to receive personnel, equipment, and financial resources worth up to 115 million euros from Deutsche Telekom over a period of five years. Up to 35 million euros was envisaged for the development of a high-performance infrastructure (VDSL, HSDPA) in the chosen city. A further 80 million euros was to be provided in the form of cash funds and technology, as well as time and expertise, for the implementation of the ideas that had been put forward and for further projects to be developed in cooperation with Deutsche Telekom.

Schwerin
Leer
Osterholz-Scharmbeck
Neuruppin
Wunstorf
Brandenburg
Frankfurt
Königs Wusterhausen
Gütersloh
Lemgo
Ahlen
Rheda-Wiedenbrück
Wernigerode
Hoyerswerda
Kamp-Lintfort
Unna
Arnsberg
Nordhausen
Velbert
Iserlohn
Meschede
Görlitz
Sundern
Radebeul
Wermelskirchen
Gotha
Weimar
Wesseling
Bad Honnef
Fulda
Ilmenau
Andernach
Bad Homburg
Maintal
Coburg
Dreieich
Rodgau
Bayreuth
Bad Kreuznach
Dietzenbach
Trier
Bamberg
Heppenheim
Weiden
Homburg
Kaiserslautern
Zweibrücken
Schwäbisch Hall
Backnang
Neu-Ulm
Landsberg
Friedrichshafen
Participants in the T-City contest
Candidate
Last 10 candidates

The T-City contest was carried out as a two-tier qualitative selection process. Out of the fifty-two applications received, the jury of ten—comprised of representatives from different social spheres and from Deutsche Telekom—initially selected ten cities, whose applications corresponded most closely to the objectives, criteria and core themes of the contest. The selection of the finalists was a majority decision by the jury, based on the accompanying scientific research and the evaluation tool that had been developed.

In the second phase of the contest, the cities and municipalities were given the opportunity to substantiate the projects and to develop suggestions regarding the organization and implementation procedures. As several of the cities had not really involved their residents, businesses, and other civil society organizations in the first phase, it was a key requirement of the second phase to strengthen information and participation channels and to document these. Suggestions for the further support of their application documents were sent to the cities by a project group within Deutsche Telekom and the consultant social scientists, who visited all the cities at the end of 2006 and spent a day discussing the strengths and weaknesses of the application with the organizers in the respective municipalities.

In a concluding jury meeting in February 2007 the city of Friedrichshafen was declared the winner following a secret ballot, on the basis of the social-scientific evaluation. In order to recognize the efforts of the unsuccessful cities and to mitigate their disappointment over not winning, Deutsche Telekom awarded all second-round contestants 50,000 euros with which to implement their project ideas. Furthermore, the city of Arnsberg received a special award for the best social project with "E-childcare," for networking their childcare facilities.

arnsberg.cityandict.de

Working towards the future—
the vision of Deutsche Telekom

The corporation itself considered T-City to be a trial for the future regarding innovative, customer-oriented, and user-friendly product developments and services, which an entire urban society was invited to participate in. The corresponding development of new marketable products was also intended to contribute to safeguarding the future of the corporation, as stated in the application documents. With T-City, and by involving user groups from the outset, Deutsche Telekom wanted to try out a new form of demand-oriented innovation management, which goes beyond the supply-oriented approach of the development and market launch of new technologies.

A central element of the T-City vision, from the point of view of Deutsche Telekom, was the particular understanding of the concept of a city. This concept comprised not only the political decision-makers or the administrative bodies. Instead it presented a very wide understanding of this concept: in the context of the contest it denoted the entire city as an urban living and business space. This meant that all members of the urban society—i.e. individual residents and social establishments as well as local businesses, scientific and public institutions—were to work together to develop creative concepts for the optimal networking of their city. This didn't mean detached, individual, and isolated projects, but a comprehensive and coordinated overall project (Deutsche Telekom 2006; Hischke/Jänig 2010).

The application documents formulated as a T-City key objective that: "*… the opportunities to use innovative broadband information and communication technologies are made visible and usable through concrete applications.*" The development and introduction of innovative ICT applications should therefore always aim to facilitate daily life and the daily coexistence of the various user groups and to generate practical uses in as many spheres of life as possible. Raising the quality of life for the inhabitants and increasing the attractiveness of the location were therefore formulated as the overriding developmental objectives. Deutsche Telekom had also defined project objectives to be realized in T-City. The planned projects were to create added value both individually and in combination with each other, conducive to the further development of the city as a living and business space. A further important objective of the project was extensive networking, meaning the integration of as many public and private sector offers and services as possible, alongside the participation of a wide range of social groups. The planned projects should therefore aim to strengthen the communication and cooperation between the participating parties (Deutsche Telekom 2006).

With T-City, the corporation was pursuing the aspiration that as many of the city's project ideas as possible would be developed further and put into practice after the conclusion of the contest, so that after the end of the planned five-year period, they would be able to demonstrate the improvement in people's interconnection, and that the performance and future viability of the city as a living and working environment can be increased.

A project involving the entire urban society

The T-City concept was laid out as a continuous process on the part of Deutsche Telekom, in which new solutions were constantly being developed in conjunction with the entire urban society—i.e., local businesses, administration, politics, and citizens—and converted into options for the civic population. This

also meant that possible difficulties and hurdles during the implementation were discussed openly and that both cooperation partners—the corporation and the chosen city—should learn from them.

Apart from this procedural aspect, the T-City project is characterized by further unique features compared with other Smart City projects, which are or were also carried out in existing cities. One of these special features was the complex, bottom-up approach taken by the T-City project, and another was the corresponding cooperation model between the two unequal partners. The project was the first comprehensive long-term partnership and cooperation agreed on between a corporation and an entire urban society. While many innovation projects focus on individual fields, the T-City project attempted to take into account all of the important aspects of daily life (Hischke/Jänig 2010). The T-City project had been purposely conceived for mid-sized cities between 25,000 and 100,000 inhabitants, in order to guarantee its visibility and to make the most of the still manageable decision-making processes.

Integration of topic areas and partners

T-City was not only a pilot project for the corporation itself, but its scale and timeframe make it one of the largest Corporate Citizenship programs in the world. Furthermore, the Deutsche Telekom project is distinctive because of the independent scientific research, which evaluated the entire course of the project using social science methodologies.

The vision of the city of Friedrichshafen

In their application for the project, the city of Friedrichshafen defined its overriding objective as the endeavor to strengthen its position as a commercial, touristic, and residential location. The application was therefore aimed at extending the central strategic fields of action that had already been established during the urban development process. All spheres of urban life were incorporated: education and research, business, retail, tourism, social life, senior citizens and family, population development and living, transport and security, culture, leisure and sports (City of Friedrichshafen 2007).

The vision of the city of Friedrichshafen included creating new opportunities for all members of urban society by means of the new information and communication technologies. Hitherto separate and isolated technologies and data were to be merged to improve the interconnection between people, organizations, and businesses within the city with the help of broadband technology.

Apart from this vision, realistic scenarios were formulated in the city's application. On the one hand, they described a day in the life of a family in Friedrichshafen; on the other hand, they gave an account of "transients," for whom the city provides various orientation and information facilities. Furthermore, the application outlined the various benefits for individual user groups, for example stating that T-City improves people's quality of life in the city and in the region, owing to the many applications that facilitate everyday life. For the administration, T-City represents greater efficiency and productivity, and for the local businesses, T-City enables more efficient procedures.

After nine sub-projects were defined in the first phase of the application, designed to achieve the objectives, the second application contained a wide range of practicable and attractive projects covering many areas of urban life and was oriented towards urban fields of action. The implementation of the broadband technologies VDSL and WLAN were named as the core projects, as was the setting up of a service platform for citizens. Basic requirements were set out for individual projects, representing their essential functions and conditions, such as multichanneling, mobility, and interactivity.

In addition, the city of Friedrichshafen set out in their application that participation and the involvement of important knowledge carriers, decision-makers, and executive bodies was of key importance. The participation strategy applied to the entire city, under the premise that participation is an important component in the success of communal policies. Participation was to ensue in various stages according to the field of action.

***The city of Friedrichshafen's fields of action
put forward in the T-City contest***

**Project areas / spheres of life /
municipal fields of action**

Education
Platform for education
and science

Educational opportunities through
E-learning, Blended Learning,
knowledge transfer via Partnerpool,
educational and academic management

The economy
Mobile work and
business networks

Mobile knowledge workplace,
virtual project spaces,
mobile infrastructure control center,
E-services

Health
Networked healthcare services

Diagnostic portal, teleconsultation /
telecooperation, Mobile Clinic and
healthcare services, administrative
efficiency in financial management

Administration
Service-oriented and
efficient administration

Customer-friendly access to the
administration, online administrative
services, IT-based modernization
of administration, online participation

Transport

Traffic control system, real-time
information for public transport
passengers, Shared Crisis Network

Media portal

Local information about all types
and functions of terminal devices

*Personalized and
mobile services*

Information and services for tourists,
citizens and businesses

Internet service platform for citizens	Comprehensive and integrated information and services
Marketing and training	Showroom, information booths, training opportunities
Future Home	ICT applications for residential construction and housing technology

Google can do it, too— the city contest as a platform

Deutsche Telekom is not the only enterprise using the platform of city contests in the context of the propagation and usage of ICT in cities. The global corporations Google, Philips, and IBM have held city contests in recent years with somewhat differing objectives and philosophies, serving the purpose of generating and using new ideas for dealing with future social challenges, as well as of cooperation with cities and municipalities.

Google, based in the USA, initiated a contest there in 2010, in order to install high-speed Internet connections in the chosen city. After a year, Kansas City emerged as the winner of this contest, which around 1,100 cities had participated in. The realization of this project is set to start in 2012 (Medin 2011).

Google brings fiber optics to Kansas City.

From 2010 to 2011, the large Dutch electronics corporation Philips held a worldwide contest with the title "Livable Cities Award." This initiative was launched to generate practical and practicable initiatives that contribute to improving the healthcare and well-being of those living in cities around the world. A jury evaluated 450 ideas from twenty-nine countries in the three categories: "Well-being outdoors," "Independent living," and "Healthy lifestyle at work and home." The jury nominated eight finalists who were then subject to a public vote. The first prize went to a project for dealing with water shortage in Yemen. Two further winners were awarded cash prizes (Philips 2011).

Philips seeks individual ideas for improving the city.

While Google's contest focused primarily on providing infrastructures and Philips was concerned with rewarding new ideas for urban development, the IT and consulting company IBM held a contest in 2010 that dealt with the subject of Smart Cities. This contest is similar to the broadly defined business scheme "Smarter Planet." With the "Smarter Cities Challenge," the company set themselves the objective of supporting a total of a hundred cities worldwide over three years in their key challenges for the future. To this end, IBM is providing technologies, but also time and expertise worth 50 million US dollars (IBM 2010).

IBM supports cities through consultancy.

The winner benefits significantly from the corporation sending its experts from various business sectors to the respective city for three weeks, in order to draw up recommendations in close cooperation with the municipal partners as to how the municipality can be made more intelligent and efficient. Last year, twenty-five cities received this sponsorship worth 250,000 to 400,000 dollars—among them, five European cities. No German cities were among the sponsored cities. The application process for 2012 is already closed, but the cities awarded sponsorship have not yet been announced (IBM 2012a).

While the approach of IBM involving the allocation of funds adheres to a diversification strategy, and the focus is on providing the cities with consulting for a fixed period of time, the priority for Deutsche Telekom is a clear geographical focus on an individual city. Deutsche Telekom's idea was that the products and applications should be able to make use of the newest, state-of-the-art broadband and wireless infrastructure. This was and is still not the case in all German cities. It also means that if the solutions had been spread across different cities and municipalities, it would have been necessary to meet the infrastructural requirements in each of them. The geographical concentration of technical possibilities in one city was intended to create synergies and added value, as well as an innovative environment in its own right.

IBM focuses primarily not only on the development of intelligent structures and systems, but also on the creation of an environment in which cities all over the world can learn from each other. With the T-City project, Deutsche Telekom pursued a similar objective on a national level in cooperation with the German Association of Cities and Municipalities. Innovation-oriented municipalities and their administrations, along with further participants from business, science and society, came together via a "future city network" to discuss new ICT applications for the development of cities. This initiative was directed by the German Association of Cities and Municipalities. Deutsche Telekom supported this network and acted as a partner, providing expertise in the area of information and communication technologies.

A common feature of the Deutsche Telekom and IBM approaches is that global corporations initiated the city contests. Unlike city contests initiated by the public sector, the private sector corporations don't act purely out of a spirit of goodwill, but also pursue their own business interests. While this objective is set out openly in Deutsche Telekom's application documents, it can only be assumed of IBM, owing to their extensive efforts to present their own solutions for smarter cities.

Deutsche Telekom implements Smart City ideas in a city in an exemplary way.

ibm.cityandict.de

netzwerkzukunftsstaedte.cityandict.de

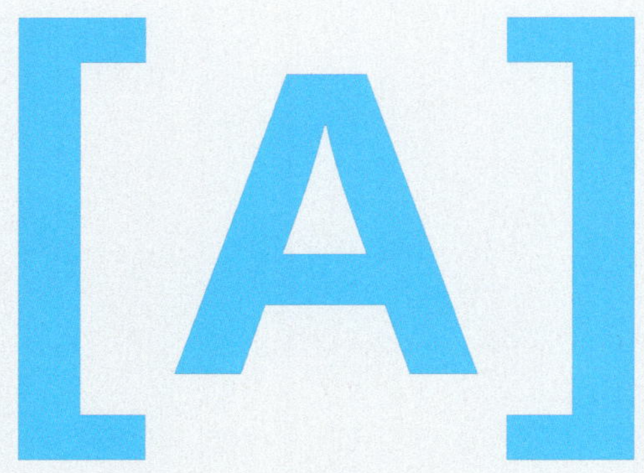

Citizens become pioneers

by René Obermann,
Chairman of the Board of Managment of Deutsche Telekom AG, Bonn

Successful innovation requires more than just a good idea. There are two sides to innovation: developing the new and implementing the new. In Germany, we are good at thinking up new ideas, especially in the field of information technology. Let's take for example the computer, developed by the German Konrad Zuse, or the MP3 format for compressing music data, researched by the Fraunhofer Institute. However, the German economy was not in a position to sell these ideas on the market. Others were ahead of us in this.

Telekom would like to deal with innovative product ideas differently. We would like not only to develop them, but also to market them successfully. For this reason, five years ago we began the search for a testing ground for the future, where we could test our product ideas in a real-life setting. Many cities and municipalities applied at the time, and in the end an independent jury decided on Friedrichshafen. There, the city administration, businesses, and especially the inhabitants were curious right from the start about the new opportunities Telekom had to offer.

Friedrichshafen was equipped with state-of-the-art infrastructures with the highest level of broadband connection. Furthermore, the citizens were given the opportunity on many occasions to act as pioneers. In Germany, they were the first to try out many of our product ideas. The secure De-Mail had its first reality check in the city at Lake Constance. Hiking trails guided by GPS were tested in Friedrichshafen and the surrounding area. Modern electricity meters were installed for the first time among the "Häfler", as the local inhabitants call themselves. Many of the projects tested there have long since progressed beyond T-City. For example, we now sell Smart Meters nationwide in our Telekom shops. The hiking trails are now available all over the country, and De-Mail will soon be launched nationwide.

For us, the T-City experiment was worthwhile. Many ideas enjoyed extraordinary success. Some good ideas failed unexpectedly and had to be fundamentally reworked. We learned a great deal in T-City, especially from our customers, who gave us valuable suggestions. As a result, the products now on the market are even better.

For this reason, the conclusion of the originally agreed five-year term does not signify the end of the cooperation between Friedrichshafen and Deutsche Telekom, and certainly not of this method of product development. We will continue to carry out such reality checks in many locations including Friedrichshafen, where we will conduct targeted tests of our products in growth areas such as energy or healthcare. Furthermore, we will continue to step up the pace of innovation within our corporation.

"Compact Innovation" in one of Germany's strongest economic regions

by Andreas Brand,
Mayor of the city of Friedrichshafen

The T-City project was and is a great success for the city of Friedrichshafen. Innovative initiatives were developed cooperatively to find better ways of dealing with the challenges faced by our city— such as an ageing population, transparent administration, energy transition, and linked transport systems—by employing modern information and communication technology (ICT).

We are looking back over five years of cooperation, during which many successful projects have been established. Today, these are being used nationwide in public administration, by utility companies, other commercial enterprises, and residents. One of the consequences for the city of Friedrichshafen is that it has become renowned not only in Germany but internationally, and is perceived as an innovative business location. This is proven by the numerous national and international delegations consisting of representatives of politics and economics, or of institutions and interest groups, who have visited the city of Friedrichshafen to gather comprehensive information about the T-City solutions. Furthermore, the city of Friedrichshafen has a stronger media presence through the T-City project—an important advertising effect for the trade and tourism city of Friedrichshafen and the entire Lake Constance area. We have proven to all German cities that it is possible to create a future in innovative cities worldwide, which incorporates information and communication technology.

However, the road was not always easy. Both project partners had to adjust to each other and get to know each other's ways of working. It is of course to be expected that in the course of such an extensive project as T-City, areas were developed that did not ultimately lead to success, just as it is of course necessary to engage with the partner and learn from one another. Therefore, the restructuring at the beginning of the second half of the project was beneficial to all parties:

existing structures were modified and procedures were streamlined. This gave the project a second lease of life and turned the second half into a success story.

The cooperation with Deutsche Telekom was an instructive and significant time, during which pioneering structures were put in place. By dividing the project into six topic areas, all of the essential aspects of a city were taken into account. The different areas were managed by our municipal project field supervisors, who are highly specialized and well connected in their fields. In addition, the city set up elaborate project management within the municipal project association FN-Dienste. In doing so, it was important to form the right structures under the right leaders. With the managing director Stefan Söchtig, they had found someone who had extensive project experience in the areas of ICT, law, and energy—with a background in business management—and he applied this to the city. He was supported by the innovative "go-between" to the city, Mr. Schraitle, responsible for the citizens' service, security, and the environment. This equipped the city for meeting the requirements of working with an important DAX corporation, which demands municipal project management. Consequently, a team of just two assistants successfully handled the project management for at times up to thirty projects at once.

FN-Dienste Ltd forms the central interface between administration, enterprise, and citizens. It transforms ideas into products that provide clarity and increase efficiency. An important aim of the municipal administration was to make their procedures transparent to residents, and to ensure and simplify access to information. We have achieved a lot in this respect with the projects in the realm of "citizen, city, state." Another of our ongoing main objectives was to involve the local economy. Internationally active and leading companies are located in Friedrichshafen, which not only have their headquarters here, but were also founded here. Alongside well-managed and innovative small and medium-sized businesses, they form the basis for a successful business environment, and at the same time foster an understanding of the city and the local requirements. The incorporation of the local economy (up to seventy-five enterprises) was a significant factor in the development of promising solutions, which add real value to the

city and contribute to the promotion of Friedrichshafen as a business location and of the whole Lake Constance region.

On the basis of these positive experiences we will continue the co-operation in the areas of energy, health, and transport, and would like to build on what has been achieved so far. In addition, the city will continue to work on other areas in future, in order to solve the challenges it faces. In this, we will benefit from the experiences gathered so far and from the developed structures, so that the continuation of the project has the potential to be at least as successful as the second phase of T-City.

Infrastructures get smart

*by Franz-Reinhard Habbel, Press Officer and Policy Director
at the German Association of Towns and Municipalities (DStGB)
and Director of the Innovators Club, Berlin*

The large-scale strategies for developing cities are called Smarter Planet, Living Planet, or City of the Future. In Cairo, Dubai, Yokohama, and Songdo, they are an integral part of the urban policy. Sustainability, resource efficiency, creative industries, and intelligent city are the catchphrases. The cities that systematically seek to conquer the twenty-first century armed with Smart City concepts are located mostly in Asia and in the Arabic world, where urbanization is in full swing. There are some individual Smart City initiatives also in Europe, such as in Amsterdam, Stockholm, northern Portugal, and Hamburg. As a rule, it is larger cities or metropolises that consistently implement new technologies for urban development. However, there are more than metropolises in the world. The so-called rural areas are also crucial for the viability of a planet with seven billion people. This makes the T-City project in Friedrichshafen even more remarkable, with smart infrastructures already being tried out in a medium-sized German city. The T-City contest organized by Deutsche Telekom, supported by the German Association of Urban and Local Authorities, is one of the most ambitious urban development contests ever held in Germany and Europe. In the more than fifty participating cities, hundreds of citizens took part in preparing their city for the future. It became clear that medium-sized cities in particular are suitable for the transformation of structures and functions.

Germany is a country with one of the best infrastructures in the world and was well-equipped for the twentieth century. However, this is no longer universally applicable to the postindustrial economy and society. Europe-wide, for example, Germany is not in the top bracket of high-speed broadband networks. There is enormous, still largely untapped potential to increase energy efficiency. In education and healthcare, the implementation of modern technologies is still very

limited. Friedrichshafen shows what can be done differently. T-City is already providing answers today to all these challenges.

These challenges are a consequence of the constant fluctuation that cities are subject to. These changes are influenced by many factors. The new information and communication technologies (ICT) play an important role. They are rapidly gaining in significance and have a substantial influence on how we work, learn, and live. The information society has long been a reality.

Because of the Internet, all local authority infrastructures will become smart and able to be monitored. Locations and objects will be fitted with sensors, which feed information about their status into an information system and open up new possibilities for their monitoring and maintenance. This applies to public facilities such as sports and leisure complexes as well as to theaters and schools.

In this context Smart Cities use ICT to carry out a forward-looking urban policy, which is resource-efficient and sustainable. They are cities in which social innovations are launched. In Smart Cities, all information systems in the areas of business, health, mobility, education, and E-government communicate with each other and provide residents and businesses with integrated services. It is not about centralization, but about a decentralized monitoring system with linked information and communications.

Smart ICT-based networks and applications reduce energy consumption, electronic calculators provide efficient monitoring of machines and cars. Networked houses and telemedicine provide answers to the demographic change. The digitization of administrative processes will lead to the disappearance of hundreds of thousands of tons of paper from administrative offices. However, this form of sustainability will only work in conjunction with greater awareness of the need to take environmental, health, and cost factors into greater consideration.

Information and communication technology and the accelerated pace of life

by Dietrich Henckel, *Professor for Urban and Regional Economics at the Institute for Urban and Regional Planning at the TU Berlin*

Even though it was already anticipated at the end of the nineteen-seventies and beginning of the nineteen-eighties that information and communication technology (ICT) would have a big impact, the effects of the "new media" are much more far-reaching than was initially expected. This is especially owing to the rapid diffusion and tremendously fast development of technologies and their corresponding services, which open up new possibilities that were previously unforeseen, such as mobile communications and the spread of computing.

In the meantime, it has become evident that ICT has contributed massively to increasing the pace of many areas of life, even if in some cases this is not immediately obvious. To name just a few examples:

— With the immediate access to information everywhere and one's ubiquitous availability, expectations regarding response times have changed significantly—as a rule an immediate reply is expected. There is no longer the time lapse that was the case with letter post. It is only recently that counter movements have been developing—such as email-free days or switching off devices.

— As a result of this, ways of working have also changed: the boundaries between different tasks are dissolving, the number of concurrent ongoing tasks (actually arranged or as an expectation) is increasing, which can lead to being on permanent latent on-call duty. The currently fashionable burn-out syndrome can also partly be seen as a consequence of this development.

— With these technologies and services, additional information becomes available that can and must be processed. The multitude of new applications (e.g., apps), which are often useful, demand one's attention and decision-making. How a greater number of options can lead to a lack of time was portrayed in the nineteen-seventies by Staffan Linder in his book, *The Harried Leisure Class* (1970).

The available technology is a precondition for the increase in the pace of life, but not the only catalyst or cause, instead it is embedded in a multitude of interdependent determining factors. As a rule, technology is created in the course of social changes to offer a solution to social problems (Beniger 1986). Amongst these social changes, for example, are the internationalization and globalization of economic relations, which are connected to and are carried out with a high degree of deregulation and flexibility, as well as increased competition.

The far-reaching changes in daily life and in working life are coupled with a significant impact on the spatial configuration of the economy and society, on the pattern of expectations, and the perception of space. It is to be expected that the accelerating effects gain momentum, so that attempts to slow them down are pretty much in vain. Thus, the increase in the pace of life continues to be one of the dominant trends of our society (Rosa 2005).

How does the new come into being?

by Matthias Wefer, independent communications and strategies consultant, and Jens-Rainer Jänig, executive partner of the brand agency and PR consultancy mc-quadrat, Berlin; External consultants for the T-City project

"Everything that is complete and perfect is admired; evolving is underestimated."
Friedrich Nietzsche

Do good and talk about it. This public relations catchphrase was taken literally by Deutsche Telekom AG in 2006. The company wanted to demonstrate what it is achieving in society as Germany's largest telecommunications provider, by showcasing it in one location. After all, information and communication technology (ICT) is shaping our future more than any other technology. However, contrary to many "showcases," taking long-term action was to precede all talk.

The focus was not on a quick image boost, but on achieving recognition. From today's perspective, the decision-makers at Telekom proved to be just as visionary as they were daring. With a Public-Private Partnership (PPP) on this scale, they were entering completely new and uncharted territory. Never before had an entire urban society been called upon to participate on so many levels, never before had there been such a large budget for joint projects (albeit not as cash funds, but generally as non-cash benefits and personal development incentives, in return for which the urban partners were at least expected to contribute commitment and good ideas).

The contest between the applying cities proved to be a significant challenge in itself, with regard to communication, management of expectations, and evaluation of the applications. When Friedrichshafen was proclaimed as the winning city, the number of participants, ideas, expectations, and goals increased again dynamically. The city had to become networked with itself (some of the organizers had never sat at the same table before), the city with the Telekom corporation (two alien galaxies), and even the corporation with itself ("If only Telekom knew what Telekom knows").

And what about Friedrichshafen? There was considerable skepticism in particular among the elected city representatives (and to a certain extent there still is up until today): What do they want from us? Is it a publicity gimmick, a Greek gift, infiltrating an entire city with a magenta Trojan horse?

Perhaps the potential gains were too great, the opportunities presented by the project too remote, and the demands it placed too unusual to be gauged accurately from the outset. In particular, the lack of a fixed overall plan and the way each subsequent step was determined individually by the city's organizers while the project was already in full flow, presented the sort of unusual freedom that is sometimes more inhibiting than motivating.

And how about the citizens, who ought to benefit the most from the advantages of modern ICT? First of all they were cautious. This is understandable, considering that the projects often seemed abstract until they were implemented into daily practices, and that not all technical innovations are met with universal enthusiasm.

However, hadn't the city just applied successfully for the well-remunerated title of T-City? Indeed it had. And hadn't the city been the first to be equipped with the most modern high-speed wireless and landlineinfrastructure, alongside large cities such as Hamburg, Frankfurt, or Berlin? Indeed it had. However, few had expected the victory, or the consequence that particularly in a PPP there have to be both give and take. For T-City was by no means a bountiful sponsoring project, but an opportunity offered to a city to develop cooperative new ICT solutions or to adapt existing ones, intended to increase the quality of life for residents.

A great deal was achieved with and in T-City. Even the experiments that are often incorrectly deemed as "failures" were an integral part of the project that was conceived from the outset as experimental, in which things were occasionally allowed to fail. Gradually, the network of projects and initiatives came together, so that today visitors come from all over the world to experience in Friedrichshafen what is often still only theoretical in Smart Cities elsewhere in the world.

To sum up one can say: the new doesn't come into being as easily as goodwill would like. The points of view and cultures differed too much, the constellations of participants were too complex, maybe the opportunities and freedoms were too unaccustomed and the mutual expectations of politics, media, residents, and partners on all sides often too negative.

Taking all of this into account, one must conclude: congratulations T-City! Congratulations to all those who repeatedly committed themselves constructively, even in the face of resistance and impasses. They all succeeded in making T-City a national and international flagship for real-life ICT applications and for the efficiency of Deutsche Telekom.

03

Install

Since 2007, the city of Friedrichshafen at Lake Constance is the T-City. With this award, the global telecommunications corporation Deutsche Telekom together with the city of Friedrichshafen wanted to develop a Smart City at Lake Constance. New ideas and applications were to be integrated into the city over the course of what was initially agreed upon as a five-year cooperation in the form of a Public Private Partnership (PPP). The objective was to improve the quality of life of the citizens, to increase the locational advantages for businesses, and to create a higher degree of networking within the city. This chapter shows how the new infrastructure was implemented and how the individual projects were carried out, which were enabled by new information and communication technologies (ICT). Numerous ideas were realized. It will become clear which challenges had to be overcome in order to integrate the individual subprojects, and thereby the entire project, in both the city on Lake Constance and Deutsche Telekom. There were general, specifically regional, and intra-corporate hurdles, not all of which could be overcome.

www.t-city.de
T-City
Friedrichshafen

Converting ideas into reality— grand visions and manageable work packages

"The implementation of these systems is not so straightforward, and can only be achieved through 'smarter governance.'"

Zoe Green, Royal Town Planning Institute (RTPI), London

globalurbanist.cityandict.de

When the development of a Smart City project idea has been completed, the efforts to implement it on-site begin. Grand visions have to be divided into smaller, manageable areas that require further development. Partners have to be sought and found, work packages set out and executed. Objectives and the intended procedures have to be agreed on and communicated.

The cooperation presented in this chapter between the telecommunications corporation Deutsche Telekom and the city of Friedrichshafen has a very distinctive configuration. A large telecommunications company and a mid-sized city are fundamentally different, and the Smart City project has to be integrated into both spheres in order to ensure overall success. Each of the partners is used to following established and different procedures in their own particular worlds when handling projects. The two partners have differing internal structures and basically pursue different objectives. Deutsche Telekom has to maximize profits for its shareholders; and as a public regional administrative body, the city of Friedrichshafen is duty-bound to public welfare.

Specifics of the implementation

These fundamental differences prompt the question of how a cooperation can succeed given these circumstances. What challenges present themselves when integrating the T-City project into the city and the corporation? How can different objectives with regard to a Smart City project be harmonized to benefit both parties? Which organizational structures and procedures enable efficient cooperation between the two partners? How can they develop trust, which is an essential foundation for the project lifespan? How can additional Smart City partners be gained and integrated into the existing structures?

What are the challenges?

Following a brief presentation of the particular characteristics of the two partners—Deutsche Telekom and the city of Friedrichshafen—this chapter explains how the basis for the infrastructure was created and how the project organization and individual sub-projects were developed and put into practice. The challenges that presented themselves during the implementation and how they were dealt with are also presented, along with the activities designed to promote the public image of the project.

070

The city of Friedrichshafen—
a small city at Lake Constance

In February 2007, Friedrichshafen was declared as the T-City. An independent jury selected the city as the winner out of the remaining ten candidates in the T-City contest. Friedrichshafen had prevailed in the contest ahead of nine other contestants from all over Germany and succeeded in bringing the project to Lake Constance. Thus, a new phase in the realization of a real Smart City was ushered in.

The announcement of the winner of the contest also meant that the Deutsche Telekom corporation had to relocate certain functions for the design of a Smart City from its company headquarters in Bonn to Friedrichshafen. The corporation and the city were faced with the challenge of harmonizing the numerous ideas developed in Friedrichshafen during the competition phase, with the equally diverse visions of the large corporation, in order to conceive a Smart City and put it into practice over a set five-year period. T-City was to be established and developed collaboratively in the city at Lake Constance.

The project partners had to engage themselves with a specific urban situation. Friedrichshafen was founded fairly recently in 1811 and thus is a relatively young city, which is today characterized not only by its special location on the shores of Lake Constance, but also by its unique economic situation and traditions. Therefore, the T-City project had to be integrated into this unique city environment, a topic currently being discussed extensively in urban studies research under the concept of "the idiosyncrasies of cities" (Löw 2008). As a consequence, it was important for the corporation to get to know the "city's personality"—i.e., the "structural logic of the city" and to take it into consideration.

The large telecommunications corporation with nearly 250,000 employees encountered a mid-sized city with nearly 60,000 inhabitants; a city with a young but eventful history. They represented two very unequal partners, who entered into a Public Private Partnership in order to set up and implement the project and who were distinguished by two differing systems.

Idyllic and cosmopolitan

The city of Friedrichshafen is the regional capital of the Lake Constance area and is the second largest city of the region after Constance. After being heavily destroyed in World War II, the city grew enormously in the second half of the twentieth century, almost doubling in population . This significant growth was due to its amalgamation with small neighboring municipalities, and above all to the immigration of a workforce for the large industrial enterprises.

Friedrichshafen occupies a remote location in Germany at Lake Constance. While the landscape in the tri-border region surrounding the lake is undoubtedly attractive, it has relatively poor accessibility:

042

For more details about the Deutsche Telekom's city contest, see the chapter "Develop"

"For us, T-City is a unique, innovative flagship project, with particular significance, in which the whole of Deutsche Telekom corporation is cooperating with an entire city. We are making T-City to demonstrate the collective efforts of an innovation-friendly, integrated telecommunications corporation."
René Obermann during the award presentation of the T-City contest

The idiosyncrasies of cities

"It is maybe precisely this combination of idyll and Weltbeachtung that is still shaping Friedrichshafen's character today: high technology, a cosmopolitan attitude, and sedate provinciality at the 'Swabian Sea' merge within the city to a fascinating amalgamation of modernity."
Renz 2008

Located in the tri-border region …

Accessibility by car has been improved in recent decades
due to the construction of the highways as far as Singen to
the west and Lindau to the east, but the city lacks an effective
bypass after plans for a motorway to Lake Constance were
shelved at the beginning of the nineteen-eighties.
There are deficits regarding the transregional train connection
with the German National Railway. Friedrichshafen lacks
an electrification system and lies in the so-called diesel hole
(Poggenpohl et al. 2012)
On the other hand, there has been significant improvement
in the last ten years regarding accessibility to the airline network.
In Germany, there are hardly any other towns of this size
that can boast a regional airport dealing with nearly 600,000
passengers per year.

However, a successful Smart City needs a further link: a broadband Internet connection. This aspect didn't play an important role in Friedrichshafen before the city contest though, because many citizens were more concerned with solving the problem of inner-city traffic. Still today, most people consider the extension of federal highway 31 more important than high-speed Internet access. This was evident, for example, in the municipal elections, when none of the candidates for the position of mayor mentioned the latter in public debates.

... but with deficiencies
in terms of its accessibility

friedrichshafen.cityandict.de

Looking at a map of Germany, Friedrichshafen lies in a southern German growth region, which lacks a definitive center. The region is characterized more by the juxtaposition and coexistence of fairly equal mid-sized towns.

This hardly played a role though over the course of the T-City project. As delineated by the contest, the project was tailored specifically to the city as the political and administrative center of the region and it didn't go beyond the boundaries of the municipality. While the daily lives of many people living in the city are regionally oriented, this wider living and working space of the inhabitants and businesses was not taken into consideration in the T-City project.

The Zeppelin's high-altitude flight and the three phases of industrial development

Apart from the particular location and its role within the region, the city is characterized by an unusual and almost unique economic profile. Very few mid-sized cities in Germany have so many prospering industrial enterprises side by side, and such flourishing tourism. Today, the city lacks a historical center because it was almost completely destroyed in World War II. The airline industry was the reason for the heavy bombings by the Allies. In the post-war era, it was rebuilt in the spirit of the nineteen-fifties. Thus, the city is not a pearl on the shores of Lake Constance, despite all of the urban development initiatives in recent years.

The rise of the city in the nineteenth century can be attributed primarily to innovations in transport engineering in the areas of steam navigation and railroads, as well as to its becoming a popular and fashionable spa town and royal residence. At that time, the town at Lake Constance was already referred to as "the Swabian Nice" or even "the second Interlaken" (Poggenpohl et al. 2012)

The industrialization of Friedrichshafen started unusually late—at the end of the nineteenth century. The catalyst that sparked a new era for the city was the high-altitude flight of the Zeppelin. The construction of airships brought about radical economic restructuring of the city, which had hitherto been a lower middle-class spa town and royal residence (Rieger-Benkel 2008). Even though airships were not constructed for a long time after World War II and manufacture has only been resumed in recent years, the Zeppelin shapes the image of the city almost mythically, representing a significant flagship that was also incorporated into the public image presented in the T-City project.

The industrial development experienced three growth spurts in the twentieth century. In the first phase, which lasted until the end of World War I, numerous subsidiary companies emerged following the founding of Zeppelin Ltd in 1908. Owing to the increasing military importance of airships, the company experienced rapid growth during World War I (Trischler 2002), which came to an abrupt end after the war ended, because of the disarmament agreement set out by the Treaty of Versailles.

In the second growth phase in the period between the World Wars, companies turned to new areas of production—from automobiles to textiles. The construction of airships for civilian air transport was resumed until the Hindenburg disaster in 1937. At the same time, production was shifted to military equipment (Köster 2008). The consequence of this development was the almost total destruction of the city in World War II.

The second phase of industrialization

In the third phase of economic development, during the period of rebuilding, the city recovered relatively quickly from the devastation of war. As the Zeppelin Foundation (ZF) could not fulfill its actual purpose because of the aviation prohibition imposed by the Allies, its assets were transferred to the city of Friedrichshafen. In the third growth phase, the city had therefore gained a significant influence on the reshaping of its industry (Semmler 2008). The enterprises stemming from the Zeppelin Foundation experienced a rapid boom and they continue to shape the urban economic structure:

The economic development after World War II

ZF Friedrichshafen Ltd established itself as a leading enterprise in the areas of driveline and chassis technology. It operates at 125 locations in twenty-six countries and has over 60,000 employees, of which more than 7,000 are in Friedrichshafen. The Zeppelin Foundation, with a share of more than 90 percent, is the main shareholder in this company.

MTU Friedrichshafen Ltd, which evolved from Maybach-Motorenbau Ltd, is a globally networked company, manufacturing driveline and system technology, especially large diesel motors for commercial vehicles and industrial purposes. The company has around 6,700 employees in Friedrichshafen.

Cassidian and Astrium, the two corporate divisions of EADS, develop and manufacture high-tech products in the field of defense technology and aerospace. EADS has around 3,200 employees in Immenstaad, which neighbors Friedrichshafen.

Tourists and workers

The second mainstay of the economy is tourism. After World War II, the city could also draw on old traditions in this area. Around 550,000 overnight stays per year represent an important source of income and of employment in the food service industry, local retail, and other local trade. The "spa tourists" shape the urban image especially during the summer season . With about two-thirds of the overnight stays, they are still the largest group, but there are increasing numbers of "trade fair tourists" and "conference tourists."

The great importance of the high-tech firms in automotive manufacturing and aviation has led to more than half of the workforce in Friedrichshafen being employed in the production sector—an unusually high proportion, significantly higher than the average of 40 percent in the highly industrialized region of Baden-Württemberg. Correspondingly, there is a significantly lower proportion employed in the service sector, especially in business-oriented services. Small and medium-sized businesses are relatively poorly represented.

Friedrichshafen's urban society is characterized by the dominance of large enterprises, industry and skilled workers, many immigrants and new citizens. Thus, in Friedrichshafen, there is no bourgeois elite and little evidence of an intellectual milieu. The founding of a private university, Zeppelin University, several years ago has done little to change this. In addition, Friedrichshafen has a noticeably high number of tourists and pensioners. Owing to the steady arrival of pensioners who have settled here over many years, the proportion of elderly people is higher than that of comparable cities and regions.

Population growth in Friedrichshafen after World War II

Year	Inhabitants
1950*	25,048
1970*	51,220
1987*	51,808
2008	58,848
2010	59,002

*census results
Source: Land Statistical Office Baden-Württemberg

Age distribution of he population (Persons per 1,000 inhabitants)

Age	FN	KN	BW
under 18	163	135	175
65 and over	214	188	194

FN: Friedrichshafen
KN: Constance
BW: Baden-Württemberg

Source: Land Statistical Office Baden-Württemberg

Deutsche Telekom— a large global corporation

If a city like Friedrichshafen received its town charter 200 years ago and is still considered quite young, then Deutsche Telekom is extremely young as a company, established only about twenty years ago. As a result of the privatization of the German Federal Post Office with its telecommunications and signal-service branches, Deutsche Telekom was founded in 1995 as a limited company. Today it is one of the so-called DAX 30 companies, the thirty largest companies listed on the Frankfurt Stock Exchange. Deutsche Telekom is also the largest telecommunications enterprise in Europe, with nearly 240,000 employees worldwide. Only a little more than half its workforce is employed in Germany. More than half of its revenue, totaling 62.4 billion euros in fiscal year 2010, was generated abroad. This distribution of employees and turnover figures across domestic and foreign markets indicates the high degree of internationality of the corporation, represented in around fifty countries worldwide.

In Germany, Deutsche Telekom is one of the largest telecommunications providers on the market. At the end of 2011, the Deutsche Telekom's networks had around twenty-four million traditional landline and more than twelve million DSL broadband connections, representing a market share of about 45 percent. In the area of mobile communications, Deutsche Telekom operates—alongside Vodafone D2, E-Plus, and Telefonica Germany (best known under the brand name O$_2$) — one of Germany's four mobile networks, with a market share of around 31 percent at the end of 2011 (Federal Network Agency 2011).

Although Deutsche Telekom is still very young, the corporation's organizational structure has changed significantly in recent years. The development of the corporation has seen frequent internal restructuring, which affected the management of the T-City project in Friedrichshafen. Before the T-City project was launched, the corporation was divided into four main business sectors until the end of 2004. The landline division T-Com, the mobile communications division T-Mobile, the Internet division T-Online, and the systems house T-Systems each had their own management board and operated autonomously to a large extent. At the beginning of 2005, a restructuring phase started, with Telekom Deutschland Ltd being established in stages under the motto of "One Company," which united all of the consumer businesses in the areas of mobile communications, landline networks, and Internet protocol television (IPTV).

During the course of the T-City project, there were frequent discussions about the possible sale of parts of the T-Systems business or even of the whole corporate sector, which currently serves mostly private key accounts and the public sector. Furthermore, the new focus on key accounts from the end of 2008 shifted many responsibilities within the corporation (Welt Online 2007; Handelsblatt 2008).

telekom.cityandict.de

A young global market enterprise …

… with an already checkered history …

As a global corporation, Deutsche Telekom has to assert itself on the telecommunications market in the face of fierce competition. Therefore, by its own account, the corporation is evolving from a traditional telephone company into a service company, which is incorporating new sources of revenue alongside its core business of installing and operating networks and connections. The corporation hopes that this will open up new growth opportunities in the future. The T-City project is an initiative that supports the preparation and shaping of these changes.

… is seeking new business sectors

Broadband infrastructure— landlines and mobile communications

By winning the city contest, the city of Friedrichshafen was to be awarded the most state-of-the-art broadband technology. This includes wired VDSL connections and mobile HSDPA connections from Deutsche Telekom. The municipal area is of course also served by other suppliers.

The wired connections from Deutsche Telekom were extended in Friedrichshafen from April to December 2007. In addition, hundreds of kilometers of fiber optic cables were laid across the entire urban area. This represented an investment of tens of millions of euros and involved significant construction work. Roads were dug open and cables were laid in the ground. At the same time, around 140 control boxes were installed for servicing the domestic connections, thus overcoming the "last mile." A central and high-performance fiber optic cable connection was installed as far as the switch boxes. From the control boxes, the individual house connections connected to the individual houses via copper telephone wires.

The mobile HSDPA connections depend on the availability of additional mobile base stations. Hence, a further fourteen transmitter stations were installed in the urban area, in addition to Deutsche Telekom's already existing ones. In a densely populated urban area, a single transmitter station covers an area with a diameter of 300 to 500 meters. In the countryside, the diameter can be significantly larger, depending on the topography. Therefore, coverage in the hilly hinterland of Friedrichshafen was more challenging than in the immediate vicinity of the lakeshore. At the beginning of the building process, there were isolated protests against the transmitter stations, however they were not of continued significance during the unfolding of the project.

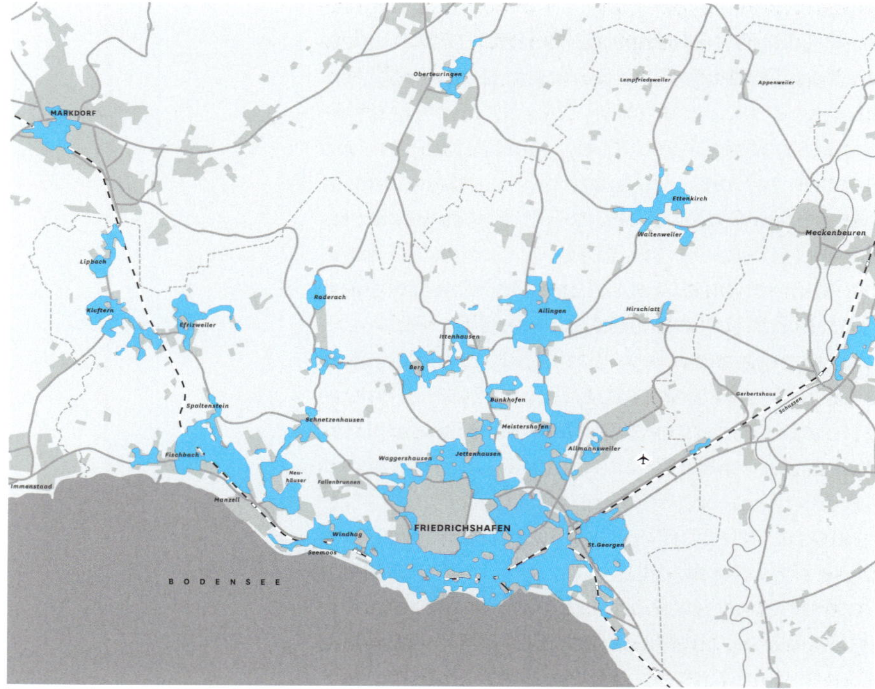

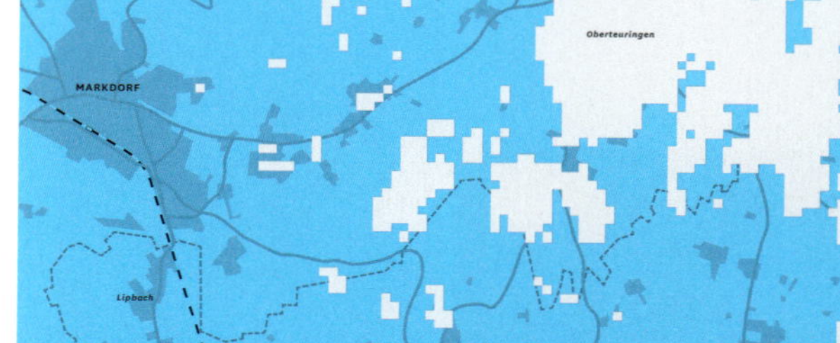

VDSL network coverage

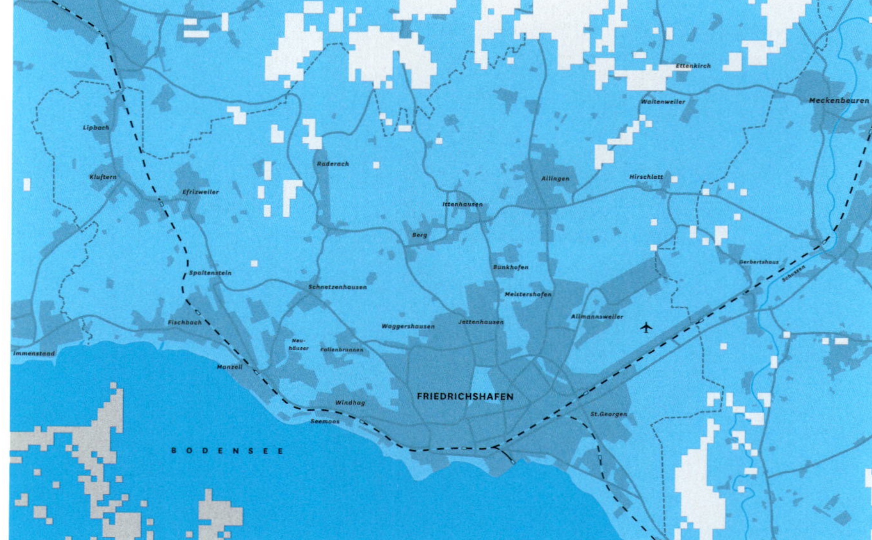

UMTS / HSDPA network coverage

Deutsche Telekom's wired connections reach 98 percent of households in Friedrichshafen. The maps show that all the built-up areas are covered. Only a few buildings in the open spaces between individual districts are not covered. Furthermore, the maps show that a wireless broadband connection is also available in virtually the entire urban area. Since the beginning of 2012, a total of eighty-two transmitter stations in fifty-four locations provide wireless mobile reception in Friedrichshafen. There are hardly any areas without reception in Friedrichshafen, except for the northern municipal area.

Apart from the Deutsche Telekom networks, there are other wired connections operated by alternative providers in Friedrichshafen, such as Kabel BW and TeleData, the city's own subsidiary company of the municipal utility provider. This company planned to extend its fiber optic network at the beginning of 2012. In the mobile communications sector, the three competitors Vodafone, O2, and E-Plus, who supply their own networks, cover almost the entire urban area offering various levels of broadband usage.

The T-City project thus resulted in providing the residents with improved access to broadband technology. The technical measures were installed in 2007 after the city won the contest, so that the high-speed cables would already be available in the year the project was due to start. However, only Deutsche Telekom customers were able to take direct advantage of this new infrastructure—in other words, only part of the urban population. In addition, all users of the individual projects benefitted from the infrastructure, even without being or becoming Telekom customers.

080

Public Private Partnership— the basic rules of cooperation

In spring 2007, at the same time as the broadband technology was being installed, the fleshing out of the T-City project content began with a so-called dialogue phase between the city of Friedrichshafen and Deutsche Telekom. The two new partners in the Public Private Partnership first had to agree on common objectives and the division of responsibilities, as well as an organizational structure and an operational procedure over the course of the five-year project.

As a result, a framework agreement between the city of Friedrichshafen and Deutsche Telekom, which set out the basic rules of the co-operation between the two unequal partners, was drawn up in summer 2007. On one side, there is the city of Friedrichshafen with the mayor, the town council and the municipal administration, as well as many additional partners from urban civil society. On the other side, there is the large international telecommunications corporation with a chief executive, who has to juggle responsibility for a wide range of business sectors. In the beginning, there were the three strategic business sectors T-Com, T-Mobile, and T-Systems, by the end of the project term it became Telekom Deutschland Ltd and T-Systems, after frequent restructuring. Thus, the framework agreement set out how the cooperation in this collaborative project between these two very unequal partners was to be organized, operated, and financed.

Project fields and their content

The framework agreement also gave first indications of the thematic organization of the overall project that encompasses so many areas of life. As with other fixed-term urban or regional development projects aimed at the comprehensive development of entire cities or even regions in recent years (Ibert et al. 1999), in Friedrichshafen various topic areas were defined when the project started, to which the individual sub-projects were assigned as the project unfolded. In summer 2007, several conferences were held in order to jointly develop the content-related structure and the first individual projects between the new partners.

Initially, five topic areas emerged from these discussions: "Citizen and State," "Lifelong Learning and Research," "Tourism and Mobility," "Business and Services," and "Healthcare." The topic areas were named "project fields" and each individual scheme could be assigned to one of these fields. These project fields include the various aspects of everyday life, which in other ICT contexts are also frequently labeled "E-themes": "E-government" which stands for politics and administration, "E-health" for healthcare, "E-learning" for further education, etc. The T-City project decided to forego these rather technical terms, which prevail in specialist discussions.

This content-related structure—i.e., the various project fields—guided the daily working life of the project organizers over the five-year course of the project, even if they were somewhat modified along the way. At the end of the project term, six project fields had been established:

Six project areas

      "Education and Research"
      "Mobility and Transport"
      "Tourism and Culture"
      "Citizen, City, and State"
      "Business and Work"
      "Healthcare and Medical Assistance"

The contentual structure of the project areas not only served the public image of the T-City. It was equally important to organize the internal division of workload and responsibilities according to these six project fields. Therefore, responsibilities were allocated within each one and project field managers were nominated from the city of Friedrichshafen and Deutsche Telekom.

tcity.cityandict.de

Responsibility for
the project areas

      The six municipal representatives came from various social spheres. Over the course of the project, there were several changes of staff, such as in the areas of "Healthcare and Medical Assistance" and "Education and Research." Apart from the municipal administration, leading representatives of the larger, local businesses were involved in the project field "Business and Work." In the project field "Education and Research," the city was represented by the new research institute Deutsche Telekom Institute for Connected Cities (TICC), which was established at Zeppelin University in Friedrichshafen in 2008 as part of the project and funded by Deutsche Telekom. The purpose of this institute is to support research regarding applied computer science and the modernization of administration. The link to the new local private university also gave rise to the hope that external impulses could be imported into the project.

ticc.cityandict.de

      On the part of the corporation, the six project field managers came from different business sectors of Deutsche Telekom, mostly from T-Systems. This was not always completely transparent for the municipal representatives, given the degree of fluctuation among the field managers from the corporate headquarters. Furthermore, the corporation was restructured several times during the course of the project, which made orientation more difficult. A further factor is that various parts of the business don't always pursue the same objectives. Employees from corporate product development have a different approach from sales and marketing employees, and these ways of thinking don't always correspond to the aims of colleagues from corporate communications. Thus, a large telecommunications corporation is just as heterogeneous a unit as a city administration, a municipal parliament, or even urban society as a whole.

Shared administrative bodies and offices

In order to achieve good results in the project in Friedrichshafen—despite the differences in objectives, organization, resources, and corporate culture between Deutsche Telekom and the city—the partners set out a project structure in the framework agreement that included joint decision-making and operational authorities, especially, for example, the so-called Advisory Board and respective project headquarters (Lobeck 2010).

The Advisory Board is the project's highest decision-making authority. It consists of four members each from Deutsche Telekom and the city of Friedrichshafen, and independently filled. The Advisory Board convenes four times a year and is responsible for the strategic management of the project. Decisions can only be made unanimously.

The project headquarters of each of the partners are located in Friedrichshafen on the same premises. In addition to the office in Friedrichshafen, Deutsche Telekom runs a project office at its headquarters in Bonn. In close cooperation, the project headquarters develop, agree on, and coordinate the local workflows. Furthermore, they are tasked with public relations and prepare the Advisory Board conferences.

In order to put the T-City project into practice, the city of Friedrichshafen founded a subsidiary company called Virtual Marketplace of the Friedrichshafen Region Ltd and rebranded it as FN-Dienste Ltd in 2008. Initially with two managing directors, FN-Dienste Ltd oversees the T-City municipal activities. Since 2008, there is an advisory board composed of representatives of the council factions, which co-determines the project guidelines.

The Deutsche Telekom headquarters in Bonn was comprised initially of a project manager and five sub-project leaders (finance, legislation, communication, innovation, and technology). The workforce of the sub-project leaders was only partially dedicated to T-City. The head of the project office in Friedrichshafen also had a coordinating function. Apart from the common administrative bodies of the two partners, Deutsche Telekom also had its own executive committee, composed of representatives of the various corporate sectors, who made the internal corporate strategic decisions.

Fluctuation and new elections

As the project unfolded, the project management was subject to change. The initially hierarchical structure of project managers and sub-project leaders that had been set up by Deutsche Telekom was dissolved in favor of the more network-like structure of a Steering Committee. Within the municipal FN-Dienste Ltd, the two full-time managing directors were exchanged for one part-time managing director after the change of mayor in spring 2009.

Apart from the structural changes within the project, several of those responsible on the part of the city and of Deutsche Telekom also left the project while it was still in progress. This applies to all areas of the project. On the part of the city, a new mayor was elected during the term of the project and the management of FN-Dienste was changed. As regards Deutsche Telekom, the chief executive changed at the beginning of the project. The overall responsibility then lay with the various members of the board. There was also a series of changes within the Steering Committee and among the project field managers. It can therefore be considered a considerable achievement of the project that the many changes went relatively smoothly. Ample documentation of the project contributed to this. Another advantage was certainly the continuity in the running of the project headquarters in Friedrichshafen.

Organizational changes

Changes of staff

084

Projects in practice—
solutions for everyday life

Friedrichshafen's T-City application already included a number of project ideas. As with all the other applications in the city contest, the overall concept put forward by the city of Friedrichshafen consisted of many individual projects that were partly interconnected. In these individual projects, the very varied spheres of life of the inhabitants, businesses, the city administration, and the municipal public services were to be supported in their challenges and functions by new information and communication technology.

In summer 2007, some of the city's original ideas were taken up by Deutsche Telekom together with the municipal organization FN-Dienste Ltd and developed into the first thirteen individual sub-projects of the overall T-City project. Up until the beginning of 2012, a further thirty ideas for individual projects followed, which were presented and discussed, but not all of which were ultimately put into practice. There were suggestions that could not be executed for a wide variety of reasons and were shelved.

In total, the responsible organizers worked on more than forty individual sub-projects. Since the beginning of 2012, thirty-one of these are being presented on the website t-city.de. They were implemented within different timeframes during the five-year period, in other words not all the sub-projects ran for the whole duration of the T-City project. Some of them were discontinued after a trial period. This was in line with the purpose of T-City, which was to develop and test project ideas collaboratively. Hence, the projects were in operation for different lengths of time and the extent to which they contributed to improving the quality of life in Friedrichshafen varied. Other individual projects weren't launched until the later phase of the T-City project.

As part of the accompanying research study, six individual projects were analyzed in more detail. The selected projects were:
- "Mobile Clinic"
- "Tumor Conference"
- "Independent Living"
- "Edunex"
- "Kindergarten Online"
- "Smart Metering"

These projects were chosen according to various criteria, whereby the project area they belonged to only played a subordinate role. The selection criteria included a certain number of users, the use of broadband technology, and a special added value. Not all of the six projects fulfill each of the criteria. The projects "Tumor Conference" and "Edunex" are dependent on broadband connections, "Smart Metering" and "Edunex" aim for high user rates and "Mobile Clinic," "Independent Living," and "Kindergarten Online" generate special added value for the respective target group.

046
The city's project ideas can be found in the chapter "Develop".

The first project ideas

090
There is an overview of the first thirty-one individual projects.

"Mobile Clinic" is a project from the area of telemonitoring, in which the patients are directly involved and consulted as partners (Gödderz 2011). The implementation of ICT enables patients with chronic heart conditions to regularly transmit monitoring data such as blood pressure and weight from home to the telemedicine center at the hospital. The data is transmitted via the Internet or cell phone to the hospital or doctor in charge (Bruhn et al. 2009). This allows for the continuous monitoring of the patient's health condition and the early identification of potential risks. Individual feedback and targeted advice for dealing with their illness can help patients apply the treatment themselves and reduce the number of hospital visits. Patients from Friedrichshafen and the Lake Constance region are saved the trouble of regular hospital visits to measure their blood pressure and weight, which can raise the quality of their everyday lives.

"Mobile Clinic"

The participating partners in the development and execution of this project (the municipal hospital in Friedrichshafen, the health insurance companies, and the two companies Philips and T-Systems) aim to provide more intensive care for patients with chronic heart disease. The remuneration for the telemedicine center staff at the hospital and for local doctors was set out in an "integrated care agreement" between the various health insurances, the network of doctors in the Lake Constance region, the General Practitioners' Association, and the Friedrichshafen hospital. The motivation of the health insurances was to reduce the overall cost of treatments. Further contracts that were a prerequisite to launching the project were drawn up between T-Systems and Philips—the medical technology partner—to regulate the supply and service framework.

The **"Tumor Conference"** is an active sub-project concerned with improving therapy options for cancer patients. This project was part of the city's contest application and evolved out of a municipal initiative. The hospitals in Friedrichshafen and Constance wanted to extend their preexisting cooperation with a jointly certified Breast Center. The municipal hospital had the idea of improving simple teleconsultations and telecooperations through the digital exchange of clinical pictures, and thereby also include doctors in private practice.

"Tumor Conference"

The participating doctors share information and experiences online via the new diagnostic portal and give advice about the best courses of treatment, with the aid of the digitally transmitted clinical pictures. Previously, the doctors had convened alternately in Friedrichshafen and Constance for such consultations. The web-based telemedicine solution "Tumor Conference" now makes it possible to do this via video conference and to save the doctors the weekly journeys. Broadband technology is an essential prerequisite for such a diagnostic portal, because certain bandwidths are necessary for transmitting the digital pictures. For Deutsche Telekom, the project was of interest because of its development of business models that deal with communications via video-telephony, with the possibility to send and view pictures at the same time. A collaboration like this one between doctors is also becoming increasingly important in other professional contexts. The project is in pilot operation since the middle of 2009.

A further sub-project being put into practice is **"Independent Living"**, which reflects the phenomenon of our increasingly ageing population. It is a residential project for people with restricted mobility. The objective is to facilitate the home assistance services within the region. The residents should be able to continue living in their own homes for longer with the help of ICT, thereby becoming more independent. A service portal installed in the home can make using certain services easier for those with restricted mobility, such as pharmacy delivery services, caretaking, or delivery services for shopping and meals. The sub-project "Independent Living" was launched at the beginning of 2011, initially for a year, in a so-called innovation house with nineteen residential units. In order to receive a broader spectrum of feedback from the tenants, the organizers had consciously chosen tenants representing a mixed age range.

This sub-project was developed as a collaboration between a local housing association, Fränkel AG, Deutsche Telekom, the Value-Added Services Center (ZMD), as well as various local service providers, a pharmacy, and a senior citizens' center in Friedrichshafen. The participating partners have differing reasons for being involved in the project (Steinbach 2011). The motive for ZMD was to develop a

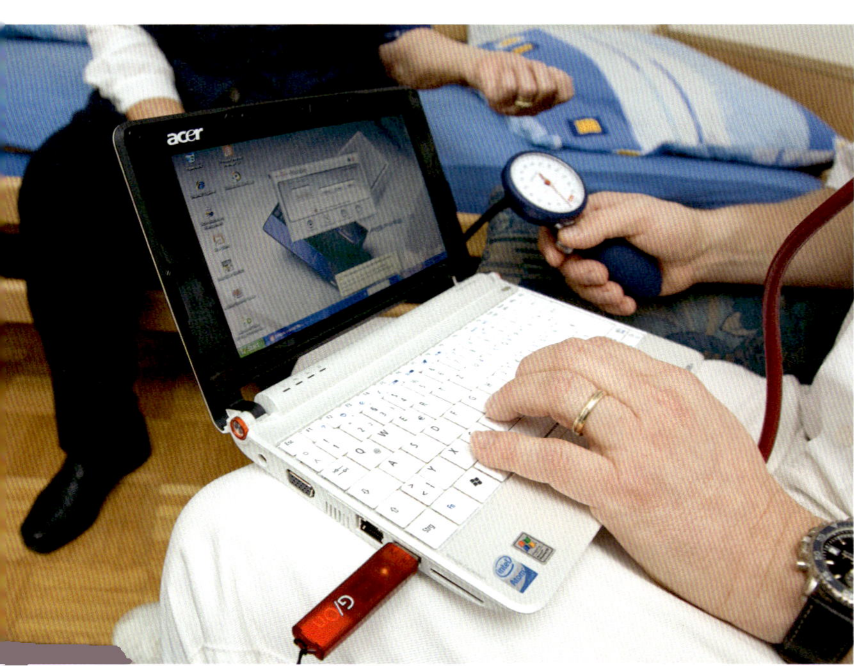

new business sector for Deutsche Telekom. The future viability of such a business model was to be investigated and the software used in the project was to be technically improved. The housing association wanted to find out how its residential units could be upgraded, in order to be able to be more adaptable to changing demands in the future. A service portal can enable elderly tenants to stay in their homes longer, through the facilitation of errands and shopping. The participating pharmacy expects new information about the behavior of its clients from the project. Senior citizens are the pharmacy's most important target group, which it also wants to provide with a good service in the future.

The senior citizens' center seeks to maintain the quality of life and the independence of the tenants for as long as possible. ICT can provide assistance for coping with life in one's own home. At the same time, it is about relieving the future shortage of skilled labor and increasing care needs through the innovative use of ICT. In this sub-project it was possible to harmonize the differing interests of the participating partners.

The sub-project **"Edunex"** is a web-based educational platform for schools in Friedrichshafen. Deutsche Telekom wanted, among other things, to create such an educational platform in cooperation with the publishing partners Cornelsen and Klett. Pupils and teachers were to have access to educational material via the Internet and to be able to work with it interactively. This would increase their flexibility in terms of space and time. Pupils who were ill, for example, would be able to look at learning materials from home, teachers would be able to upload these materials onto the platform from anywhere. Modules are made available for the development and carrying out of specific individual learning schemes. Tools such as E-mail or chat forums for pupils to communicate among themselves or with the teacher are also provided.

According to Deutsche Telekom, the use of "Edunex" can help teaching staff to prepare, carry out, and follow up on their lessons. It facilitates the internal differentiation and support of groups and individual pupils. Finally, long-distance communication is conceivable. For example, it could be used in foreign language lessons in cooperation with partner schools abroad.

The sub-project **"Kindergarten Online"** is an example of how applications in this field can benefit customers and suppliers. On the one hand, the project seeks to help parents by facilitating the registration of their children at kindergarten. On the other hand, the project is intended to help the kindergarten management and the city administration to organize these registrations. Project partners included the city's kindergartens, the city administration, and T-Systems. The ideas behind this sub-project originated when T-City was launched, but it could only be put into practice in summer 2009. The launch was delayed by a number of staff changes among the developers of the project.

"Edunex"

"Kindergarten Online"

kiga.cityandict.de

The aim of the electronic registration is to improve, both for parents and for the kindergartens, the procedures for the allocation and organization of places. The project is based on an Internet portal for the online registration of children for a kindergarten place. Since the end of 2009, thirty-seven kindergartens are linked to this system. Parents can gather information about the various kindergartens in Friedrichshafen via the Internet. There is information about the location, the opening hours, and the educational concepts of the establishments. Parents can list a maximum of three kindergartens in order of preference. The advantage for the kindergartens is that the planning processes, such as the formation of groups or the allocation of staff, are made faster and easier using this system.

The sub-project **"Smart Metering"** was put into practice as a cooperation between Deutsche Telekom and Technische Werke Friedrichshafen (TWF). The aim of the project, launched in 2008, is to save energy in private households. With the help of new electricity meters, so-called Smart Meters, consumers can monitor their own individual energy consumption via the Internet. They can make targeted savings if they change their habits as a result of this new information. Initially, the Smart Meters were installed in around 350 volunteering households across the whole urban area. Since the end of 2009, the development has focused on the two city districts of Oberhof and Windhag, in order to be able to assess the costs of a comprehensive roll-out. In spring 2011, both districts were fully equipped with the new intelligent meters.

With this pilot scheme, TWF is seeking to assess the potential economic consequences of a comprehensive Smart Meter rollout. Processes in terms of the reading, analysis, and accounting of consumption data are to be made more efficient. Furthermore, it is hoped that insights will be gained into how to influence and control load patterns to avoid load peaks. The end-user, the customer, is more informed about personal electricity consumption and about the energy costs involved. Consumers are able to identify power guzzlers and to improve their energy efficiency by replacing them. The first major studies of the installation of Smart Meters, however, show that the savings impact for end-users is very limited.

The new electricity meters transfer the data in real time via cell phone or DSL connection to the energy provider. There the information is processed and made available to the customer via a personalized internet portal—the so-called Clever Counter Portal. Using a computer with Internet access, customers can monitor their consumption at quarter-hourly intervals, provided they have signed a corresponding user agreement.

"Smart Metering"

200
Regarding the question of data protection issues in Smart Metering, see the chapter "Avoid Crash"

2007   2008   2009

Education & research
- 5 *Edunex*
- 6 *EduKey*

Tourism & culture
- 8 *Digital Picture Frame*
- 9 *CityInfo*
- 10 *Multimedia Stations*
- 4 *Media Hotel*
- 11 *Telephones for the hearing impaired*
- 12 *SZ News*
- 13 *Tourism Portal*

Mobility & transport
- 3 *KatCard*
- 1 *GPS distress signal*

Business & work
- 7 *Smart Metering*
- 15 *dDesk*
- 14 *G/On*

Healthcare
- 2 *Mobile Clinic*

Citizen, city & state

2010 2011 2012

19 *suchen.mobi*

27 *Interactive Hiking*

29 *flinc*

26 *HomeNetwork 2.0*

21 *Mobile Worker Bundle*

20 *Tumor Conference*

30 *Independent Living*

25 *derBUTLER*

16 *T-Mobile emergency number*

28 *BIGkidscoach*

18 *BodyTel*

22 *D115*

23 *De-Mail*

31 *Sag's doch*

24 *Kindergarten Online*

17 *City Portal*

1   In an emergency, water sportsmen can send a **GPS distress signal** by touching their cell phone, to alert the rescue services on duty.

2   The **Mobile Clinic** system enables the interactive monitoring of patients with chronic heart conditions. The participants in the project transmit their health data from home to the hospital or doctor in charge. The data is evaluated at a distance. Mobile Clinic contributes to restoring the patients' personal responsibility and quality of life.

3   The **KatCard** E-ticketing project enables the non-cash purchase of tickets for catamarans operating in the Lake Constance region.

4   In the **Media Hotel** "Goldenes Rad" ("The Golden Wheel") in Friedrichshafen, guests can use state-of-the-art multimedia technology. Entertainment and information services can be accessed via a media center. The device can also be used as a digital video recorder and as a work station.

5   **Edunex** is a web-based educational platform for schools in Friedrichshafen.

6   The Edunex educational platform is accessed via the biometrically secured **EduKey.**

7   **Smart Metering** provides customers with information about their electricity and gas consumption. Sensors transmit personal consumption data and the results are presented via a web portal. This helps customers to control their consumption. The project helps energy providers to gain insight into potential future energy infrastructures.

8   The **digital picture frame** has an integrated wireless module and receives digital photos via the Deutsche Telekom network, displaying them automatically on the screen.

9   Short infos on various topics can be requested via the **CityInfo** SMS information service. Businesses, municipalities and associations also provided their own information services.

10 The touchscreens of nine **Multimedia Stations** in Friedrichshafen provided information and services free of charge in the areas of city, tourism, events and short-range public transportation.

11 The multi media stations in Friedrichshafen give deaf people access to a sign language interpreting service, using special video **telephones for the hearing impaired.** An interpreter translates the conversation spontaneously in both directions.

12 **SZ News** / Schwäbische.de on Entertain adds a local dimension to the IPTV (Internet Protocol Television) information services. The user can choose options according to personal preferences, such as filtering information from different cities in the Lake Constance region, selecting topic areas, and whether they are presented as text, video or photo.

13 www.friedrichshafen.info compiles all important information required for a stay in Friedrichshafen. The **Tourism Portal** enables the booking of accommodation and research about events. It also provides leisure time tips.

14 With **G/On,** employees can access their work stations securely from anywhere in the world. Users have access only to approved applications. Access to the company network is declined, preventing infiltration by hackers or malware.

15 Using **dDesk,** applications and data are stored on the cloud on a central server. Users can access their programs and data from anywhere in the world, without installing them locally.

16 The **T-Mobile emergency number** supports the coordination of rescue services in Friedrichshafen. Apart from the analog notification system of the rescue forces, the lifesavers also receive automized calls and SMS messages on their landline and cell phones. The receiver responds by pressing a key, to communicate whether he will arrive at the scene immediately or whether he will be delayed.

17 The **City Portal** www.friedrichshafen.de provides official information quickly and clearly. Many municipal services, such as managing appointments and providing forms, are available online.

18 **BodyTel** enables patients with chronic illnesses to record physical data, such as blood pressure, weight or blood sugar levels, in an internet diary. If the values deviate from the norm, the doctor or person in charge is notified via SMS, e-mail or fax.

19 The »location based service« **suchen.mobi** provides users with relevant information about the nearest restaurants, shopping options, banks and tourist sights, according to their location. The service also provides suggestions for city tours in Friedrichshafen.

20 The telemedicine project **Tumor Conference** enables communication and cooperation between doctors that is independent of location. The sharing of medical findings is integrated into the system and they are discussed via video conferencing. Tumor Conference is intended to contribute towards improving communication between medical staff and raising the quality of patient care.

21 The **Mobile Worker Bundle** enables the transmission of handwritten information to a server. The data are recorded with a pen, sent to a company server, converted into typescript and finally archived.

22 The public services hotline number **D 115** brings together all questions about public services centrally. Simple questions are answered immediately or are forwarded directly to the relevant department.

23 Messages can be sent securely, traceably and reliably with **De-Mail,** Sensitive data such as contracts or invoices can be sent via the internet, saving time and money.

24 With **Kindergarten Online,** parents can obtain information about various educational establishments in Friedrichshafen and register their children for three kindergartens, in order of preference. The portal also helps to assess the demand for places.

25 The mobile device **derBUTLER,** for making emergency calls, helps senior citizens and high-risk patients to stay mobile. In an emergency, an alarm is triggered and transmitted manually or automatically (in the case of a fall). A speaker phone, a tracking function and the transmission of vital data also support the safety of the user.

26 With **HomeNetwork 2.0,** domestic electrical appliances can be monitored and controlled from anywhere, using mobile terminal devices (laptop or smartphone).

27 **Interactive Hiking** enables the downloading of hiking maps onto a smartphone. A solar charging device makes it possible to use the maps beyond the usual battery lifecycle.

28 **BIGkidscoach** is a nutrition platform that encourages children and young people to exercise more and have healthier diets. After various tests and analyses, the participants receive a personalized training program, guided by a 3D trainer.

29 **flinc** communicates spontaneous car sharing possibilities. Using a sat-nav and a smartphone, routes are communicated between the driver and the passenger. Fares can be paid via an integrated payment system.

30 The **Independent Living** project is designed to help people to live in their own homes for longer. By providing various services (pharmacy, caretaker, shopping, public transport etc.) via a touchscreen, senior citizens and people with restricted mobility are supported in their everyday lives.

31 **Sag's doch** is a portal for reporting issues in Friedrichshafen. Requests and suggestions can be communicated quickly and easily. The current status of their handling can be followed at any time, thereby making the process more transparent.

096

Complexity—
the limits of controllability

It wasn't possible to convert some of the individual projects into pilot schemes, or else they were unsuccessful and were abandoned in agreement with both partners. This exemplifies the nature of the future workshop of the T-City project in Friedrichshafen—that new products in the Smart City will also be tested. While some people in the city felt like guinea pigs, others pointed out the corporation's honesty in being able to admit to failed initiatives.

In some cases, there were overriding reasons that caused difficulties when putting individual projects into practice or led to their being abandoned after a trial period. These overriding reasons included technical inadequacies, such as with one of the first T-City sub-projects, the "KatCard." The project was introduced at the end of 2007 and abandoned in April 2009. The idea was for passengers on the catamaran connection between Friedrichshafen and Constance to be able to pay the fare via their cell phone, instead of using cash. It was intended to make the ride on the catamaran easier and more comfortable for casual passengers, avoiding waiting times and the search for coins. However, buying the ticket via cell phone required a device with Near Field Communication. Today, they are in wide use, but in the early stages of the project, the launch was delayed repeatedly by the manufacturers, so that the E-ticketing project was shut down. The project partners were simply ahead of their time.

The second E-ticketing project, "Easy Air Travel Services," could not even be launched. The aim of this project was to enable an automized check-in of passengers already on the way to the airport. The boarding card was to be sent directly to the passenger's cell phone, which would have saved time for the passenger and simplified the check-in process for the airline. However, the change in circumstances brought about by the international economic crisis meant that they were unable to find the originally planned thirty volunteers for the trial run. Businesses had cut their travel budgets. As a result, the execution of this T-City project idea failed due to general economic circumstances beyond its control.

A healthcare project, "Transition of Care," also had to struggle with technical difficulties. The idea behind this project was the smooth transfer of information on patients who had been referred from the hospital to the outpatient or in-patient departments. This project would have enabled the care facilities to handle patient data more efficiently. By receiving information quicker, the care attendants could have provided the appropriate patient care immediately. However, the many different software systems used by the care facilities lead to a very high expenditure during data exchange. It seems that a solution that standardizes the various systems is not yet in sight.

Ahead of their time

Economic crisis

Incompatibility
of systems

Other obstacles were presented, for example, by the official authorities in some project areas. Teaching materials were supposed to be uploaded centrally onto the educational platform "Edunex," which had either been provided by publishers in return for a fee or developed by the teachers themselves. The attempt to set this up on a municipal level in cooperation with individual schools failed, because in Germany the federal states are in charge of the educational policy. The state of Baden-Württemberg prefers an alternative competing product for such platforms. "Moodle" is an educational platform based on open source software, which a number of teachers in Friedrichshafen were already familiar with. They were not prepared to change their tried and tested platform.

Finally, Deutsche Telekom also ran up against local competition. Apart from transregional competitors, the subsidiary company of TWF, Teledata, also provides data links for private households and smaller businesses, as well as for the global industrial enterprises in Friedrichshafen. TWF tried to assert itself against Deutsche Telekom on the strength of its local presence: "the network with the home advantage" or "not on the stock exchange, but on location" were slogans that could be read on posters and buses. A certain ambivalence arose for TWF. On the one hand, it competed with Deutsche Telekom in one of its business sectors; on the other hand, it was one of Deutsche Telekom's partners, for example, in energy supply projects. Furthermore, its Chairman of the Supervisory Board, the mayor of Friedrichshafen, is also an essential cooperation partner of Deutsche Telekom in the joint development of the Smart City.

Schedule of responsibilities

165
Regarding how the project was received, see the chapter "Open"

Local competition

teledata.cityandict.de

098

Idiosyncrasies—unique features of Friedrichshafen

Putting the T-City project into practice as a comprehensive Smart City concept was for a long time hampered by difficulties resulting from the particular urban structures (Hatzelhoffer et al. 2010b). From the outset, the project was regarded cautiously by the city. This applies to large parts of the population as well as to many businesses and some local politicians. At times, the implementation of the project was even regarded as an imposition (Poggenpohl et al. 2012).

Even five years after the official start of the project, it is evident that a large proportion of the urban society still has reservations about T-City. Only the users of selected individual projects, who are directly benefiting from their applications, are convinced by their particular sub-project. For a variety of reasons, in Friedrichshafen there is still widespread skepticism and a poor perception of the overall project—in other words the idea of a comprehensive Smart City.

The ambivalences and contradictions of the city of Friedrichshafen play an important role. It is an urban society which, on the one hand, is characterized by high-tech companies with high investment potential, but which on the other hand also enjoys such a high quality of life that there is hardly any motivation in daily life to participate in initiatives designed to improve living conditions. "World-class by day, complacent by night," as it is summarized pointedly by the authors of a book about the city (Poggenpohl et al. 2012).

Where is the innovative and creative city?

The highly innovative companies in the city of Friedrichshafen were an important reason for being selected as the T-City in the contest. The companies have their own research and development departments, which would indicate a creative and innovative city milieu. Therefore, when the city was declared the winner of the contest, there was the understandable expectation that Deutsche Telekom would be able to develop and implement innovative projects in Friedrichshafen together with the whole urban population. The jury had banked on the traditionally close link between high technology and urban society within an economically prosperous region.

There is a historical connection between the city and its enterprises, expressed in particular by developments and activities that raise the general level of prosperity in Friedrichshafen. The city's Zeppelin Foundation, as the major shareholder, benefits from the ZF dividends and passes this money on to social and cultural areas in Friedrichshafen. While the city and industry are strongly intertwined in this way, the innovative milieu driven by the high technology enterprises has barely taken root in the urban society.

Wide skepticism

156
A detailed portrayal of the inhabitants' perceptions can be found in the chapter "Open".

"For more than a century there has been a cultural chasm in Friedrichshafen and as its inhabitants, we are living in a kind of schizophrenia: on the one hand, we accommodated and still accommodate pioneers, on the other hand we are skeptical towards new ideas. On the one hand, we are cosmopolitan, on the other hand, we deliberately shy away. On the one hand, we are proud of our economic success, on the other hand, inhibited and overly self-critical."

Poggenpohl et al. 2012

High technology and urban society exist independently side by side.

According to the recent insights in the field of economic geography, a creative and innovative milieu depends primarily on urban qualities. New ideas that emerge in the "creative, innovative city" (Florida 2001; Landry 2000) require encounters with the unfamiliar and with the unknown. They are characterized by spontaneous and unplanned interactions between various social groups. The prerequisite for such an innovative milieu are urban density and interaction, which enable communication and contacts in the first place. A feature of such creative cities is therefore a diverse population structure, openness, and tolerance towards others and the unfamiliar (Florida 2001; Florida/Gates 2001). It is unclear whether and to what extent such urban qualities and an innovative and creative milieu are sufficiently on hand in Friedrichshafen (Hatzelhoffer et al. 2010b).

Instead, one can observe that the innovative activities unfold within the individual participating businesses and their transregional and worldwide networks, so that the scientific and technical progress is made independently of the urban qualities. In this sense, the innovations in Friedrichshafen *"… are implemented within autonomous enterprises, which for a century had been used to organizing their innovation procedures themselves, strictly in accordance with internal interests"* (Poggenpohl et al. 2012).

In the case of the inhabitants of Friedrichshafen, one can hardly talk of a creative and innovative milieu that is rooted in urban qualities, with the corresponding diversity and openness towards what is new and unfamiliar. The employees of Zeppelin University, which was founded in 2003, share a similar experience. The private university is hardly integrated into the urban society, despite numerous efforts on the part of the scientific establishment to be involved with the citizens of Friedrichshafen.

Thus, while there is a high level of technological dynamism within the large enterprises, this does not carry over into the daily lives of most inhabitants. The city is therefore characterized by a tension between "high-flying cutting-edge technology" and "a pusillanimous Upper Swabian backyard mentality," as a resident put it pointedly in an interview. The innovative aspect of the enterprises is isolated and not connected with the city. The globally significant technical solutions for automotive manufacturing and aviation are developed behind the factory gates of the large enterprises, while on the lakeside promenade, it's just cappuccino and the view of the lake.

Lakeside promenade and
Alpine panorama

Apart from the particular circumstances regarding innovation, which do not concern the inhabitants of Friedrichshafen in their everyday lives, the particular living and working conditions in Friedrichshafen also play an important role. In the urban population, there is a high degree of satisfaction regarding living and working conditions, for which there are two important reasons: the attractiveness of the landscape and the economic prosperity. Both of these explain why from the beginning, inhabitants were not particularly enthusiastic about the T-City project.

First of all, the city enjoys an extraordinary location at Lake Constance, which is perceived as particularly advantageous by the inhabitants and is highly valued. From the long promenade, one can observe changing lakeside atmospheres at different times of day and in different seasons. On many days of the year, one can even see the Alpine mountain range on the opposite shore. The lake also provides possibilities for active or passive relaxation. These qualities were mentioned in nearly all of the discussions with residents. Hence, the technology-oriented T-City project, with its aim of improving the local quality of life, found it difficult to secure the enthusiasm of the inhabitants and to achieve its high ambitions.

Secondly, Friedrichshafen has a strong economy with low unemployment and an above-average earnings potential. Building on the still relatively young industrial tradition, the proportion of employees in industry is very high and significantly above the national average. Only few cities like Ludwigshafen, Leverkusen, or Wolfsburg—with their large industrial enterprises — have a comparably high proportion of industrial workers.

81%
of the inhabitants consider Friedrichshafen as an attractive place to live.
(our own survey in 2007)

An attractive landscape and...

... and economic prosperity

The employees in Friedrichshafen's industrial enterprises are generally well-paid. The city also has excellent social and cultural facilities. The Zeppelin Foundation—which became an important financial resource for the municipal budget after World War II and the cessation of its original purpose—supports these initiatives in numerous ways. Since the transfer of the foundation's fortune to the city of Friedrichshafen, the funds have been used for charitable causes. Important contributions are being made to high-quality care for children and youth work, to the areas of literacy and education, healthcare and social services, as well as the sponsorship of art and culture, which bring considerable benefits to the inhabitants in their everyday lives.

The Swabian mentality, the lack of an "elite," and of local patriotism

Ultimately, after winning the T-City contest, there was a widespread expectation in Friedrichshafen that Deutsche Telekom would sponsor the city financially. It was barely stipulated in the city council and among the inhabitants that the new cooperation involved a financial contribution on the part of the city. This was made even more problematic by the much invoked Swabian thriftiness, which apparently still shapes the urban mentality. At the same time, some of the decision-makers within the city were increasingly disappointed that Deutsche Telekom assigned only few tasks to the smaller enterprises in the city, and for the implementation of the project brought along mostly their own staff or external business partners. Thus, there was reluctance in the city to contribute financially to the development of the Smart City.

Another reason for the difficulty in developing the T-City project can be found in the particular makeup of the urban society. Sections of a possible "elite" are not based in the city of Friedrichshafen. Many highly ranked employees from the large enterprises don't live in the city, but in the modest little surrounding municipalities or in the more attractive neighboring towns of Lindau, Meersburg, or Ravensburg. The inhabitants of Friedrichshafen also frequently visit these neighboring towns for shopping, as they are much more attractive and have a more pleasant atmosphere.

"Grand schemes have long become run-of-the-mill in this city: the airport, the trade fair, T-City. We have a mixture of fluctuating identities: famous and provincial, progressive and conservative at the same time."
Renz 2008

High expectations in the city

In an interview, one resident drew the following conclusions: that Friedrichshafen has in many ways a rather negative image and that no outsider finds the city really great; that it conveys an image of wealth and prosperity and has everything conducive to a good quality of life, but that especially newcomers lack clear identification with the new city, whose history is still so young. Furthermore, highly qualified employees in Friedrichshafen mostly find it difficult to integrate themselves into the existing urban society and didn't attend the local summer festival Seehasenfest, didn't celebrate Carnival, and were seldom active members of local clubs and societies. The newcomers lacked "local patriotic duty." Consequently, the city was not a suitable breeding ground for the development of a Smart City, which was not just targeted towards sub-projects with restricted individual uses, but sought to integrate the new solutions of information and communication technology comprehensively into urban society.

The particular makeup of the urban society

Heterogeneity and dynamics—challenges for Deutsche Telekom

For Deutsche Telekom, as a large global telecommunications corporation, putting the T-City project into practice was also a new challenge. The corporation sought to fulfill two key objectives with the project: first, to raise the reputation of the corporation through positive reports about the innovative T-City; second, for the various corporate sectors—T-Com, T-Mobile, T-Online, and T-Systems—to learn how to work more closely together on a joint project.

The division of Deutsche Telekom into these various strategic business sectors was also noticeable for the partners in the city of Friedrichshafen over the course of the project. In some project fields or sub-projects, the contact persons changed when the business sectors were restructured. During the project, for example, T-Com became T-Home in 2007. In 2008, 160,000 medium-size customers were transferred from T-Systems to T-Home, so that T-Systems could focus on large corporations. Finally in 2010, T-Mobile and T-Home were merged into Telekom Deutschland Ltd.

During the project, some of the responsible project partners in the city gained the impression that the original objective of the project, with its focus on innovation and communication, had shifted in favor of an orientation towards sales and applications. It appears that over the course of the project, there was a reduction especially of those developments that corresponded to special wishes on behalf of the city of Friedrichshafen, which Deutsche Telekom could not market in other locations later on. The city—as a partner in the PPP—had no influence on such decisions, which resulted from internal corporate considerations.

Other decisions were also imposed by Deutsche Telekom. From the outset, the fulfillment of the pledge made in the contest of an investment of up to 80 million euros into the implementation of projects by Deutsche Telekom didn't mean the allocation of disposable financial resources. Instead, this financial input was to be provided mostly in the form of consultancy and implementation services on behalf of Deutsche Telekom staff. On the one hand, this greatly restricted the contest winner's freedom to channel the funding; and on the other hand, it caused a certain resentment on the part of the city, as business enterprises in Friedrichshafen could hardly profit directly from the budget. In particular, some small or medium-sized IT companies were disappointed by the purely "in-house allocation" of the Telekom corporation's funds.

The experts from Deutsche Telekom, who developed and executed the projects together with partners from the city of Friedrichshafen, were hardly ever present in the city themselves. They traveled to Friedrichshafen mostly for just one working day to attend their appointments. As a result, they could not gain deeper knowledge of the city, nor forge and foster personal contacts, which would have formed the basis for a deeper mutual trust. The division of the project management between the headquarters in Bonn and Friedrichshafen also did nothing to improve the understanding between the project partners.

The two objectives of the project

Repeated organizational restructuring

Compromises within the city

This, by all means professional handling of personnel resources on the part of Deutsche Telekom, reflects an organizational philosophy and a company culture that were the source of further aggravations and misunderstandings. For example, after launching certain public relations activities, it took a while before the city was able to comprehend Deutsche Telekom's requests that it use Deutsche Telekom's corporate design. The city did not want to be monopolized by the public image of the corporation. Deutsche Telekom's "magenta" was not to dominate the city. Here, Deutsche Telekom also had to learn how to consult with an equal partner.

   Finally, some of the municipal organizers reacted partly with irritation and partly with humor to Deutsche Telekom's meeting notes. The documentation of objectives, procedures, research, project status reports, etc. was sometimes so extensive that those involved could hardly process them. These comprehensive summaries, however, contributed significantly to ensuring the continuity of the project despite the numerous changes in staff and responsibilities.

Mutual misunderstanding

Public relations—
do good and talk about it

The project's decision-makers were very aware of the difficulties in conveying the T-City project to Friedrichshafen's inhabitants and in fostering enthusiasm for the idea of a Smart City. Consequently, there was a string of imaginative ideas on how to promote the project within the city and to convince the inhabitants of the benefits of the various Smart City sub-projects. At the same time, the public relations work served the purpose of presenting the project nationally and internationally.

The public relations initiatives in Friedrichshafen were met with varying degrees of success. In the initial phase of the T-City project, there were ideas for a dedicated showroom within the city, a sort of permanent trade fair with which to present the project's innovative applications to the wider public. Several locations within the city were considered, in order to find a location as central as possible from which to inform inhabitants and the many Lake Constance tourists about the project. This sort of permanent trade fair was to demonstrate how T-City can improve people's quality of life. Already in the mid-nineteen-nineties, large construction sites had relevant information points, such as the red box on Potsdamer Square in Berlin, which had led to great interest in the construction project, as well as to a greater acceptance of the undertaking. However, it proved impossible to implement such an accompanying measure in the city of Friedrichshafen. Instead, a very modest information panel was erected in a not very prominent public space.

Information panel instead of showroom

Conveying the purpose—
a wide range of measures

The project's first awareness campaign was launched in summer 2007 under the slogan "Action?!" The idea behind it was achieving good publicity in a three-stage procedure: first attracting attention to the project; then asking and gathering questions about the project; and third, providing the inhabitants with answers to their questions. A blue question mark acted as a symbol for their questions, a magenta exclamation mark was the symbol for Deutsche Telekom's answers. There were advertisements in regional daily newspapers and on public posters within the city to build momentum and increase awareness. However, the response from the people in terms of asking questions about the project was relatively limited. This was the first indication for the decision-makers that it wasn't going to be easy to foster enthusiasm for the project.

A second measure to anchor the project locally was the election of the so-called ambassadors in spring 2008. Initially, they were comprised of twenty-six inhabitants from the city or the surrounding region with very differing professional backgrounds. Their task was to inform the local population and visitors in Friedrichshafen about the projects, services, and innovations within the T-City project. Thus, their purpose was to convey the project to the urban community and to help to make it as easy to understand as possible for their fellow citizens. They were the transmitters and the translators between the project and the civic population and were available free of charge for individual information events. The idea behind it was that it would be easier for citizens to win their fellow citizens' trust, compared to representatives of the corporation or of the city.

A further strategy for advertising the project among the local population, as well as to increase its profile within the city, was the "Futurists Initiative." This meant that ten different households in Friedrichshafen were to be equipped free of charge with state-of-the-art information and communication technology and allowed to test numerous T-City project applications within their own four walls. To become a Futurist, citizens had to take part in a selection contest. Futurists Initiative

As many as 548 households, about 2 percent of households in Friedrichshafen, aspired to be Futurists. A jury selected ten Futurist households—including two apartment-sharing communities and a kindergarten—from the many applications in June 2009. They were purposely chosen to represent very differing population groups within the city (young, old, with or without children, communities, and single people). Initially for a year, later extended for a second year, they received the most cutting-edge technological devices. At the same time, some individual projects were installed in their homes. In return, they allowed the media or the researchers involved in the project to question them about their experiences with the devices and projects. They gave honest accounts of the various possibilities and limitations of the applications in their various daily lives and documented these clearly via blogs and interviews on the website.

The internal and external communications frequently made use of a so-called "Futurists Living Room". This room-sized installation, comprised of a seating area and a television with web TV, a Smart Meter for energy metering, and modern networking of electrical appliances via a "Home Network" presented the idea of networking an array of activities in a vivid and tangible way. This "Living Room" was set up for example at trade fairs and other events such as Deutsche Telekom's general assembly. "Futurists Living Room"

Finally, there were further advertising and information events, such as the T-City Days, which were held annually in Friedrichshafen from 2008 and attended by Federal Chancellor Angela Merkel in February 2011. The "Hotspot Summer" events held annually for a number of years were especially popular, with inhabitants and visitors to the city center enjoying free WLAN Internet access for several weeks. More than thirty hotspots enabling wireless access for mobile devices are now permanently installed in the city. On the bicentenary of the city, the project provided a city beach and set up on the promenade, which was well received by the majority of inhabitants.

Apart from the numerous events, there was also traditional project information and advertising. The claim "We are living the future" focused on the connection between the prospects of ICT and its applications within Friedrichshafen. They tried to increase local identification with the T-City project by using the Zeppelin as an advertising medium. The airline company Intersky—which is based in Friedrichshafen and flies from the Lake Constance area to locations such as Düsseldorf, Berlin, and Hamburg—was chosen as the advertising partner.

Of course, there was a German and English language website, as well as an online presence on Facebook, YouTube, and Twitter. Films, podcasts, and news bulletins were to provide information about the overall project and the individual sub-projects. A project magazine, a radio broadcast, a TV format, leaflets, and flyers promoting various sub-projects reveal the scope of the communications strategy. At the end of 2011, the entire communication was transferred to the project's Facebook page, where there are new daily updates about aspects of the project and information about general ICT issues.

A project magazine called "T-City Spiegel" was issued nine times—from the beginning of 2009 to the beginning of 2011—presenting the project areas, the project partners, the Futurists and general ICT topics. The "Connections" broadcast on the university radio station Welle 20 ran from January 2009 until December 2011, introducing a different sub-project or special ICT topic every two to four weeks with studio guests. From January 2010, the program "T-City Magazin" on the regional TV channel regioTV broadcast similar items.

spiegel.cityandict.de

magazine.cityandict.de

Local news coverage— providing benevolent backing

To gain a perspective on the public relations work surrounding the project, it is interesting to take a look at the news coverage in the two local daily newspapers Schwäbische Zeitung and Südkurier. The greatest number of project-related news items was issued when the Federal Chancellor Angela Merkel visited in February 2011. The number of news items had already risen in March 2010 when the event was announced. The volume of news reports continued to be influenced by local political events. For example, the change of mayor at the beginning of 2009 was reflected in the volume of T-City news items. Generally speaking, over the entire course of the T-City project, the local press reported benevolently about it; 1,234 articles in two local newspapers from June 2007 to December 2011 represented an average of five articles per week.

The illustration shows a so-called "Word Cloud". The cloud contains key words that are arranged in order of how frequently they are used. This representation analyzes various news items relating to T-City, taken from the Friedrichshafen newspapers *Schwäbische Zeitung* and *Südkurier*. The larger the key word is printed, the more frequently it was mentioned in the newspapers. Therefore this illustration reflects what the local press was most interested in over the course of the project. It shows that it was not individual projects that attracted the attention of the press at Lake Constance, but events such as the visit of the Federal Chancellor Angela Merkel on the occasion of the T-City Day in 2011, or general topics relating to information and communication technology, such as criticism of mobile communications. Certain projects, such as "Independent Living" or the platform "Kindergarten Online", were mentioned very rarely in the press. As they were hardly reported about at all, it was only very attentive newspaper readers or those who had heard about these projects from other sources who were aware of their content and purpose. On the other hand, the press reported frequently about the development of the broadband network, E-metering and the "Futurists". It is also interesting to note that the city beach, which T-City gave as a gift to Friedrichshafen for its anniversary in summer 2011, but which was completely unrelated to the new communications technologies, was reported about significantly more often than the T-City project's objectives of improving Friedrichshafen's quality of life and locational advantages.

ng

work 2.0 T-City Day data security

rists T-Home Entertain

Kindergarten Online

UMTS/HSDPA

Smart Home

E-Health

of the

Smart Grid

Chancellor GlucoTel

Independent Living

Quality of life and

sm of of the location

communications

VDSL Digital Divide

ach E-Metering

Government De-Mail

City ICT Costs Media partner

E-Mobility

roadband

otection Telephone for the hearing impaired

Mobile Clinic

T-City review—
the roles of citizens and businesses

by Josef Büchelmeier,
Mayor of the city of Friedrichshafen from 2001 to 2009

Initially, it was the municipal administration of Friedrichshafen that took the initiative to participate in the T-City project. The administration modernizer Jürgen Kegelmann and the IT officer Andreas Roth were very interested in this project. As the mayor at that time, they each presented me with the general outline of the contest and argued in favor of submitting an application. The primary focuses were on administration, the optimization of internal IT processes, and increasing citizen participation through information and communication technology (ICT). Apart from seeking the support of the administration, participating partners were also sought among the local inhabitants and businesses. Clear interest was soon expressed by company representatives, the hospital, the utility provider Technische Werke, tourism, the airport, transport companies, and city marketing. However, a public event for informing or even enthusing citizens didn't elicit much of a response. On the other hand, the representatives of the companies and commercially operating establishments, such as the hospital and public utilities, recognized the potential of the opportunities on offer. This resulted in the implementation of a string of useful ideas. The application was also discussed in the city council and considered potentially beneficial to the city.

The review shows why the project developed as it did later on: the information given in bulletins, brochures, daily newspapers, etc. didn't really make an impression on the average citizen, or only in a distorted form. It was almost impossible to convey to the inhabitants how such a joint project involving the municipality could be compatible with a large corporation and its interests. Thus, there was widespread belief that the city or individual residents were to be the recipients of "gifts" from the corporation. In my opinion, this reflects the typical attitude to funding from Brussels, Berlin, or Stuttgart, with the receiving of donations and gifts as a basic feature of local politics. It works in a similar way to the marketing and product promotions of major corporations. There is no real requirement for what is being offered, but the municipality sees an opportunity to snap up a "bargain," so to speak, as customers do with product promotions.

In the field of education, for example, as long as alternative organizational structures and new ways of learning and thinking do not become the norm, students do not need new ICT applications to enable different ways of learning. There is no demand here for the well-intentioned and sponsored offers, so they come to nothing or are reduced to marginal niceties. The same applies to the Citizens' Wiki or the iPhone App for the city that never materialized. The "Futurists" initiative also had more of a promotional character than that of a genuine search for solutions.

Alongside this, there was and is the world of business with its clear work procedures in the T-City project. Companies and establishments oriented towards success or profit, such as the hospital, are already familiar with other forms of cooperation owing to their commercial aspects and they approached the project with quite different interests. What mattered to them was the demand, the competition, the financial and organizational benefits, and finally also the image of progressiveness. Therefore, it was right to integrate these areas of the city more comprehensively. In these areas, participation and interest were determined by usage and genuine demand. In contrast to civic society, there are positive reports of satisfaction from the areas of medicine, Smart Metering within the field of energy, and other concrete applications. T-City succeeded in implementing new solutions based on ICT for the benefit of such participants. For these partners within the city, the T-City project was useful and beneficial. Deutsche Telekom also gained valuable experience that can be helpful when putting other such initiatives into practice in the future. As with every project, there was objective criticism regarding the details of individual procedures, but no fundamental discontent or misunderstandings, which I can see is a misconception about the T-City project that has taken root in the minds of some in the wider political world.

My conclusion is that T-City was well received by those partners and users in the city who had concrete requirements or demands. On the other hand, the project never really took hold in those areas where this market-oriented context didn't apply.

The challenge of project management— why communication is so important

by Jörg Bollow, BMC Bollow Management & Consulting, Münster; T-City Project Director at Deutsche Telekom from 2006 to 2009

In my view, the basis for a collaborative project and work platform was created on the one hand by the project communities provided by the city and also on the part of Telekom, by implementing the fully functional joint procedures, as well as providing the Telekom staff. Furthermore, it was Telekom's communications budget and materials that were the prerequisite for the project-related dialogue with citizens and the communication surrounding the projects. In addition, alongside the project ideas, Telekom initiated and then partly also carried out local advertising and other valuable cooperations (Zeppelin NT, Zeppelin University, Volleyballverein, Seehasenfest, Dornier Museum, Intersky). Overall, the setting up and opening of the project headquarters in Bonn and Friedrichshafen worked well in all departments.

Laying out the basic framework agreement with the city, the initiation of the projects, and the project governance went less smoothly. Now that a few years have passed, my perception today with hindsight is that the projects were implemented too quickly, in the interests of visibly achieving quick results, at the expense of quality. Therefore, I would by all means now wait for at least six months between signing the framework agreement and actively carrying out the first project idea.

This wouldn't have been a problem if a provisional timetable had been agreed on internally and communicated in the application conditions when the T-City concept was launched. For example, after February 2007 when the chosen T-City was announced, there should have been a further time requirement of six months (from May to October 2007) for setting up the framework agreement. The first project implementations following the applications should have been put on hold for another three or four months (from January 2008). Overall, we were too optimistic regarding the synchronization of structures and the speed

of implementations and decisions. From the outset, we should have built an additional project phase into the time period between the announcement of the chosen city and the first project implementation, specifically allowing for a development and transition period to take place.

In my opinion, all further challenges that presented themselves were, to a greater or lesser extent, consequences of this central "birth defect." Retrospectively, it is clear that the timetable of the originally planned project phases was accelerated at some point and that goal posts were shifted. This occurred at various stages as the projects progressed.

Apart from the aforementioned potential for improving the framework and the corresponding lessons to be learned, I would also like to mention the political aspect. Apart from setting out the project framework, I think that the diversity and complexity of the various interests and motivations behind the project are a key factor influencing its success. This factor needs to be evaluated realistically from the outset, as it directly affects how the strength of communication within the project unfolds.

T-City—success and failure

by Jürgen Kaack, STZ-Consulting Group, Erftstadt; Managing Director of the municipal project association of T-City Friedrichshafen from 2007 to 2009

T-City is remarkably successful as an innovation project. During the course of the project, more than forty individual project proposals were planned and implemented by Deutsche Telekom together with various partners in the city of Friedrichshafen. Considering the breadth and complexity of the five spheres of innovation—health, education, administration, economy, and transport—the cooperation established with many partners worked well. The wide range of project areas and partners presented a challenge to the project management.

With hindsight, the project management could probably have been simplified if there had been an integrated project organization between the city and Deutsche Telekom, instead of two organizationally separate project offices, with an occasionally complicated decision-making and voting structure. Furthermore, the city's local communities didn't have formal authorities set up for dealing with all of the project themes involved. Overcoming most of the operative difficulties can be regarded as another component in the project's success.

Despite the strong commitment of the partners, not all project areas were successful, as some could only be implemented limitedly with the city partners. This applies, for example, not only to the area of education, which is governed nationally in the first instance, but also to healthcare projects, which must first be entered into the catalog of benefits of health insurances. Although some projects never went beyond the testing phase, which is to be expected within a bold innovation project, the sum of successful individual projects is impressive.

However, the majority of projects have one thing in common: they hardly have any impact on other project areas or even on the city as a whole. Indeed, most of the projects could have been carried out in completely separate communities. Nevertheless, the degree of innovation and of usage will certainly guarantee the majority of the projects a lasting influence; this includes projects such as Smart-Grid, Smart-Metering, Tumor Conference, Mobile Clinic, the standard public services hotline D115 or the optimization of administrative processes. On the other hand, the great expense of the information events accompanying the projects and of the support structures for target groups achieved only partial success. Of the latter, only the "senior citizens' Internet assistance network" set up during the course of the project has the potential to continue running independently after the project has ended. The media literacy seminars held in all school classes will probably also have a longer-term influence.

Comprehensive success was limited by the "construction fault" that the project could not be driven by the civic population from the outset. The project didn't succeed in being "taken over" by the people with their own initiatives and project ideas. Individual technical solutions are only of use to selected target groups, despite their high degree of innovation. It seems that more communal initiatives—rather than the sum of limited individual applications—are necessary in order to launch a wide movement. In addition, people's assumption that they were dealing with an advertising or sales campaign by Telekom blurred the perception of the project. The constant technical approach also limited how it was perceived. For a comprehensive Smart City project to have succeeded, perhaps additional project leaders with different approaches would have been required.

Civic participation projects (traditional or online) as preliminary and accompanying measures would perhaps have stimulated the necessary "movement" among the civic population. Whereby e-participation should not be launched and regularly practiced in relation to complex and overburdened areas such as the municipal budget. If the project themes are relevant for a sufficient number of citizens and the

results of the subsequent evaluation are taken into account in their implementation, many promising starting points emerge. Unfortunately, over the course of the project it wasn't possible to set up any e-participation schemes in Friedrichshafen, presumably because politics and administration were concerned about the potential resulting demands and wishes of the residents, while not yet having the organizational setup to action them; although an efficient and clear implementation would have been possible precisely through the use of modern communication technology. This could have led to ideas for innovative schemes with a better chance of wide appeal and attractiveness. It would be worth venturing a new attempt and to use the lessons learned from the T-City project as the basis for a new Smart City project scheme.

T-City Futurists sum up their experiences

*by Hans-Joachim Bachmann and Family,
T-City Futurists, Friedrichshafen*

Since 2009, the Bachmann family from Friedrichshafen has been given the opportunity to try out technological applications that might only be available to the wider public in a couple of years. After three years of field testing, the Bachmanns evaluate these applications and report on their day-to-day usage and their experiences of the T-City solutions.

Mr. Bachmann, what expectations did you have when you applied to be a T-City Futurist more than three years ago, and in what ways have these expectations been fulfilled?

"After our successful application to be futurists we didn't harbor any concrete expectations, but assumed it involved the usual means of telecommunication, such as the mobile phone, the Internet, and so on. It soon became clear that the project went far beyond this. It surpassed our expectations and we were provided with more equipment than we anticipated. Projects were immediately implemented in our household that we wouldn't have associated with Telekom. To name just a few: Smart Meter, the monitor for electricity-water-gas consumption. Home Network 2.0, the intelligent house control panel and monitor for electrical appliances. Bodytel, the health portal. Over time, we gained an insight into potentially new business segments for Telekom, we were able to try things out that were not yet available to other users. These products, which we would not want to do without from now on, provided revealing and exciting experiences, which were mostly positive for us."

*As a "technology pioneer," what was your experience of
the various projects and applications?*

"Certainly there were also some projects that proved to be unsuitable
for our household, but of course it is also part of the purpose of a pilot
project to find out which areas of application are more useful than
others. Telekom was open to this, welcoming our honest reports about
our experiences, even if there were aspects that some of the project
leaders weren't keen to hear. However, more than 90% of the components we tested were so positive that we will continue to use them
in future, even if it costs us money."

*What changes has the futurist project brought to
your daily lives?*

"Our current use of ICT has changed significantly compared to before
the project began. We are benefitting as a matter of course from the
entire spectrum of available, and in many cases, not yet available
options. Our life has not been turned upside down, but in some areas
it is taking on a different direction through the extensive use of the
technologies."

*And in what ways have the project and your role as a
T-City futurist changed over the years?*

"One aspect of the project became increasingly prominent: the sharing
of our experiences at all sorts of events, for example at various trade
fairs, at Telekom events, or various groups visiting us at home. These
will always be recalled by all of our family members. Of course, we all
learned over the course of the project to deal with different situations
and groups of people, to gauge the expectations of these groups cor-
rectly, and to react to spontaneous changes in the planned procedure.
We very much enjoyed this and never found it a burden that more than
a hundred people sat in our living room over the course of the project
to hear about our experiences."

*Now when you evaluate the two to three years of field
testing, what were your personal highlights and how will
you remember the project?*

"I can say the following as a summary of the last two years: we have
never regretted taking part in the project, every family member was
involved and had their own favorite projects. However, we all agree
that there were some unforgettable highlights. For example, an abso-
lute highlight was the T-City Day in Friedrichshafen with the visit by
the Federal Chancellor."

The transformation of public places through the technical enhancement of sensory perceptions

by Rainer Kazig, Professor of Social Geography with a focus on sustainability, Ludwig Maximilian University of Munich

Public life has become more talkative! This describes the perhaps most significant current change on a sensory level brought about by the use of new information and communication technology (ICT). This development, linked to the spread of mobile telephony, is especially prominent on public transport and at its stops, where a new form of public communication has emerged. One is excessively exposed to snippets of dialogue that individuals are having with absent family members, friends, or business partners. In large cities in particular, this has in certain places created a new dimension of sensory overload. The problem of sensory overload as a feature of large cities was pointed out already at the beginning of the twentieth century by the sociologist Georg Simmel, who advised switching off and ignoring it as a protective mechanism against this situation. However, all this public communication with those who are physically absent is difficult to ignore. Consequently, in the places prone to this kind of disturbance—such as long-distance trains or restaurants—regulatory measures in the form of cell phone prohibitions are gradually being implemented.

At the same time, mobile ICT has widened the options for avoiding unwanted acoustic impressions, enabling the immersion into a private musical sphere by means of headphones. The introduction of the Walkman at the end of the nineteen-seventies paved the way for this, while the advent of new storage media has opened up a whole new range of options, now enabling
one to carry along an almost unlimited number of music tracks and to determine one's own playlists. However, listening to music while on the move serves a much greater purpose than just shielding oneself against ambient noise. Almost anyone who has jogged while listening to music is aware of how it alters the experience of running. Similarly, listening to music on mobile devices enables a conscious link between one's sensory life and public places.

In comparison, the transformation of the sensory through the mobile Internet has only just begun. Nevertheless, it leads to what can be experienced being extended beyond our immediate surroundings. Those who are traveling equipped with the corresponding devices and apps can access information at any time about the shortest routes, tourist sights, restaurant ratings, available rental cars, or which friends are in the vicinity. The immediate sensory impressions of public spaces are therefore coupled with an already processed and technically mediated perspective on our surroundings. On the one hand, this increases one's confidence in public places and possibly also the enjoyment of exploring them. On the other hand, the mobile Internet demands one's full attention while being used, so that the immediate experience fades into the background. However, the sensory will continue to impose itself through smells, light, and noise, so that even in future we will not only have a second-hand experience of public places.

04

Open

New information and communication technologies (ICT) pervade many areas of our lives. The use of these technologies opens up new opportunities that shape our daily lives: communication and access to information are possible virtually anywhere and anytime. At the same time, information and communication technologies are clearly not without limitations. Furthermore, our norms and values can be disturbed by new patterns of public or private behavior brought about by using the technologies. The Smart City concepts and initiatives also promise cities new ways of shaping the present and future through the use of technological applications. Apart from questions about the daily use of information and communication technologies and their impact on our daily lives in urban environments, this chapter also deals with how a Smart City, in this case the T-City of Friedrichshafen, is perceived and experienced by urban society. It is particularly important to take the inhabitants into consideration, since ultimately it is they who live in the city and actively bring it to life.

Everyday life—new possibilities and new limitations

"Everything's amazing right now and nobody's happy."
Louis C.K.

When the American comedian Louis C.K. touched on the topic of new information and communication technology (ICT) in a talk show in 2009, he mentioned the great possibilities their use opens up. Many of our daily tasks can be dealt with quicker and easier than ever before in human history. The only drawback in all of this is that people are unable to appreciate it: the technological achievements in recent years are taken for granted. We are constantly complaining because we expect too much of the technologies and are then disappointed.

New information and communication technologies are increasingly pervading many areas of our everyday and working lives and we can no longer do without them (Hatzelhoffer et al. 2011a). The technological developments have opened up new ways of communicating and sharing information, which have an effect on time and space (Henckel 2011). At the same time, the use of new technologies has its limitations and can lead to frustration.

As we stroll through town taking not only our phones but also the Internet with us wherever we go, the new generation of cell phones have made it possible for us to be "phoneurs," rather than Walter Benjamin's (1982) flaneur.

Web-based map services such as Google Maps, Bing, or Google Street View provide new assistance for orientation and navigation around cities, with portals where we can read or write reviews about specific places. Furthermore, social networks such as Facebook, MySpace, and Google+ provide us with other options for face-to-face communication, telephoning, and worldwide networking.

These new tools—whether we regard them positively or negatively—also have certain limitations or can be a source of frustration because they affect user behavior. As we all know, cell phone conversations can suddenly be cut off on train journeys upon entering a tunnel or when leaving the city limits behind. It can also be irritating to be forced to listen to the private telephone conversations of fellow passengers in a crowded train compartment. The traditional understanding of the boundaries between the public and the private has been blurred by the use of ICT (Rauterberg 2001). Other spheres of everyday life that used to be clearly delineated also seem to be dissolving and recombining in new ways, if, for example the laptop on the sofa functions as a mobile office in the evening. And finally, one has to conclude that telephone conferences between continents can only partly replace face-to-face contact between colleagues or business partners and are complicated by different time zones.

louisck.cityandict.de

186
The subject of dealing with concerns related to the use of ICT is dealt with later in the book (chapter "Avoid Crash").

New possibilities and new limitations through the use of ICT

The quote at the beginning of this section underlines that technological innovations in themselves are not enough to bring about changes in our everyday lives or in society. What causes change is how new ICT are applied, the ways in which the technologies are incorporated actively into daily life, and how they can be used. After about five years of empirical research in T-City Friedrichshafen—with many interviews on the subject of new ICT usage—this chapter presents the correlation between the range of technological applications available and daily life in the city: how is ICT used and how does it affect everyday life? What expectations are there of the new technologies and to what extent are they met? What possibilities and limitations are perceived? And maybe the key question: who actually uses the new ICT, and indeed who is capable of using them?

For more about social change and ICT usage, see Hanson (2007)

Urban society—the interplay of urbanity and virtuality

The new ICT applications can affect how we live, work, consume, organize ourselves and obtain information. What is in fact the relationship between ICT and cities?

Cities—meaning the inherent characteristics and strengths of European cities—are regarded as places of transformation and change. Apart from the historical architectural forms, providing localized frameworks for the phenomenon of urbanity (Wüst 2004), people living in cities can also experience a virtual network that enables alternative forms of social exchange, companionship, and organization. The new applications that pervade and influence daily routines seem to change the way we live within the city and thereby the city itself (Hatzelhoffer et al. 2011a und 2011b).

While until the nineteen-nineties many academics who studied the subject of virtual and real space—such as the French philosopher Paul Virilio (1993)—stipulated that cities would dissolve because particular locations would lose their meaning through the superimposition of technology, nowadays this argumentation is obsolete. The anticipated effects didn't manifest themselves in our cities. Today, it is believed that the use of ICT, society, and the city influence each other mutually and that location and urban life do not become obsolete through the application of technology. In this context, Stefan Schmitz (2010) speaks of a "parallel urbanity," in which urbanity and virtuality complement and enhance each other. Crang, Crosbie, and Graham (2007) emphasize that physical and virtual space shouldn't be viewed as separate from or in opposition to each other, as our life in the city is produced and reproduced actively in daily routines with the incorporation of new ICT.

This short digression into the discourse about the correlation of ICT and cities shows that today the new technological applications are no longer regarded as a threat to cities. Instead, the application of technological solutions is seen as helping to overcome challenges that cities currently face and undoubtedly will face in future. This is why technological applications, which form a part of Smart City concepts or initiatives, are currently being tested around the world in the most wide-ranging spheres of life.

Such a concept was also implemented in Friedrichshafen with the T-City project. The primary objective of T-City—through the application of technological solutions to six project areas—was to demonstrate how the use of technology within the city can improve the quality of life and of the location and can increase the interconnection of urban society (Lobeck et al. 2009a, 2009c). The series of projects ranges from a telemedicine application that enables patients with heart disease to transmit their vital data to the hospital in charge, via an interactive educational platform with teaching materials made available online, to an intelligent electricity meter designed to enable better monitoring and management of electricity consumption.

The city vs. technologies?

016

More details about Smart City initiatives and schemes can be found in the chapter "Develop".

Apart from general questions about how the use of ICT affects our daily urban lives and the way we go about things, in this chapter we would also like to present how a Smart City, more specifically T-City, is perceived, focusing on what it means to live in a T-City. How do the inhabitants experience the T-City? What changes does the project bring about in the city and in the lives of people living in Friedrichshafen?

090
More details about the T-City project can be found in the chapter "Install".

Information and communication— what's new?

The applications and the technologies that they are based on have developed at a phenomenal rate over the last few decades. A whole host of brand new devices, infrastructures, and applications are available to us. Their social importance and their spatial significance could hardly be foreseen at the beginning of the nineteen-nineties (Lobeck et al. 2008).

These new technologies do, however, stem from preceding innovations. For example, the cell phone and the Internet developed from wired communication, such as the landline telephone. We have now arrived in the so-called digital age (Negroponte 1998), characterized among other things by the increasing digitalization of information and communication processes. Nowadays, more information is stored digitally than analogically, owing to ever greater storage capacities and the ever higher performance of communication networks, which now enable not only the transmission of speech and text, but also of pictures, films, and music. Furthermore, the ways in which technical devices and applications are interconnected with each other and with their environment have changed in recent years. They operate together increasingly automatically and adapt themselves intelligently to the individual modes of behavior and requirements of the users, which we have come to expect.

Whereas in the beginning the Internet could only be used from a fixed location, recently it is also advancing rapidly in its mobile form. The increasing number of W-LAN hotspots in Germany has contributed to this. These localized transmission networks located in hotels and cafés, or at airports and train stations, enable wireless Internet access for those with a transportable web-enabled terminal device. The further development of wireless transmission technologies and hardware has greatly widened the scope of mobile Internet usage. The tablet PCs and smartphones, which enable mobile Internet access and whose functions are increasingly comparable to those of a normal PC, have heralded a new era of Internet usage.

New possibilities regarding usage

There is a huge range of applications in the area of telecommunications that transform previous processes and procedures. Shopping, healthcare, education, and contacting the local government (Hatzelhoffer et al. 2010a) are just a few examples of areas in which new ICT is increasingly being used. The new ICT opens up three basic realms of usage (Lobeck et al. 2009b):

negroponte.cityandict.de

For more details and mathematical aspects of the development of digitalization, see Hilbert and López (2011)

Unilateral access to a wealth of information on the web
Since the World Wide Web was launched in 1993, the Internet has become a worldwide information system, in which wide-ranging and comprehensive information about current events in all spheres of life is provided often free of charge. Search engines such as Google have contributed significantly to users being able to navigate fairly easily through the vast array of information. In recent years, the Internet has become the largest library in the world.

Direct communication and the instant sharing of information between individual users
The Internet is a quick and cheap means of worldwide communication and of sharing information. This includes the transmission of simple text-based messages via E-mail, which in recent years has significantly transformed private and business communication and can already be considered a standard communication medium. Furthermore, it is possible to share data such as music, pictures, and videos. Other changes have resulted from being able to telephone cheaply via the Internet using Voice over IP (VoIP), which also led to the breakthrough of videophones.

The distribution and the sharing of content that users produce themselves and post on the Internet
The really new phenomenon regarding what is possible on the internet is "Web 2.0," also called "Social Web" (regarding the term: Kooptech 2008) with a multitude of blogs, wikis, and social networks such as Facebook, Google+, Twitter, Tumblr, or the VZ networks (StudiVZ and SchülerVZ). Owing to these, the network society (Castells 1996) has reached a new level of development. Web 2.0 enables a *"self-organized interaction and communication by users through the creation, sharing, and processing of user-based contents"* (Meckel 2008), opening up a new form of communication and affecting our social coexistence: anybody can be an author.

Thus, the new ICT leads to new ways of sharing information and of communicating and these new possibilities have an impact on space and time. Communication and sharing information are possible virtually anywhere and anytime. It is also referred to as being "always on," leading to new forms of coexistence, which can be perceived as either a blessing or a curse.

Who uses what?

The technological developments have changed the spread and the usage of the technologies, as well as their applications. According to the International Tele-communication Union (ITU), the number of Internet users increased worldwide by 12 percent in 2010 to 2.08 billion. This means that a good 30 percent of the world's population is online, whereby in industrial countries, the figure is 71 percent and in developing countries 21 percent of the population. If one takes a closer look at the worldwide distribution, one can see that for example 44 percent of all Internet users in the world are in Asia, about 23 percent in Europe, and 13 percent in North America. With more than 420 million people online, China has the greatest number compared to other countries. In Germany, around 80 percent of the population is now online, with further increases expected. Germany ranks seventh in Europe, so not quite at the top but higher than average.

The Internet boom could not be foreseen at the beginning of the nineteen-nineties. The broad dissemination and use of personal computers (PC) as part of the general computerization contributed to this. At the beginning of 2009, around 79 percent of all households in Germany had a PC, stationary or mobile. The PC is also of increasing importance in working life. In 2010, 61 percent of employees used a PC regularly in their jobs, as opposed to just 44 percent in 2003.

It is the use of mobile terminal devices, in particular, that has spread rapidly in recent years. While at the beginning of 2005 only 17 percent of households possessed a laptop, in 2009, it was already 40 percent. The use of cell phones was more of an exception at the beginning of the nineteen-nineties and was restricted to business relations. The situation is quite different today. With the introduction of digital wireless transmission in 1992, the decreasing costs of mobile telephony, and the enormous technical advancement of terminal devices, the use of cell phones has spread rapidly in Germany—especially since the end of the nineteen-nineties—and is now also fully established in the private domain. In the middle of 2006, the number of cell phone contracts already exceeded the number of inhabitants. In the meantime, smartphones and other mobile web-enabled terminal devices have reached the mass market.

At present 16.9 million Germans use the mobile Internet. 63 percent of the trend users, who constitute around 26 percent of the total population, take the opportunity to access the Internet from anywhere. At least 20 million people in Germany own a smartphone and the number of tablet PCs is also increasing. Moreover in Germany in 2010, the number of downloaded Apps increased by more than 112 percent compared to the previous year.

More figures relating to the use of technology: Initiative D21: (N)Onliner Atlas 2011

80%
percent of Germany's population is online.

The figures are taken from studies by Bitkom and the National Statistical Agency.

Germany goes mobile.

The figures in these sections are taken from the National Statistical Agency, the D21 Initiative, the newspaper *Süddeutsche Zeitung*, and various Bitkom studies.

136

The Digital Divide—
gaps are opening up

However, what do these figures relating to the incredibly rapid development and spread of new ICT really tell us? What is certain is that the technologies pervade wide areas of our society. On the other hand, as the quote from Gunter Dueck (former Chief Technical Officer at IBM Germany) highlights, the Internet has not yet completely infiltrated our society. Free and ubiquitous Internet access is not yet available in Germany, nor is there an infrastructure that covers all regions and social areas and could therefore function as a *"social operating system"* (Dueck 2011). The number of users may be increasing, but upon closer inspection a differentiated picture presents itself: far from everyone has the possibility or the ability to use what is theoretically available.

This is referred to as the Digital Divide. It signifies the inequality between different groups with regard to access to and opportunities to use the new technologies and to what extent they shape their daily lives, which in turn has an impact on their social opportunities and social coexistence. This divide can apply to countries on a global level or on a smaller scale to different regions, city districts, households, or individuals, according to certain demographic aspects such as age, sex, or income. Therefore, it is debatable to what extent the new ICT can in fact infiltrate our society and act as a *"social operating system."*

Regarding computer usage, a study by Bitkom drew attention to a Digital Divide within Germany according to sex, age, and level of education. The representative surveys in Friedrichshafen, carried out annually over the last five years, also reflect a Digital Divide referring to different levels of ICT usage by women and men: women are clearly more skeptical towards the new technologies than men and use them less. A similar Digital Divide can be discerned in relation to age. While among those surveyed over the years, there was an increase in the number of Internet connections for those aged between 50 and 65, it is still a smaller number than in the younger age groups, which increasingly take Internet usage for granted and consider it an important feature of daily life. While this younger age group, up to age 29, views ICT as something normal and habitual, those over 66 in particular were less familiar with the new technologies. Their opinion regarding the usefulness and significance of ICT in relation to the quality of life is thus noticeably more reserved.

gunterdueck.cityandict.de

More details regarding the Digital Divide: Crang et al. (2006) and Kubicek/Welling (2000)

The Digital Divide runs through Germany …

… and Friedrichshafen.

What the results of the survey reveal is reflected in a more differentiated way in the qualitative interviews carried out with people living in Friedrichshafen. A Digital Divide was evident in relation to sex and age. Furthermore the social divide—in terms of education, income, and the ability to use ICT—was considered an important issue by our interview partners.

The structure of the T-City accompanying research

The work group Urbanism and Regional Science at the Department of Geography of the University of Bonn conducted scientific research during the five-year T-City project. The purpose of the accompanying research was to evaluate the three project objectives:

— to raise the quality of life for the citizens
— to improve the locational advantages for businesses
— to increase networking between the
participating partners in the urban society.

The accompanying research was divided into the two areas of *impact research* (what did the project achieve?) and *procedural research* (how was it achieved?). Both the overall project and selected individual sub-projects were evaluated applying a combination of qualitative and quantitative methods.

The purpose of the *impact research* was to find out whether and to what extent the T-City project affected the quality of life of the inhabitants and the locational advantages for the local businesses.

The impact on the *quality of life* was analyzed by a research panel by means of qualitative and guided interviews. The term "quality of life" is understood as a subjectively perceived concept in this case. Four surveys were carried out at yearly intervals, each comprising interviews with up to thirty people living in Friedrichshafen. Subsequently they were transcribed and evaluated according to an open coding system supported by theory. The interview partners were specifically selected according to age, sex, and nationality. By interviewing the same people at yearly intervals, the development of experiences and perceptions of the project could be tracked as the project unfolded.

In addition to the research panel, one particular group of citizens, the "Futurists", was also studied by means of qualitative and guided interviews. The participating households in this group had been equipped with various technological solutions and were part of numerous T-City projects. This initiative provided insights into their experiences and evaluations of the implementation and usage of new technologies in everyday life, by means of seven waves of qualitative interviews with thirty-one discussion partners in eleven households.

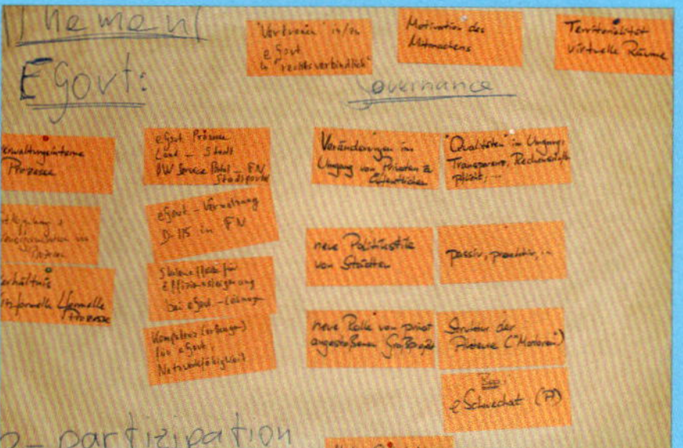

The qualitative interviews were supported by a representative telephone survey in the form of a standardized questionnaire, carried out annually from 2007. This involved randomly selecting a thousand people living in Friedrichshafen, aged fourteen and upwards. At the same time, the research team carried out a parallel survey of comparative groups, comprised of a representative selection of five hundred people from all other German cities with a population of 25,000 to 100,000.

The impact on the *locational advantages* for businesses was analyzed similarly, with a mixture of qualitative interviews and quantitative surveys.

The *procedural research*, on the other hand, was carried out differently. The purpose of this research was to evaluate how Deutsche Telekom and the city of Friedrichshafen interacted with each other, how local projects were developed and implemented as a cooperation between various partners, how the project and its products were conveyed to their users, and how the project was communicated externally. In this context, around 250 qualitative interviews were carried out over the course of the project with the responsible partners in the city of Friedrichshafen and at Deutsche Telekom, as well as with a wide circle of participants from the administration, city council, committees, press, and other experts who were directly or indirectly involved with the project.

In addition to the interviews and surveys involving citizens and business representatives, the local press coverage, the minutes of the local council meetings, and the public relations work of the project were continuously assessed. This was supplemented by participatory observations of committee meetings and observations regarding the usage of ICT in the public sphere.

Finally, the following six individual sub-projects from different project areas were studied:

— "Kindergarten Online" from the project area "Citizen, City and State"
— "Mobile Clinic," "Tumor Conference," and "Independent Living" from the project area "Healthcare and Social Services"
— "Smart Metering" from the project area "Business and Work"
— "Edunex" from the project area "Education and Research"

The overall project and individual sub-projects were observed and analyzed as longitudinal studies over the course of the project. Four specialist conferences with professionals in the relevant fields were held to discuss the results of the research. In the conference titled "e-motion," the general relationship between urban development and ICT, as well as the project's objectives and the status of its implementation in Friedrichshafen were discussed with experts in the theory and practice of these fields. The accompanying research was also supported by an interdisciplinary network of experts in various specialist disciplines.

e-motion.cityandict.de

Differences between women and men

Women often consider themselves less competent in the use of ICT and men also tend to not credit women with as much competence in this area. Presumably, the specific gender roles that still exist in Germany play a part in this. Some women state that they struggle with technology and turn to their brothers, boyfriends, or husbands for help, who in their view can handle technology better and with greater ease. The reluctance to use technology is caused by a lack of knowledge about the application and operation of technology. In the interviews, it was almost exclusively women who mentioned this reluctance.

Apart from the divide according to sex, one can also ascertain a divide according to age. Especially older women consider their technological competence to be very low and are dependent on assistance. An older female interviewee said on this subject: *"… and I myself never bothered about technology, because I always had men around me […] I'm not familiar with all the functions on my telephone. I can only telephone and reply to calls, that's all."* However, the younger female interviewees also mention the discrepancy in user competence between women and men. One of the younger female discussion partners said that she can only use the Internet to obtain information and to communicate via E-mail. Beyond that, she has to resort to assistance: *"I can't do it. My brother has to help me out. Well, sometimes I do watch films and stuff on the Internet. But I wouldn't know how to set it up."* While one female interviewee remarked that she prefers to rely on her husband's help, *"I suppose I could have attended a course, but I had my husband at home,"* others reported that they taught themselves how to use technology or attended a course.

Apart from the discrepancies in user competences, it also emerged that women use technology in a different way and for different purposes. One female interviewee said on this subject: *"Yes, for us women it has to be something specific and meaningful, rather than clicking and surfing around, sometimes perhaps ending up on something and flitting around here and there. It has to be targeted: what am I looking for and how do I get there?"*

The interviews reveal that women often adhere to a targeted use of technology. Especially among young people, girls use the technologies less for games and more for communication purposes, compared to boys.

Women and men

Unless otherwise indicated, the quotes that follow in this chapter are statements made by interview partners.

See also: Morley (2000)

Differences between
Germans and migrants

There doesn't appear to be a Digital Divide based on the migrant background of the interviewees, in terms of the intensity and frequency of usage. The people we interviewed who have a migrant background use the technologies widely and merely report an age divide among fellow migrants.

According to some people with a migrant background, the language barrier makes ICT usage more difficult for some of the more inexperienced users, as the software products available in Germany or German websites generally have default settings in the German language. One female interviewee remarked on this: *"His daughter in Turkey has an Internet connection with a webcam [...] while they live here and he and his wife just want to see their grandson and their daughter, too. It's all possible via webcam, you just push a couple of buttons and then it works. But it doesn't work for him to write an E-mail [...] The programs are all in German."* A female kindergarten teacher states that parents with a migrant background often have problems registering their child using the standard procedure via a German webpage. They often don't have sufficient knowledge of German to fill in the forms. The teacher helps the parents by carrying out a personal registration at the kindergarten, in order to work around the language barrier more efficiently.

Migrant backgrounds

Differences between
young and old

The Digital Divide with regard to age doesn't apply only to senior citizens, but also to middle-aged people. Their knowledge and usage of media is limited compared to the younger age groups. Younger people in particular ascribe less ICT competence to the older generation, but they themselves also consider their ability to adopt and use technologies to be limited.

"It's no good to me that it's available, I don't understand it anyway. Especially for older people who don't really engage with it, most of the information available isn't very comprehensible," reports an older gentleman. Many older interviewees stated that they are by all means willing to use new technologies, but that in many cases learning the application—which comes much easier to the younger generation—is difficult for people who are more advanced in years. Older people lack practice in handling ICT, and help provided by younger people is often insufficient or difficult to follow. According to a middle-aged housewife: *"... the young people know a lot, but they mostly show you too quickly, they grew up with it."*

Young and old

The various age groups also differ with regard to the usage of individual applications. It was primarily younger users who said that they use chat forums. Out of the five interviewees over the age of sixty, only one uses this application. On the other hand many of the older people interviewed have a cell phone for emergency situations, with its use restricted in most cases to the telephone function.

Some of the older interviewees feel limited in their daily lives because of their lesser knowledge and use of ICT, since a certain level of competence in the use of ICT is widely assumed. For example, they feel excluded from communication processes in their personal sphere, or else these are only possible with difficulty. An older gentleman said: *"… but as long as we aren't connected to the Internet we can't send anything. It has become apparent that other people communicate almost exclusively by E-mail and they send photos, etc. We are the only people in the chain who haven't got it."* The younger interviewees are also aware of this gap in the means of communication with respect to older people and they have to avoid certain communication media and resort to "traditional" ones. A middle-aged gentleman commented on the possibilities of video telephony: *"The only use I might have for it would perhaps be to connect with my relatives, whom I haven't seen for a long time. But the other problem is that they don't know how to use it […] Well, it's really mostly about my aunts and uncles, who are already quite elderly, therefore it is not an option."*

Furthermore, older people can perceive it as annoying to have to learn from younger people and to admit to their limitations with regard to using technology. One female interviewee saw this as the loss of the authority of age and reacted with a reluctant attitude accordingly: *"Somehow I didn't want to have anything to do with it […] There were the young ones, they could already do it all and I was supposed to be above them as their senior. I was quite frankly disgusted that I had to listen to these young whippersnappers."*

Once the Digital Divide had been partly overcome and certain technologies adopted, many of the older interviewees spoke in positive terms about the possibilities they open up. According to the motto that practice makes perfect, one female interviewee described how easily and cheaply she can now communicate with her daughter who lives in the Netherlands. Another female interviewee tells of an elderly lady she met on her computer course. Regarding the advantages of using ICT to support restricted mobility later in life she said: *"She also has a computer, because she said she doesn't get out and about much these days, so it helps her to communicate with others and in a sense bring them into the home […] She says that it makes her feel like she is part of the world, she's also in contact with people in lots of countries, I think that's great."*

Trying out fosters enthusiasm

144

Always on— global on location

As already mentioned in the first sections of this chapter, the usage of new ICT has an impact on aspects of space and time in our everyday lives. It influences how we perceive time, construct space, and experience distances. In relation to this, overcoming distances and the independence of location are often mentioned as a consequence of the new information and communication applications. Using ICT leads to a new independence of location and in a social context it changes the role of co-presence, meaning communication at the same time in the same place, as described by Christian Stegbauer (2008). While exchanges with conversation partners all over the world or access to spatially independent information sources used to be much more limited or else restricted to one's residence, place of work or even a temporary location such as a café or a hotel, today access to information is increasingly global and also mobile.

Impact on the spatiotemporal dimensions of everyday life

"Always present" anywhere in the world

In the qualitative discussions with citizens in Friedrichshafen, the phenomenon of ICT usage creating a networked space covering great distances was often mentioned. The multitude of communication media—whether E-mail, Internet telephony, or social media—make it possible to stay in contact on a personal level with relatives and friends or on a business level with colleagues and business partners who don't live or work in the immediate vicinity. Global communication through new media is perceived as easier and also cheaper.

Globally networked space

For many interviewees, whose friends or relatives live abroad, ICT enables them to take part in the lives of others, creating a sense of proximity despite the distance between them. An interviewee from Italy says that owing to the new media he is "always up to date" with his family in Italy. For example, he is regularly sent photos of his niece's children, which gives him the feeling of *"always being present."* A female interviewee, who is in contact with many friends abroad via Facebook, explains that it enables her to *"take part in their lives."*

In this regard, the visual options of VoIP usage with a webcam play an especially important role, apart from communication via text and speech. One interviewee said: *"One of my acquaintances' sons went back to Italy. And she speaks to them nearly every day via the computer. They can see each other. Her children's children showed her the whole apartment through the laptop. That's great."* A female interviewee, whose family lives in Romania, explained that it is important to her that with Internet telephony and a webcam it is possible to see each other, with facial expressions and gestures. This makes the contact more personal and less anonymous.

Many discussion partners find that using ICT links places that are geographically far apart. It creates a mentally constructed interconnected space. Some interviewees have the feeling that it reduces or even dissolves distances. One interviewee explained that the world has become smaller in recent years because of the new technologies. He went on to say that he can now even read the newspaper *Schwäbische Zeitung* online when he is at home in Italy, enabling him to follow what is happening at Lake Constance when he is away.

Embedded in a local context

Despite the independence of location and global interconnection, it becomes clear in the interviews that the use of ICT also has a local dimension and is inextricably entwined with the circumstances of local daily life. Technical issues, individual daily routines, and local or global relationships that might operate in different time zones are not all detached from the respective location and the way daily life unfolds there. The interviews reveal interesting intersections between local technology usage, overcoming distance and time gaps, and locally ingrained ways of operating, which bring about (new) routines and strategies in the organization of everyday life.

Global as well as local networks are not completely detached from one's current or former place of residence or whereabouts. In most cases, ICT is used for communicating with relatives or friends who have moved away or maybe even still live in Friedrichshafen or the area. Many discussion partners also reported that new ICT makes it possible to maintain contact with people they met abroad, who were visiting Friedrichshafen, or who no longer live in the immediate vicinity. One female interviewee told how she communicates with friends — in Sweden, Hungary, Italy, France, and Switzerland — whom she met when they were trainees in Friedrichshafen and who still regularly visit Lake Constance. The interviewees rarely mention longer-term communication with people they met in "virtual space." In most cases, these are not so much personal contacts as a sharing of specific in-

Regarding the local integration of ICT usage in neighborhoods: Hampton/Wellman (2003) and Crang et al. (2007)

formation or exchanges of expert knowledge in special forums. For example, one interviewee regularly visits an English language forum on the subject of fishkeeping, where he receives valuable advice and tips. This type of communication and interconnection via the web provides a new opportunity to access knowledge and experiences that are not available locally in Friedrichshafen.

It is noticeable that some interviewees use the new ICT extensively to communicate with friends or relatives who live in the neighborhood or in the immediate vicinity. One female interviewee chats after work in the evening with her friends who live in the same city district, because she doesn't feel like leaving the house. It makes her feel less alone. Another interviewee reports that in the evenings he doesn't feel like telephoning friends, because he has to make a lot of phone calls during the day in his job. Therefore, he also prefers to chat about the day via chat.

These patterns of behavior show that the use of ICT is bound up with our individual daily habits and can be strongly bound up with local circumstances. Furthermore, with the various ICT applications, one has the choice of using them whenever it's suitable. One interviewee said: *"I like writing E-mails at midnight or one o'clock in the morning, as I simply work through my to-do list."* The advantages and disadvantages of synchronized (e.g., telephoning) and unsynchronized (e.g., E-mail) communication are raised by many interviewees. One female interviewee said that she always uses the telephone to deal with spontaneous matters that have to be resolved quickly, since an E-mail may not be read in time. Another interviewee prefers online chatting, because telephoning would take up more time. Furthermore, he can see who is online and available at that moment. The users who mention the differences between the various media apparently use these in a very targeted fashion, according to the situation, the purpose, or whom they are communicating with.

The new media are also used for organizing regular local activities with friends or acquaintances. Many interviewees use E-mails, SMS, or chat forums to arrange meetings with several friends or within clubs or societies. Even if this is sometimes seen as a complicated procedure, it helps with setting up appointments, sharing information, or arranging meeting places. The sourcing of information— apart from gathering information for presentations, recipes, etc.—has a strongly local dimension. Most interviewees source information on the Internet for activities within the city, whether it is a cinema program, reviews of certain localities, or finding directions. This applies to people who have a smartphone and increasingly have a mobile connection while in the city. Information from the interviewees was also transmitted via the new media. Apart from posting event dates, some interviewees also wrote reviews of places they had visited, posted event notifications online, modified groups on certain platforms, or tweeted. For most interviewees, the active posting or circulation of information was restricted to a small circle of people, comprised of friends or acquaintances.

Communication within close social circles

Using ICT as and when it suits you.

Organizing local daily activities

Apart from the local aspect of ICT usage in terms of communication, organization, and information, usage is also perceived as locally bound and globally restricted because of the tariff structures and policies of the telecommunications providers. Many interviewees report that they restrict their ICT usage as soon as they cross regional borders on holiday or on business trips: *"... and then perhaps there is the negative aspect of traveling abroad. It really is unbelievable, as soon as you enter Switzerland [...] and then there is a great risk, actually you should switch the device off, otherwise you get your bill and the cost of your holiday has doubled [...] Communication ought to have fewer boundaries."* Especially the location of Friedrichshafen in the tri-border region, with the frequent crossing of national boundaries, has led many interviewees to experience this limitation with regard to ICT usage. It has made them realize that unlimited mobility, overcoming distances, and independence of location—which they are able to experience in many situations through the use of ICT—can also become an illusion in relation to the reality of a city close to national borders.

Locally bound, globally restricted: tariff structures for ICT usage

Competing with the city?

Thus, the new ICT usage has a wide and ambivalent impact on our perception and construction of (urban) space. The sections above have shown that among the interviewees, the ICT applications lead neither to the complete irrelevance of distance nor to the structuring of daily life in a way that is completely independent of location. While many discussion partners perceive the use of new media as extending their options within the city, others view the new technologies as competing with the city. Many people do not consider the new communication options as a replacement for co-presence. In terms of worldwide and also local communication, the use of technology serves to maintain contacts and arrange or prepare personal meetings. One interviewee observed, for example, that it is sufficient to communicate with acquaintances or friends by E-mail for long stretches of time. However, it is then necessary to meet again personally after a while, to maintain the closeness and the friendship, since the devices are not a replacement for face-to-face contact and feelings. Many interview partners emphasize that the new means of communication do not replace personal contact, as everyone still has the option of meeting face-to-face, too. The use of ICT is viewed more as facilitating communication and as complementing personal meetings. One female interviewee highlights this and explained that "traditional" means of communication such as letters are also not seen as a threat to face-to-face meetings: *"But E-mails do not replace personal contact, meaning face-to-face contact […] Letters don't replace personal contact either, do they?"* Another interviewee emphasized the free choice of the user in this respect: *"I think that they [personal contact and the use of technology] complement each other. And I think it is a question of individual personality and choice. I have said it on many occasions: I decide how to do things. I am not controlled by technology, it is still me who controls technology."* While the use of ICT is regarded as an extension of—and not a replacement for—personal communication, there are also those who are concerned that it leads to a decrease in face-to-face contact. Such concerns are often in relation to young people and children, who are growing up with the technologies and spend a lot of time with them.

The reduction or the increase of face-to-face contact through the use of new media is discussed widely in specialist literature (Boden and Molotch 2004). These issues were mentioned in the discussions in Friedrichshafen, but the daily reality of most of the interviewees is characterized by a complex mixture of virtual communication and personal meetings. ICT serves as a means of preparing or planning personal meetings: *"I really try to maintain the personal relationship. It is perfect for making some quick arrangements or plans to meet up."* The use of mobile media makes it easier to meet spontaneously or to confer en route in case of unforeseen circumstances: *"… because people can get in touch quicker, of course. You are out somewhere and realize that certain people might be able to join you, for example, and you can arrange it via SMS or a call on the cell phone."*

"Of course, it can't replace personal contact, that's for sure, but it doesn't even try to."

Apart from arranging personal meetings, the new media also serve the purpose of following up on personal meetings or of reminders—for example, the sharing of photographs of get-togethers after the event via E-mail or social networks. A further way media support face-to-face contact is mentioned in the interviews as the "rediscovery" of old friends or relatives via the web. Many interviewees reported that they had found old school friends, acquaintances, or relatives again via the Internet, which led to face-to-face meetings.

"... with friends, when we've arranged to meet in town and something comes up, then we use the cell phone, spontaneously."

In the discussions, there is no evidence of a decrease in activities in the city through the use of the new ICT. While functions such as Internet shopping and online banking are made use of, all interview partners emphasize that these usages do not replace visiting the city and experiencing its atmosphere. Some interview partners report that Internet shopping fills a gap regarding the limitations of what is available in Friedrichshafen. Nevertheless, they undertake regular trips to Ravensburg or Stuttgart. After all, some people say, the Internet doesn't offer tactile experiences; instead, it allows shoppers to compare prices and products. Certain items, such as electronic goods or books, are ordered online by the interviewees, while they consider it necessary to buy other items—such as clothing that has to be tried on—in "traditional" shops. Mobile devices are used for assistance in traditional shops: for comparing prices, checking shopping lists, or consulting recipe suggestions online. Apart from satisfying one's tactile senses in a shop in the city, many interview partners also consider the personal contact with the seller or the bank employee to be important.

"In the end we are people who prefer to get our hands on things."

The significance of the city as a place for meeting people and as a place for experiencing a particular atmosphere is also reflected by the organization of leisure time. Many people use the new ICT as leisure-time entertainment. However, according to the interviewees, spending leisure time at particular spots in the city—such as in a café, on the promenade, in a museum or outside of the city in the mountains—can't be replaced by the use of new media; at best it can complement these experiences. One interviewee mentioned that rather than traveling to a particular trade fair he can gather sufficient information on an Internet blog instead. In the majority of discussions, however, it is evident that the interviewees enjoy leaving their media-dominated daily lives for a couple of hours to visit places in or outside of the city during their leisure time.

New combinations, new places, new freedoms

The new ICT applications pervade many areas of our everyday lives and, in relation to "real life," are seen either as complementary, supporting, or competing. So much is possible anywhere and anytime these days. The new technologies that are available are incorporated into certain areas of our life. As a consequence of this, media are used in new ways in our daily routines, altering our spatiotemporal patterns of experience. This leads to new combinations of hitherto distinctive and separate spheres in the structure of daily life, mentioned in the interviews in Friedrichshafen.

Firstly, we have new ways of doing things in daily life. Whether it is online banking, with certain tasks being dealt with from home instead of at the bank, or *"dead space time"* (Crang, Crosbie and Graham 2006) being filled with new applications. It was mentioned in the interviews, for example, that while waiting for a bus one can deal with a couple of outstanding telephone calls. Habitual activities are combined or merged with new activities.

Secondly new areas of usage are opened up. Up until the emergence and increasing spread of mobile terminal devices, the use of media was restricted to fixed locations: *"For me personally, it is an advantage that I can be mobile. Before I only had Internet at home. There was a computer in a fixed place, from which one could access the Internet. Now I've always got my laptop with me."* The big advantage of a smartphone, according to another interviewee, is its bundling of many applications and functions and the greater mobility it offers. This enables the brief checking of E-mails when on the move and communication via Skype. When out and about in the city, one can also access information about certain places or use the navigation system. The interviewees become aware of the limitations of mobile usage as soon as they leave the city limits behind. There are reports of frequent network interruptions on trains or of the rather poor connectivity in the more rural areas outside of Friedrichshafen. However, in the city ICT is used in a wide range of places — whether in open spaces, cafés, restaurants, schools, at the university, or on public transport. While many people we talked to enjoy the freedom this mobile usage brings, others are annoyed or disturbed by it. One female interviewee mentions a train journey during which she was forced to listen to the *"empty"* conversations of a fellow passenger, which bothered her. Another female discussion partner talks about the use of cell phones in public places: *"Well, it even happened to us in church. Everywhere. And I find it unacceptable. Or when I go out for a meal, I think there really ought to be a cell phone restriction there. One wishes to be able to eat in peace."*

Furthermore, whole areas of life converge in places that were previously used for just one purpose, for example with the café used as an office during the daytime or the living room doubling as an office in the evening. Two groups emerge regarding the question of the separation or the merging of professional and private spheres when using ICT. The "mergers" are generally frequent users, who find it

Everyday processes and activities are dealt with differently.

New areas of technology usage

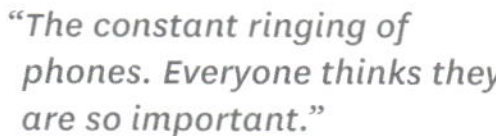

"The constant ringing of phones. Everyone thinks they are so important."

too tedious to run separate accounts or telephone connections. Furthermore, they enjoy the freedom of mobile working and combine the private and the professional as regards time and space. One interviewee explained: *"With my BlackBerry, for instance, I have the freedom to simply leave the office sometimes. To sit down by the lake and go for a coffee with friends. And if something urgent comes up I can get back to the office quickly. That's what I call freedom."*

Separation or merging of professional and private spheres.

The "separators" want to avoid their professional lives infringing on their private sphere. One female interviewee emphasized that she maintains a strict separation between her private life and working life as regards ICT usage. In her case, she finds dividing these two spheres between two different cities helpful. She considers Friedrichshafen exclusively as her place of residence and base for leisure activities, while Ravensburg is her place of work. She also emphasized that she doesn't want to work on the train using a mobile device, but prefers to use this interim period to relax and switch off. A third group is formed by people who would like to merge the two spheres—e. g., by using mobile communications or in the form of a home office—but are unable to do so because of company policy regarding data security or because the workplace is poorly equipped in terms of ICT. This leads to some interviewees using ICT to quite different extents in their private and professional lives.

A related point that came up in the interviews is the combination of spontaneity, speed, the immediate accessibility of other people and of information, and one's own availability, which affects how we go about daily life. This combination of attributes creates, on the one hand, the feeling of having more options in different spheres of life, but on the other hand it also causes a certain feeling of pressure. Anybody can be reached quickly at any time, be sent a message and receive messages. It is possible to access a wealth of information immediately and the costs are considered reasonable.

This combination of features that many interview partners experience on a daily basis through the use of ICT can be referred to as spatial, temporal and social ubiquitousness. It leads to new freedoms, but also to new dependences and sometimes also to a feeling of being overloaded. The freedoms are self-evident and can contribute to a feeling of security. One female interviewee said with regard to this: *"We've always got a cell phone with us and so we can always be reached. Especially as we also have children who don't always come with us anymore and are then at home."*

The dependences and feeling overloaded are created by the expectation, which has become the social norm, of immediate availability and prompt reactions. One interview partner says that he feels the pressure of other people's expectation that they should always be able to reach him and for him to always have to reply. Because of the resulting stress, he tries to take control and to take some time out from being available. These reactions are shared by many interviewees, even if for some, taking time out only refers to going away on holiday. Apart from the expectation of being "always on," many interview partners point to the wealth of information that is always available to them as a further reason for feeling overloaded. One female interviewee said: *"These new media expect people to more or less carve themselves up. One has to be present everywhere, one has to know everything, it is assumed that one can do anything."* When using new media, the pressure and overloading caused by expectations can cause unease. The ubiquitousness and the "anytime and anywhere" that is supposed to make things quicker and easier can become an illusion: *"I do make an effort to somehow do things quicker [...] It's always about that. Does it in fact make things faster or is something left behind in the process? [...] Everything has to go faster all the time, one has to answer quicker and write quicker."*

"... that is the most difficult thing, being besieged by information and not knowing what's really important and what isn't."

COLUMBIA
PICTURES
Sony.Com/Spider-Man
ROCA
MTV
LIVE
LIVE
SUNDAY
JUNE 3
8PM/7c
the mtv
SPELLING BEE

154

Networking—
the invisible city

So far, we have portrayed how the inhabitants of Friedrichshafen actively incorporate new ICT into their daily lives and how its use affects everyday life. Apart from the limits and frustrations regarding the use of ICT, the citizens also experience new ways of facilitating, complementing or adapting their day-to-day tasks. In the following sections, we will shift the focus onto the T-City project and consider what new opportunities the project opened up in the city and to what extent it met the ambitious objectives: raising the quality of life and of the location and increasing the interconnection of urban society through the use of ICT. With regard to this, it is of course interesting to know how the project was implemented within the city and what opportunities and challenges presented themselves to T-City as the project unfolded. It is especially important to consider the inhabitants and how they perceive and experience T-City. Ultimately, it is the citizens who reside in the Smart City and actively bring it to life.

When analyzing the implementation of ICT in the context of Smart Cities and probing into how these technological applications change life in the city, it is noticeable that ICT is virtually invisible in the urban space (Hatzelhoffer et al. 2011b). The mobile terminal devices, although they are in many cases a status symbol, appear inconspicuously small in the urban environment. In contrast to the previous urban infrastructures and networks, the new infrastructural elements are hardly visible. The small constructional changes in the form of switch boxes or transmission masts hardly alter the appearance of cities and don't fundamentally challenge the urban landscape, even if they are sometimes complained about in building culture discussions as blemishes.

Other material manifestations of ICT primarily have functions that support the usage of the new media. Owing to the short innovation cycle of ICT and the corresponding rapidly changing ways of using them, the construction elements don't have a long-term impact on the urban image. The mobile terminal devices have made services such as telephone booths, and Internet cafés—which are at fixed locations in the city—almost obsolete. Instead, there are now other visible signs of mobile ICT usage: on the walls of cafés, on shop windows, on advertising posters, and on other surfaces, one can increasingly see QR codes and indicators of where free WLAN is available or where the use of cell phones is prohibited. This signage is perhaps the most conspicuous indication that new technologies influence our daily lives in the city, along with the actual use of ICT that we can observe on a daily basis in cafés, in public spaces, in parks, or when circulating through the city.

The low visibility of ICT also has an influence on the attention it is paid by the local population. To put it pointedly, the T-City project has visible and tangible competition within the city, which can present a challenge to the public perception of the project: while anyone strolling along the promenade in Friedrichshafen can gaze at the lake and the mountains and feel a unique atmosphere there, the T-City is barely visible and perceivable within the city.

The virtually invisible ICT are the basic foundation of Smart City projects.

066

The chapter "Install" deals in more detail with the challenges faced by the incorporation of T-City into the city.

T-City—what does it have in store for us?

In the first interviews that were carried out at the end of 2007 and the beginning of 2008, at a time when the contest had been won and the T-City had already been partially installed, many expectations with regard to the future ideas for the T-City project were raised. One interviewee described his expectations as follows: *"... simply that more people become acquainted with technology, that they have relatively cheap and easy access to the Internet. And very quick. Even in the hinterland."* Another female interviewee hopes that with T-City more people with limited access to ICT usage will be supported by the project. The majority of expectations are directed towards the development of the infrastructure and quicker access to the Internet. Others emphasize the wider range of day-to-day options that T-City promises: *"... and people just come along with their laptops and plonk themselves down, in a café around the corner that has a pleasant atmosphere [...] When I think about Friedrichshafen as a T-City, it would have to be at least how I've just described. At the very least."*

In the discussions, it was clear that the interview partners have expectations and ideas with regard to the T-City project, but very little concrete knowledge about it. There was talk of new usage opportunities for the people in Friedrichshafen, but they were unclear about what they really entail.

The interviewees feel largely uninformed about planned and concrete contents of potential individual sub-projects or solutions for the various areas of urban life. Overall many interviewees have a positive basic impression, but the discussions revealed that on many levels, the inhabitants of Friedrichshafen would like to have more concrete information: *"We simply still know too little. Partly because we are told too little. The information fluctuates [...] and that makes me feel even more uncertain, it makes me even more cautious and to want to say no, no, thank you, hang on a moment."*

The only thing that is perceived as a visible and tangible change is the development of the infrastructure. Many interview partners reported at that time, but also retrospectively, about the (visible) road works during the infrastructure development, which didn't spare the sidewalks or in some cases even private land. Some inhabitants say that they didn't feel prepared for this and that there was a lack of information and transparency regarding the building work. One female interviewee said: *"At the time, we had the impression that what was being complained about was the building sites where the networks were being laid."* Many interviewees were aware that the building work was a necessary evil. Some of those who felt poorly informed were indignant though: *"Especially because we were wrongly informed, or because we weren't informed at all, and now it is costing a fortune [...] Perhaps all you can see in Friedrichshafen now is building sites, sixty masts are supposed to be erected. I don't think much of it at all."*

"If I've got a laptop, for example, I can sit by the lakeshore and enjoy the view... maybe a second or third person will join me and then one has an open-air office.... Yes, of course, these are ideas for the future."

186
Regarding concerns about the transmission masts, see the chapter "Avoid Crash"

The discussions reveal that expectations of the project were quite high after the long-drawn-out application phase and during the ensuing quiet phase while the framework agreement was being negotiated. During the first phase, however, the interviewees were lacking information and clarity about what was going to happen next. One female interviewee expressed her skepticism, seeing the lack of information as a threat to the realization of the project, even though she welcomes T-City in itself:

"What is happening here is practically unique. It is a great opportunity for Friedrichshafen [...] But a large company like Telekom also has to consider that they can't allow it to go belly-up now. Because if a project like this flops, it damages one's public image in the media. And it is well on its way to doing just that. I mean, I have to think of the people, of the majority of people [...] who have to take it all on board. The whole thing is too impersonal [...] What the people want to know is whether they have a connection when they pick up the receiver and whether they have access to the Internet. Whether they can perhaps have a video conference with their granddaughter sometime."

She emphasized that T-City has to appeal to the people in Friedrichshafen and to benefit them in some way. She explains that the usefulness of ICT applications has to be actively experienced by the inhabitants.

158

Participation— a difficult process

While over the years, awareness of the T-City was raised and the attention of experts in the field was increasingly drawn to the project, with more and more delegations from all over the world visiting the T-City, the level of awareness among the inhabitants of Friedrichshafen also increased and reached a high level as the project went on. In 2007 only 38 percent of inhabitants had heard of T-City, in 2012 it was 86 percent. At the beginning of the T-City project, it was especially the middle-aged and older age groups who were aware of the project. By 2012, there were hardly any differences in awareness between the different age groups. However, outside of Friedrichshafen awareness of the project is very low. In 2012, only five percent of the national representative population sample had heard of T-City.

As T-City unfolded many individual sub-projects were implemented and many public relations activities were carried out. As the figures show, these increased the awareness of the project. However, the results of the qualitative interviews show clearly that the content of the T-City project remained largely elusive for the interview partners even after the initial phase. Both the overall idea and the primary objectives and the concretely implemented solutions remained unclear for many inhabitants or else they only had vague knowledge and expectations. As one female interviewee from Friedrichshafen said in 2009, *"People know that we are the T-City, but they don't know what it means or what projects there are."*

The interviews over the years showed that T-City was for a long time associated with the development of the infrastructure. The results of the quantitative survey also point to the fact that no individual project was the main association with T-City in 2011. In an open survey, it was the infrastructure that was named most often as the "T-City project." Furthermore, there were often vague perceptions and no concrete knowledge of the individual projects. While some interview partners could name an increasing number of projects as time went on, many of them could only think of projects when asked specific questions, without being able to name them and without being clear about their exact content or purpose. Often, it was only activities in areas such as healthcare or school that were mentioned.

Information through advertising?

All interview partners report that they read about T-City in newspapers, received information leaflets, saw information stands, or heard of events, such as the visit of the Federal Chancellor. Despite all of this, most of the content of T-City or of the individual projects remained elusive or abstract. Several interviewees said that the lack of knowledge of many inhabitants is a result of the abstractness of the technologies, whose purpose is not immediately obvious and which form the basis of T-City. Content related to technologies is difficult to convey textually, pictorially, or linguistically and can only be appreciated by being actively used: *"But I think that it is simply because people just don't know what they are supposed to use it for later."* Those who don't have the necessary imagination or knowledge or are

86 %
of the Friedrichshafen population
have heard of T-City

105
More about public relations activities
in the chapter "Install"

"We get a newsletter and also other important information via e-mail. That's how I became aware of it [...] Apart from that, after a while I didn't hear anything else about T-City. Now T-City has something to do with higher speed on these networks.

"Yes, but most people have no idea what it is [...] Lots of people have no knowledge of it."

not particularly enthusiastic about technologies have to be reached on a level that sparks curiosity and especially that makes the purpose of the technological applications visible or tangible.

Another reason some people do not want to engage more with the T-City information sources is the commercial character of the information materials, according to the interview discussions. Some reports say that they contain too little information and that they create the impression of wanting to sell people certain products. This, according to some interviewees, is also seen as a contradiction to the aims of the overall project, which are for T-City to be a trial for the future and a joint project between the city and Deutsche Telekom. Furthermore, it is off-putting for people that the information is written in complicated technical language with abstract concepts and a lot of foreign terminology, which many people don't understand.

The interviews draw attention to a further reason for people's lack of knowledge about what T-City involves. The inhabitants of Friedrichshafen don't want to or can't spare the time in their daily lives to get to know T-City in depth. Their days are already filled with a whole array of duties and activities, so to take the time to read something about T-City or to attend an information event isn't always their highest priority.

The Ambassadors and Futurists, who are meant to bring T-City "close to the people" of Friedrichshafen, are welcomed by most of the interviewees. Many of the discussion partners rate the Futurist initiative as a good way of demonstrating how ICT usage can benefit everyday life. Although it doesn't enable the people to experience the technology themselves, the Futurists can convey the idea. Some of the interviewees, on the other hand, do not perceive the Futurists as possible role models, instead viewing them as an advertising medium with a marketing character. One interviewee explained that the Futurists, as selected trial households, don't have any *"recognition value."* On the other hand, he thought that users of the individual projects or the ambassadors were better candidates for highlighting the human and useful aspects of T-City.

"It was too much advertising with too little information."

The people in Friedrichshafen already have a daily life.

105
More about the Ambassadors and the Futurists in the chapter "Install"

Where can I try it out hands-on?

All of this shows clearly that it isn't easy to convey Smart City ideas and projects to the people by means of information material and events. One interviewee remarked: *"Of course it is difficult to get people to understand T-City. I visited the IBO fair, where there was a stand. How do you represent it? I mean like fast Internet access. This and many other things are not tangible."*

In the discussions with citizens, it is mentioned time and time again that the abstractness of T-City makes it difficult to appreciate and to understand. A Smart City such as this isn't something that people can look at or hear. Therefore it would be helpful for them if there were a venue in the city where they could try out T-City hands-on.

"… I don't think it's necessary to write so much in the newspapers about what they are doing, instead what is needed now is a venue where all these things are simply there."

The project headquarters weren't considered suitable for such purposes: *"The project headquarters aren't in a very practical location. The building is tucked away and nobody passes by there. Especially not young people."* The headquarters don't create the impression of being a place that people can turn to for information or to try something out. In their view, what is lacking is a publicly accessible venue where one can try the projects out in a hands-on way.

Technology, technology, but how about the people?

In the discussions, many comments refer to T-City as a joint project involving the urban population and show how the interviewed citizens perceive the integration of the project into Friedrichshafen and into urban society. In this context, three thematic areas in particular came up in the interviews: the joint project with the city, the possibilities for citizens to participate, and the key aspects of the orientation and implementation of the project.

Joint project: In many respects, the interviewees did not perceive T-City as a joint project between the city and Deutsche Telekom. For many citizens, the project had a commercial nature, which undermined its validity as a joint project. Furthermore, a true integration of the project into the city wasn't possible, because firstly it was to a great extent the Deutsche Telekom experts—who were unfamiliar with the living environment in Friedrichshafen—who were shaping the project. Secondly, according to the interviewees, they had observed too many changes of staff on both sides of the T-City partnership project for a joint, continuous, and consistent integration to be possible. Moreover, it was often pointed out that the city was *"not active enough,"* and that its contribution was shaped too strongly by daily politics and the general political situation.

"Well, it is not doing a good job of selling itself as a joint project."

Participation possibilities: The T-City project was not perceived as a *"join-in project"* by many discussion partners. The comments on this subject were related to the opportunities to actively participate in the shaping of the project and to actively try out and experience the T-City solutions. Despite the invitation to citizens to participate in the shaping of T-City—after all, it was a project that concerned the whole of urban society—those who put forward ideas or project suggestions had the feeling that they weren't welcome. One discussion partner reported that he sent in several project ideas, but after the initial discussions he never heard any more about them from those responsible. As a result, he was disappointed and not motivated to contribute anything else whatsoever. Furthermore, he had the impression that only a certain select circle of people was allowed to contribute to determining the individual projects.

"… not enough of a join-in project."

The second point regarding "joining in" relates to the usage of the projects. Most of the interviewees used none or only few of the solutions developed in T-City. According to many discussion partners, there was a lack of individual projects that were relevant to the daily lives of the majority of citizens and that would enable them to experience T-City. While there were projects that were conceived for a wide circle of addressees, they were rarely used or not considered very useful. In connection with this, many citizens commented that more locally targeted individual projects should have been realized—in other words projects that deal with the "real" problems within the city, especially traffic solutions.

The orientation of the project: In the opinion of many discussion partners, the project focused too strongly on the technologies or on boosting images and too little on the people. In relation to the latter point, according to an interviewee, there was too little effort to link the project with real people in the city and to connect with them on an emotional and personal level. One female interviewee described T-City as a *"profiling project"* for the city, which was only intended *"for the elite"* but not for normal inhabitants. Another female citizen mentioned the differences in the ways that women and men deal with ICT. She had the impression that the project was created by male techno geeks, who didn't take the requirements of normal residents into consideration. It was reported in positive terms that T-City succeeded in reaching the target group of senior citizens and involving them in ICT, through the support of the Senior Citizens' Internet Society, which was viewed as useful and important. Apart from the lack of attention paid to people-oriented aspects, many interviewees also missed the experience of a surprising and innovative moment, which in their opinion would inspire a real project for the future.

Some discussion partners pointed out that Friedrichshafen's culture and mentality made it difficult to integrate the project within the city. One interview partner commented that the population of Friedrichshafen was too well off to welcome a new project in the city. Other interviewees mentioned with regard to this that the *Häfler* (as the locals call themselves) are not particularly open to novelty.

"Regarding the technology everything has been done. Everything is good and great."

Advantages and usefulness— a matter of perspective

What has changed then in Friedrichshafen as a result of all the new applications introduced by T-City? Overall, the impact of the project on the quality of life of those we interviewed was perceived as minimal. The perception of the project is often limited to some of its individual aspects, which are generally not recognized as having a purpose in their own right. Nevertheless, some of the interviewed citizens attribute to the T-City project a possible positive impact on the urban situation as a whole. In relation to this, interviewees reported that the project might indeed boost the image of Friedrichshafen or that the city and its industry were experiencing a general improvement of locational advantages. As one interviewee put it: *"Certainly, it is advantageous for industry and for some businesses. According to the information I have gathered it is indeed worthwhile for them."* Another interview partner emphasized that T-City is important for the city of Friedrichshafen to be able to hold its own in competition with other cities.

In addition, T-City was seen as having potential advantages and uses in certain fields such as healthcare and education. In the field of education, the achievements of T-City were rated as modest by those who were interviewed, even if they could see great potential here for using technological applications. The field of healthcare was mentioned especially often and highlighted positively, as a result of successful and useful individual projects. While the majority of inhabitants don't experience personal benefits themselves through T-City as a result of this, the telemonitoring solutions and technological support for senior citizens are nevertheless mentioned. For interviewees, these solutions are straightforward and easy to understand.

Apart from the infrastructure, which enables better and quicker access to the Internet, in the interviews the inhabitants rarely mentioned using and experiencing particular individual projects themselves. Some of the interviewees had tried solutions such as *"Kindergarten Online"*, the electronic Citizens Registration Office, or the city portal but didn't perceive them as a great facilitation and rarely used them. Some interviewees have heard of other projects and rated the ideas positively, but haven't tried them out themselves yet. Regarding the better infrastructure, it has been noted critically that it can only be used by Telekom customers, thus excluding part of the urban population.

In the discussions, the impact of T-City on the general and individual quality of life in Friedrichshafen was perceived as limited. The representative surveys show that in 2012, only 36 percent of the Friedrichshafen population agreed with the statement, *"The quality of life in Friedrichshafen will improve through T-City."* This is a similar percentage to the first survey in 2008, hence hardly any change had occurred over the course of the project.

138
More about the notion of quality of life, according to the accompanying research, can be found in the section "The structure of the T-City accompanying research."

Positive impact on the urban situation as a whole

36 %
of citizens expect that T-City will have a positive effect on the quality of life in the city in future.

The various age groups have differing expectations for the future. The youngest (fourteen to twenty-nine years old) have the highest expectations of improvement through T-City, with 42 percent agreeing with the statement. In the group of thirty to forty-nine-year-olds, it is 33 percent and in the group of those between fifty and sixty-five, it is 36 percent.

The expectations regarding future development are more positive than the perception of the improvements that have already been achieved, according to the people of Friedrichshafen. In 2012, 28 percent of interviewees agreed that T-City had already improved the quality of life in Friedrichshafen.

Regarding whether T-City would bring personal benefits, 28 percent of those questioned expect the project to benefit them in future. A differentiated look at the various age groups reveals that the youngest age group generally has the most positive expectations of the project. 37 percent of those surveyed agree with the statement that they will experience personal advantages on account of T-City. In the other two age groups, about one quarter agree respectively.

Therefore, it is the youngest surveyed group that harbors the most optimism regarding the expected impact of T-City on the quality of life and the potential personal benefits in future.

Individual projects: using and experiencing T-City actively

The results of the survey in 2012 show that about one-third of the inhabitants expect to be benefitted personally by T-City in future, while a quarter states that they have already experienced a personal benefit. The following section focuses on how selected individual projects were experienced and presents how they were applied to people's daily lives.

"Tumor Conference"

The use of the videoconference system at the Breast Center at the Constance and Friedrichshafen hospitals facilitates the daily working lives of the hospital doctors. The external medical staff's willingness to participate is still limited because of the costs and the work involved in installing and maintaining the system.

The participating users highlight in positive terms that "Tumor Conference" is a technological innovation project that will be used increasingly in future because of the structural organization of the healthcare system. Furthermore it is regarded as positive that this T-City project idea was conceived right at the very beginning when the application was submitted. A local problem was tackled and overcome by means of a technological solution.

A particular advantage in daily working life is the timesaving aspect, with the doctors not having to travel across the lake every two weeks. However, according to the participating doctors, the personal contact and "informal" exchanges with colleagues before and after the conference has been lost.

The real advantage of video conferencing systems is only expected to reach fruition when they have become a standard feature throughout Germany and worldwide, enabling exchanges about particular issues or treatment methods with experts outside of the two hospitals. A challenging aspect of this is the problem of the lack of compatibility of various technological solutions.

"Edunex"

The interactive educational platform "Edunex" is used very little by the teachers and pupils at participating schools. According to teachers, the reasons for the limited usage during and outside of lessons are technical issues, limited functions, laborious handling, and the lack of teaching materials, as well as the better offers provided by open source solutions. The advantages these solutions offer include active exchanges with other teachers even outside of Friedrichshafen and access to a pool of teaching materials. The lack of instructions and guidance with regard to using the platform and the fluctuating support teams on the technical side caused dissatisfaction among teachers who had initially been enthusiastic. Nor did the structural framework inspire teachers to invest time and engage with "Edunex" extensively, as the financial terms and the length of the platform's availability are not ensured in the long run.

The introduction of educational platforms in schools is seen by some teachers as being difficult in general, because older colleagues struggle with the platforms. They mention teachers who don't know how to handle the new technologies and are opposed to implementing them in schools.

"Edunex": hardly used and with competition from an open source solution

097
More about the structural framework when introducing and implementing "Edunex" in the chapter "Install"

"Mobile Clinic"

According to the perceptions of interviewed patients who use the telemonitoring system "Mobile Clinic," their quality of life is strongly compromised by their heart conditions and they have to adapt their daily lives. The patients are supported in this by the use of the "Mobile Clinic," as the system contributes to their safety.

First, they have a feeling of "positive surveillance." They know that their vital data is monitored daily by the Friedrichshafen hospital and that the hospital will contact them if the results are not within the safe range. The monitoring gives the patients greater freedom in the organization of their daily lives and some of the interviewees are more willing to venture out and do things.

Second, it is very important to the patients that they are in the care of a hospital, albeit at a distance. They ascribe greater specialized competence to the hospital, compared to general practitioners. Furthermore, it is reassuring for some of the participants that they can contact the hospital 24/7.

Finally, by using the "Mobile Clinic," patients learn to assess the state of their health, which contributes to a general sense of security. In addition, it helps them to live with their illness and to adapt their lifestyle. The use of the "Mobile Clinic" thus represents a support system that encourages the self-regulation of daily life and provides the patient with important information in relation to the illness.

"Kindergarten Online"

The portal "Kindergarten Online" is perceived by the city as an administrative facilitator. For the childcare workers and kindergarten management, on the other hand, the conversion to the new system involves significant time and effort. However, at the same time it is expected that in the long run it will facilitate the organization of kindergartens and the planning of requirements. The transparency created between the administration and the kindergarten is not welcomed by all child care workers, however. There are fears of shortcuts being taken and of greater problems in daily working life as a result. Furthermore this individual project is also faced with the challenge of the Digital Divide with regard to age: the child care workers report that there is a divide within the kindergartens, because older colleagues are not familiar with the technology.

"Mobile Clinic":
a sense of security in everyday life

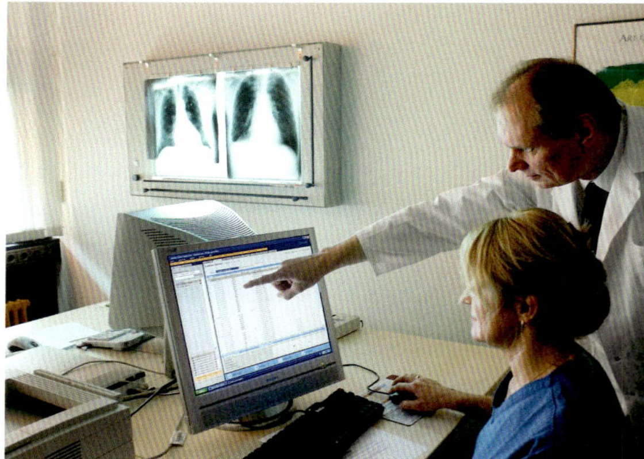

"Kindergarten Online":
initially costing time and effort,
but ultimately expected to
facilitate everyday working life

The option of registering children online is regarded critically by most child care workers. It is important to them to get to know the children and parents personally before registration.

The parents can't see many advantages to the new portal. They point to a lack of functions in terms of the usability and the menu structure, as well as to the platform's lack of information and innovation, and they would prefer a more transparent registration procedure. It wasn't possible to modify the child's registration online, nor did the portal provide an overview of free places or the child's registration status. The idea of the general overview of all kindergartens in Friedrichshafen was seen as positive though.

"Smart Metering"

"Smart Metering" is a project that attracted wide attention. The results of the survey and interviews with users provide an ambivalent picture of how it was rated. Apart from technical problems with accessing the portal or with the availability of one's own data, the functionality of the portal and of the digital meter was also seen as lacking. A low level of motivation and a lack of incentives to use the Smart Meter were also due to a lack of information about tariffs. The insight into one's own consumption is initially an incentive to use the meter, but the interest in digital meters quickly evaporates once the "power guzzlers" have been identified.

The issue of data protection is viewed by many of those who were interviewed or surveyed as an important, but also critical, issue when implementing Smart Metering. Overall, the topic of transparent and efficient electricity usage is viewed as important, and among those questioned there was a high level of willingness to take part in a similar project again in the future.

"Smart Metering": ambivalent assessment by users

"Independent Living"

The service platform "Independent Living" is hardly used by the residents of a multiunit residential dwelling in Saint-Die Street in Friedrichshafen. Most of the residents feel that the services offered don't apply to them and beyond that, technical issues made usage unattractive.

The various age groups among the residents see themselves as the wrong user groups for the service platform. Even the older residents said that they prefer to go to town or to the supermarket, instead of pressing a button.

"Independent Living": used very little, but the topic of AAL is considered very relevant

Even if the use of the platform in its current form has been minimal, the topic of Ambient Assisted Living (AAL) is widely accepted by the residents. Most of the residents are of the opinion that such a service portal can contribute to the quality of life of elderly people with restricted mobility and they consider it an important topic. The willingness to take part in a pilot project is therefore quite wide, despite the fact that it doesn't all function optimally yet.

Trying something out can spark enthusiasm

The last section showed that the application of technological solutions in individual projects can be perceived and experienced as beneficial to daily life. In the discussions with people living in Friedrichshafen, it was often pointed out that active usage in daily life is key. Several interviewees reported enthusiastically, for example, about the Hotspot Summer in 2008, when they had the opportunity to experience T-City actively for the first time. Trying out ICT applications in the daily life of a Smart City can therefore spark enthusiasm and help to convey the idea behind a Smart City. It is anyone's guess why this is isn't available as a matter of course in a city that is specifically designated as a testing ground for the future, where one should be able to try out and test things.

The results of the survey show that T-City is rated more positively by participants in the pilot projects than by non-participants. In 2011, 57 percent of those questioned had participated in individual projects, and 41 percent of users of individual projects agree with the statement that T-City will contribute to the quality of life in Friedrichshafen. Only a quarter of non-users agree with this. The potential future personal benefits of T-City are also evaluated more positively by users, with 36 percent in agreement, compared to non-users with 16 percent. The results of the representative survey also show clearly that users involved in two or more projects agree more strongly with the statement that T-City will raise the quality of life than users of just one project.

Differences exist between the users of individual projects with regard to how T-City affects their daily lives. For example, the qualitative interviews show clearly that users of the "Mobile Clinic" consider T-City's contribution to their quality of life as greater than, for instance, the users of "Kindergarten Online." It is therefore a matter of what application is involved and what benefits it offers in the structure of daily life.

Using ICT can spark enthusiasm.

Users of individual projects rate T-City more positively than non-users.

Figures from the survey in 2012

28 %
of those surveyed agreed with the
statement that they will benefit personally
from Friedrichshafen becoming a T-City.

53 %
have used social networks
in the last 12 months
14–29-year-olds **84 %**
30–49-year-olds **50 %**
50–65-year-olds **26 %**

20 %
feel that ICT is an invasion
of their private sphere.

54 %
are concerned that the protection
of their personal data is not taken
into account sufficiently when
introducing new technologies.

24 %
feel overwhelmed by the
constant introduction
of new ICT

50 %
perceive ICT as an important
contribution to the quality of life

36 %
of those questioned agree with the
statement that the quality of life in
Friedrichshafen will be enhanced.
Users **45 %**
Non-users **22 %**

58 %
say that ICT facilitates staying
in touch with family,
friends and acquaintances.

Through ICT, levels of personal
contact have increased.
14–29-year-olds **44 %**
30–49-year-olds **23 %**
50–65-year-olds **19 %**

Amongst those surveyed,
daily newspapers, TV and radio
are used less by 25%, 17% and 17%
respectively, because of the internet.

I have already heard of T-City.
(all figures as percentages)

2007
n=500

total figure	38
14–29-year-olds	21
30–49-year-olds	41
50–65-year-olds	49

2008
n=1003

total figure	80
14–29-year-olds	79
30–49-year-olds	81
50–65-year-olds	81

2009
n=1004

total figure	83
14–29-year-olds	80
30–49-year-olds	84
50–65-year-olds	83

2010
n=1000

total figure	87
14–29-year-olds	81
30–49-year-olds	91
50–65-year-olds	88

2011
n=935

total figure	86
14–29-year-olds	82
30–49-year-olds	88
50–65-year-olds	87

2012
n=1001

total figure	86
14–29-year-olds	84
30–49-year-olds	88
50–65-year-olds	85

Legend:
- total figure
- 14–29-year-olds
- 30–49-year-olds
- 50–65-year-olds

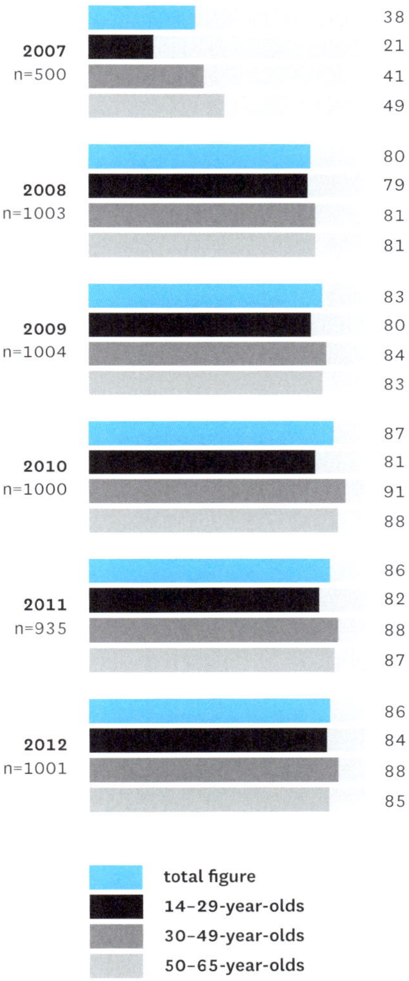

The quality of life in Friedrichshafen will be enhanced in future through T-City.
(all figures as percentages)

2008
n=803

total figure	36
14–29-year-olds	38
30–49-year-olds	34
50–65-year-olds	36

2009
n=831

total figure	33
14–29-year-olds	41
30–49-year-olds	30
50–65-year-olds	29

2010
n=872

total figure	33
14–29-year-olds	44
30–49-year-olds	30
50–65-year-olds	29

2011
n=802

total figure	36
14–29-year-olds	38
30–49-year-olds	34
50–65-year-olds	37

2012
n=860

total figure	36
14–29-year-olds	42
30–49-year-olds	33
50–65-year-olds	36

Legend:
- total figure
- 14–29-year-olds
- 30–49-year-olds
- 50–65-year-olds

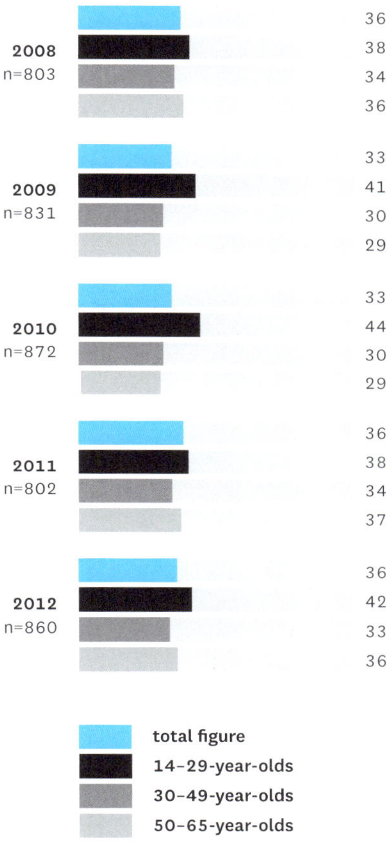

Expectations of future personal benefits through T-City
(all figures as percentages)

2008
n=803

total figure	26
14–29-year-olds	35
30–49-year-olds	22
50–65-year-olds	23

2009
n=831

total figure	29
14–29-year-olds	36
30–49-year-olds	27
50–65-year-olds	24

2010
n=872

total figure	28
14–29-year-olds	38
30–49-year-olds	26
50–65-year-olds	23

2011
n=802

total figure	30
14–29-year-olds	37
30–49-year-olds	29
50–65-year-olds	23

2012
n=860

total figure	28
14–29-year-olds	37
30–49-year-olds	24
50–65-year-olds	24

Legend:
- total figure
- 14–29-year-olds
- 30–49-year-olds
- 50–65-year-olds

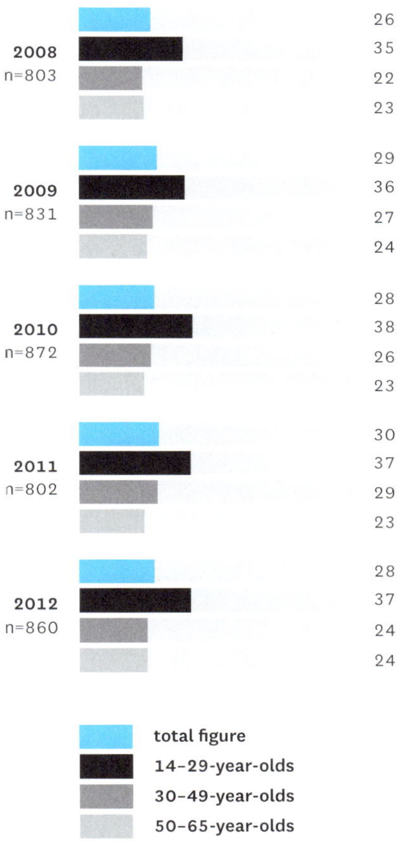

[C]

Innovation project T-City Friedrichshafen four questions—four answers

by Ferdinand Tempel, Director of the T-City representative office in Friedrichshafen

What did the T-City project achieve for Deutsche Telekom and for the city of Friedrichshafen?

As Deutsche Telekom, we clearly demonstrated our capacity for innovation and consolidated our reputation, especially in the future-orientated fields of energy, health, and mobility, since not only concepts but also "tangible solutions" were realized in the T-City of Friedrichshafen.

The T-City products thereby became the basis for the development of new strategic business segments within our corporation. For example, the Smart Metering solutions (electronic reading of electricity, gas, and water meters) developed in T-City are now marketed nationally and internationally.

Furthermore, a functioning innovation platform now links the various units of the Telekom corporation to the partners in the city of Friedrichshafen and in the Lake Constance area, who have built up relevant expertise through more than sixty projects. This led to fourteen innovative solutions in the field of information and communication technology (ICT) being developed into marketable long-term solutions, applicable within the city or as Telekom products available on the market. These are so widely successful that an extension of the project activities for a further three years until 2015 has just been agreed upon.

T-City brought about the modernization of the broadband infrastructure in the city of Friedrichshafen, with 98% of all households having VDSL access. An extensive UMTS cellular network is available and a city-wide WLAN network with thirty-seven hotspots was set up. The broadband infrastructure thereby became an important basis for the development and testing of innovative ICT solutions during the course of the project. Furthermore, it ensures the future viability of the enterprises and residents in the digital age as a "gigabit society".

The municipal administration in particular was modernized, so as to become service-oriented and efficient. This resulted in the redesign of the tourism portal, the interactive city portal, and the automation of public services (e.g., citizens' service, issue management—"just say it," management of kindergarten places), while employing national solutions such as the standard public services hotline number D115 or De-Mail.

The use of innovative solutions increased among the municipal partners (especially Technische Werke Friedrichshafen, Klinikum, *Schwäbische Zeitung*), who as a result gained customers and prominence beyond the city limits. Specific schemes and campaigns enabled new target groups (senior citizens' initiatives, small businesses, and microenterprises) to use new media in everyday life, bringing a lasting improvement to their quality of life and ability to compete on the market. In addition, within the framework of the project activities, individual spin-off companies (e.g., flinc, Giritech, Bodytel) were able to establish themselves on the market. T-City therefore boosted the municipal and regional economy and promoted the locational advantages of the innovative Lake Constance region.

Through the many visitors and the communication events that brought good publicity, the city attracted national and international attention and became more well known.

What has been your experience with regard to the co-operation with the city of Friedrichshafen over the years?

The co-operation with the city of Friedrichshafen was characterized in the first phase of the project by the high level of personal involvement and the innovation friendliness of the city's leadership, along with the incorporation of Deutsche Telekom into all municipal activities. Over the course of the project, it became clear how important it is for the city to reach a consensus on the overall policy, regarding the project

framework and the ways of cooperating with Telekom, in order to run such a project successfully over a period of five years. Furthermore, the importance of long-term support from politics and the city leadership was brought to light, especially in terms of administrative clarity regarding decisions and the provision of resources in the second phase of the project.

The setup of a successful regional innovation platform is based to a large extent on the competence and openness to innovation of the participating companies and individuals, who view ICT as contributing to the success of their business. There are many innovative solutions that seem interesting technologically or because of their media presence, but which fail to be converted into viable business models. Therefore identifying viable business models is crucial for success in developing innovations.

*In your opinion, what was the response to the project
in the city of Friedrichshafen?*

The perception of the project in the city evolved over the course of five years. Initially, the project was taken as a "gift" presented by a city contest. The upgrading of broadband free of charge and the project budget of up to 80 million euros envisaged by Telekom gave rise most of all to the expectation of gaining financial benefits from the project. After a period of disillusionment, it was the innovation-friendly partners and residents in particular who recognized the potential in information and communication technology, in terms of future products and solutions for one's own business and personal use.

*Which target groups was the project aimed at and which
groups are not represented by the project and why?*

A great deal was contributed to the innovation project by those municipal and regional enterprises and residents for whom the commercial or personal benefits became clear as the project unfolded. As a result of this commitment, the project was of greater ascertainable value to them in terms of quality of life and locational advantage. Less present within the project, on the other hand, were those groups who can't or do not want to implement procedural changes linked to innovative ICT applications, out of tradition and habit.

"Bottom up dynamics"— a contribution to the energy transition

by Stefan Söchtig, Managing Director of the municipal project association of T-City Friedrichshafen since 2009

From the beginning, energy has played a significant role in the T-City project. The starting point for this was Smart Metering. Today, the additional project extensions Smart Grid and Smart Home are being recognized as ways of helping to solve the problem of energy transition in Germany and Europe. In view of this, especially in the second phase of T-City, the project structure and the teamwork within the project organization focused on turning every idea into a project and carrying every project over into additional projects as far as possible. It was only in summer 2011 that EU Commissioner Oettinger started to take a personal interest again in the results of Friedrichshafen, which he describes as *"upward dynamics"* and views as an exemplary contribution to ensuring the future supply of energy. The Federal Environment Ministry, the Federal Ministry of Economics, and the Federal Network Agency monitored the development of the project on site.

As with all projects, the starting point for the Smart Metering project was the question of how information and communication technology (ICT) could help a city like Friedrichshafen to find better solutions to its problems. In 2007, it had to be clarified whether the city, which runs a public utility company for its energy and water supply, could ensure a better—i.e., more ecological and economical—energy supply for its residents by means of ICT. The starting point for this was the stipulation by the German legislature, which now applies to all EU states, that the use of Smart Metering can save more energy, because it makes residents aware of their consumption.

It was immediately clear upon taking a closer look at the law that it wasn't possible to proceed according to its exact wording. For instance, it didn't stipulate the technical possibility of meters being read remotely, meaning that the user would still have had to go down into the cellar to gauge their electricity or gas consumption.

Therefore, the project leaders decided "against the law" to incorporate networked meters that could be read by the customer on a PC or TV. From the beginning, the focus was on developing a solution that offered the energy user a financial incentive to reduce their consumption. However, the cost of an immediate "mass rollout" and installation of meters like those tested in 2,000 households was too high.

The follow-up question therefore was how to develop further options for the customer using the existing technology and networks, which is where Smart Home and Smart Grid come in. For example, with Smart Home one can read the meters on individual radiators via the same connection, while also adjusting the thermostat. This enables each tenant to turn up the heating remotely only when it is really needed, for example when on the way home from work. That might seem insignificant, but considering the approximately forty million German households, it represents an enormous energy savings potential.

An example: if ten million households switch on the heating an hour later on sixty cold days, the resulting energy saving is 600 million hours of heat output. In T-City, many solutions such as these are being developed.

The other option enabled by Smart Metering is the interconnection of decentralized generation systems, such as photovoltaics, combined heat and power, wind power, storage in the form of batteries, including car batteries. The goal is to link consumption more closely with local on-site generation. This reduces the expansion of high-tension power lines and the need for large power stations, which is necessary because of the shutdown of nuclear power plants.

Nowadays, this is not just a question of ecology and efficiency, but also of security of supply. Wind power and supply through photovoltaics can no longer be handled by our networks. Smart Grid is part of the solution and T-City contributed to its development, although its application will still need to be brought to maturation in the continuation of the project after 2012.

A problematic aspect of the project, as with other projects, was that in the beginning an agreement couldn't be reached on the development of a product suitable for the majority of users in Germany. There are namely more than 800 energy providers, mostly small public utilities. They have to master the often complex structures of Smart Home and Smart Grid by means of ICT that is easy to use. However, progress has been made regarding this through the open and intensive project work.

In conclusion, the implementation of this key project has drawn worldwide attention to Friedrichshafen, especially in the last two years. Ensuring the supply of energy at affordable prices is a contribution towards improving the quality of life and the attractiveness of the location.

Smart Meters — a new contribution to saving electricity

by Sebastian Gölz, Fraunhofer Institute for Solar Energy Systems ISE, Freiburg

"Are you trying to save electricity at home?"—presumably, most people would reply to this question in the affirmative. However, this mindset is not sufficient in itself to save electricity: first of all, the power guzzlers in the household have to be identified. Furthermore, members of the household have to be aware of which ingrained habits waste electricity—and therefore also money—and how to improve on this. Some time ago, a new technical device was developed that might help households to economize significantly: the Smart Meter, which records to the second how much electricity is being used when. The data is sent to the monitoring system of the municipal energy suppliers as an automatic read-out via a wireless link. The energy provider can then report back quickly to the users on their consumption—via a personalized Internet portal, SMS, Smart Phone, or posted letter.

The usage of Smart Meters gave rise to the expectation in recent years, especially among political representatives in Berlin and Brussels, that they could help households save energy. Numerous pilot projects in Germany and other European countries researched whether reporting back on electricity consumption could really lead to energy conservation. In a field trial involving more than 2000 households in Germany and Austria, the Fraunhofer Institute for Solar Energy Systems (ISE) studied the responses to feedback sent via the Internet or posted letter, drawing valuable conclusions about saving electricity using Smart Meters. Just the availability of feedback in itself led to a 3.7% reduction in electricity consumption. Households on a time variable rate achieved an additional saving of 6%, the load transfer was only 2% (www.intelliekon.de).

However, it should be mentioned that less positive results were recorded in some other Smart Meter studies. In some cases, very little or no power at all was saved and the participating households expressed their disappointment that the feedback was inconclusive about how to save more power. However, overall the studies showed that many people find the analysis of their electricity consumption very helpful and rate it highly as a monitoring mechanism, making them more aware of electricity consumption as an issue. In particular, the results emerging from the time variable rate show that, with suitable incentives, households can be motivated to take notice of the electricity supply data and adapt their habits accordingly. This could lead to households taking a more active role in transforming the supply of electricity in Germany. Combining Smart Meters with power generation through photovoltaics or CHP stations provides new product options for utility companies, service providers, and those with solar power systems.

In order to achieve further progress with saving power and energy, there is more and more research into smart measuring and monitoring systems in the home (Smart Home), which are better suited to people's individual requirements.

"Independent Living"— a T-City residential project

by Jaqueline Egger-Buck, Fränkel AG, Friedrichshafen

The project "Independent Living" focuses especially on senior citizens and is designed to enable them to stay longer in their own homes and familiar environment. For the pilot project, a residential building in Friedrichshafen with nineteen rental apartments was equipped with special technology.

In order to facilitate independent living, a simple and intuitively operated touchpad monitor screen was installed. This monitor screen depicts a virtual marketplace, comprising services that relate to daily requirements (pharmacy, bread delivery service, information services, meals on wheels, pizza delivery service, Rewe groceries delivery service, video telephony, social services, etc.). For the real estate management, this virtual marketplace represents the opportunity to reduce the fluctuation of tenants by helping to keep the tenants in the apartments for longer. It can also increase the attractiveness and the quality of the apartments. The aim of installing the touchpad was to increase the well-being of the tenants and the quality of life of people in all stages of life.

In the first instance the pilot project was concerned with the following aspects:

— to probe the degree of acceptance of the
   touchpad monitor screens and of the whole system
— to try out the selection and integration of
   service providers
— to test order and payment procedures
— to assess advantages and disadvantages for service
   providers and to make suggestions for improvement
— to prevent isolation within the home using video
   telephony and chat forums
— to ensure everyday safety through instant contact
   with the outside world
— to find out to what extent information services
   can facilitate daily life

Putting the pilot project into practice proved more difficult than was anticipated. Owing to a late launch, there was no application procedure—as was the case for other T-City projects—instead, the participants were selected. The concentration of participants in one house was seen as an advantage. However, it was difficult to convince the participants that their participation in the initiative was beneficial to them and could contribute to the success of the project. It took time to overcome the initial difficulties with the technology and the software, as well as the communication with the service providers. During the trial phase, it was not always possible to ensure the prompt implementation of technological features or to solve problems identified or complained about by the tenants. In the end, the participants occasionally accessed news and ordered their shopping, medicines, and meals via the portal.

The coordination between Deutsche Telekom, T-City, and Fränkel AG worked well. The service providers were also open-minded towards the portal and optimistic that it has a chance on the market in the future.

Social GeoWeb—participatory planning using digital maps

by Stefan Höffken, Research associate at the Technical University of Kaiserslautern (CAD)

So-called Webmaps enable new participatory applications for the planning of urban space. They open up new potential for experts, residents and initiatives, by adding a new "mobile" dimension to the scope of participation. Below is an outline of what direction Webmaps and Mobile Participation are taking.

GeoWeb—digital maps for the public: geocoded content can be viewed using online digital maps such as Google Maps or OpenStreet-Map (OSM). This Internet-based geocoding is called GeoWeb (cf. Streich/Zeile 2011). These maps are easy to use, compared to the traditional geographical information systems (GIS) intended for experts. Their usability and the fact that they are free of charge have contributed significantly to the success of these web-mapping technologies in recent years. This is supported by their performance, that is to say the quick downloading of new data, so that interaction takes place in real time. The user can select the maps interactively without a fixed sequence, determine the displayed content individually, choose the perspective, and zoom in or out seamlessly.

Social GeoWeb—communication via social networks: the added value of digital maps is that additional information such as traffic, social or geographical data can easily be incorporated. It can be integrated into websites using programming interfaces and combined with other content—creating so-called mashups (cf. Novak/Voigt 2007; Höffken 2011). Furthermore, it can be integrated into Web 2.0, enabling the easy sharing of data via Facebook and Twitter, for example. Content can be combined and transmitted in multiple media (i.e., via text, image, audio, geodata). This social sharing is an integral component of participatory strategies, as it enables a faster, more open, and wider communication about planning schemes.

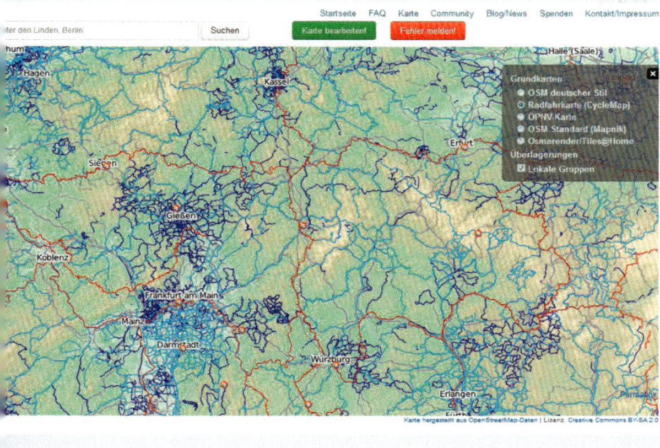

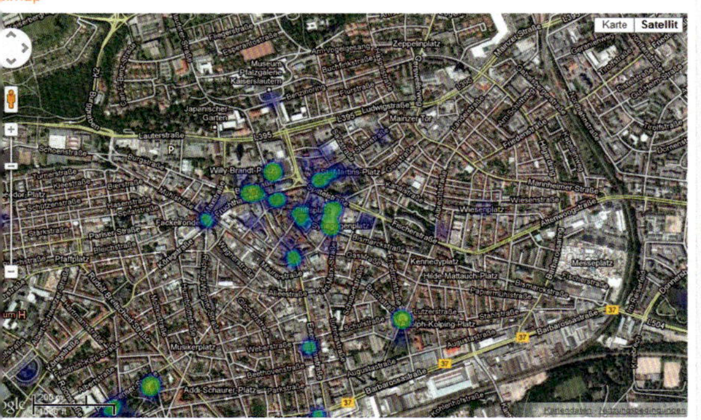

Online Mapping—the added value of digital maps: the project *Frankfurt Gestalten* (Designing Frankfurt) aims to bring committed residents together and inform them about current urban development projects in Frankfurt/Main. According to the website frankfurt-gestalten.de: *"Residents can network on the local Internet to plan their city."* On the basis of OpenStreetMap data, current projects are communicated and presented clearly so that they are easy to understand. Based on the first prominent projects, such as the web platform fixmystreet.com, a string of so-called reporting portals have emerged, through which residents can report "problems," such as potholes, broken benches, or illegal garbage dumping—i.e., they can enter it onto the maps. Well-known examples of this are the portals maerker.brandenburg.de or unortkataster.de from Cologne. Many tools are available to the contributors for drawing their own maps (e.g., via Scribble Maps), visualizing them (Google Earth), and sharing them via social networks.

Mobile participation—the next step: Smartphones have now enabled spontaneous active participation. For example on nexthamburg.de residents can use their iPhone for making suggestions for planning spaces or for reporting run-down buildings. This type of mobile participation is also being studied in the specialist area of Computer-Aided Design (CAD) at the Technical University of Kaiserslautern for assessing open spaces and cycle paths, in cooperation with the German Research Center for Artificial Intelligence (DFKI). Here the focus is also on the integration of 3D urban models, with which the information can be located and made available even more accurately. Particularly in the context of Smart Cities, this forms a starting point to complete and improve the existing data sets through the collaborative gathering process of crowdsourcing and through inductive monitoring (Streich 2011). The Social GeoWeb therefore opens up a multitude of new communication channels and enables innovative, participatory strategies.

05

Avoid crash

Over the entire course of the development of T-City Friedrichshafen—by citizens, local organizations and businesses, the city administration, and Deutsche Telekom—implementing the project proved difficult in a number of ways, although many of these difficulties were overcome. This chapter shows how the various partners coped with these challenges, thereby avoiding a "crash." Furthermore, as the project unfolded, it emerged that some of the inhabitants, as well as certain companies, were reluctant to use the new technologies. Among the most common reasons for this were the protection of personal and business data against loss and damage, and the protection of this data from unwanted circulation and utilization. The fear that these concerns would not be sufficiently taken into consideration doesn't always lead to complete abstinence regarding usage, but the latent concern that data might disappear or fall into the wrong hands makes it difficult for some people to use the new media uninhibitedly. This section shows how one can deal with such reservations constructively, thereby enabling the creation of a vibrant Smart City.

Avoiding crash—
dealing with concerns

"It is very dangerous to listen. If you listen, you can be persuaded."
Oscar Wilde

In the digital world, there is nothing worse than experiencing a technical crash. However, crashes are also feared in other areas. It also applies to the concrete implementation and execution of projects like Smart City. Thus, this chapter deals first of all with the question of how the risk of a T-City crash was avoided in Friedrichshafen. What was done to ensure the success of the project even in difficult times? How were the respective partners brought together? What mechanisms were developed to hold the very unequal partners—the city and the corporation—together for the long term?

The risks faced by the cooperation

Secondly, it became clear while putting the project into practice that—despite the opportunities provided by modern information and communication technology (ICT)—some people have reservations about using cell phones, laptops, or social networks. Is the radiation necessary for mobile communications in fact harmful, despite all the research and socially negotiated radiation limit values? Is our data really secure, or can it be lost in virtual space and read by strangers or even tampered with? Will the new technology take over and change personal relations? These and similar questions are asked by many users, not only in Friedrichshafen, but also by the wider public regarding the daily usage of new media in Germany.

Concerns and fears

This chapter presents various perspectives, resulting from the research into the procedures and the impact of the T-City project in Friedrichshafen, with regard to two issues: dealing with the difficulties presented by a concrete Smart City project, and the reservations towards the daily usage of the new information and communication technologies.

190

Project partners—differing objectives and cultures

During the planning and execution of a Smart City project difficulties can arise, which is common in collaborations between businesses and the public sector. Given that businesses in the private sector and cities as municipal administrative bodies have fundamentally differing objectives, have different organizational structures, and foster different cultures and etiquettes, it takes a great deal of time and effort to reach mutual understanding and agreements within the partnership. The pursuit of profit by businesses is often viewed skeptically by many public sector partners, while the public sector's reluctance to take risks is often derided by business representatives. Lengthy, democratically safeguarded decision-making processes in the municipalities are contrasted with quick hierarchical decisions on the part of the businesses. Such differing structures and procedures can lead to the crash of a Public Private Partnership (PPP), which has to be avoided.

The differing objectives of the public and private sector partners

PPP between complementarity and conflicting objectives

The discrepancies between the partners present both a risk and an opportunity. If mutual trust can be established, then the potential courses of action can lead to win-win situations. The city can contribute its experiences regarding civic participation or benefit the project by asserting its authority, while in return, the business can contribute its ability to market products worldwide or put its prospective financial resources in the balance. This can be advantageous for both partners. However, if trust is not developed between those involved in the partnership, every project runs the risk of being critically questioned and of incurring significantly greater communication costs. If trust does not develop on a personal and individual level—providing reassurance that both partners are taking each other's interests into account—then a great deal of energy is wasted on defensive measures that hamper the smooth operation of a project. A lack of flexibility regarding roles and the inability to adjust to different and unfamiliar approaches can make it difficult to form trust on both sides.

Beyond role expectations, the partners in the project are fundamentally bound to different objectives. The corporations under private law have to make the investments of their shareholders more profitable, while the cities governed by public law have to increase public welfare for their inhabitants. However, joint projects run the risk that each partner only pursues their own interests. Regarding the city, this could be an individual project that focuses exclusively on one of the city's own unique problems; for the business, it could be the prioritization of the mass marketing of a particular, single product. For a cooperation to succeed, ideally both partners have to agree on common objectives, or at least on individual objectives that are not detrimental to the other.

Apart from the discrepancies between their fundamental objectives, private and public partners also differ in other respects. Their decision-making processes are set up differently, different employment laws are applied, the regulatory authorities have different roles, and finally they have different cultures, affecting how they deal with risks and how these are communicated internally and publicly.

More about PPP, see Sack (2009)

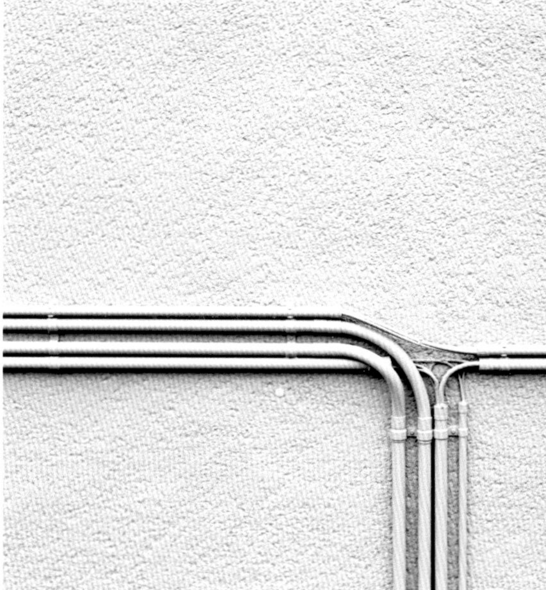

Dealing with a long-term project

Large-scale projects often run over a long period of time. The longer the term of the project, the more likely it is that changes in personnel will occur during that time. In general, Smart City project partners are professional enough to ensure that staff changes do not disrupt coherence and continuity of content, by means of a well-organized project management. Considering the differing system logics and the mutual reservations of the partners, it is essential to provide sufficient resources for the fostering of individual contacts between the personnel. It has often been pointed out that projects depend on people and constellations of people with *"the right chemistry."* This cannot always be created, but it can nearly always be improved if the issue is recognized and dealt with.

Integration of technological solutions into social contexts

In contrast to the traditional approaches to cooperation by public and private sector partners, the PPP in Smart City projects has a distinctive makeup. Smart Cities seek technological solutions to social problems. However, within the complexity of a Smart City, such solutions are inextricably entwined with the basic social circumstances. The technologies implemented in Smart Cities influence the social organization of the project and vice versa (Mayntz 2008).

The following examples will clarify and substantiate this theoretical point. The cost of sending an SMS in a T-City project is "perceived" as higher than in other parts of Germany by the Upper Swabians, known for their thriftiness. Therefore, the projects that were based on people's participation by sending an SMS—for example a project idea for voting in a concert contest—placed greater demands on the perception of its usefulness than it would have done otherwise. A rather different angle is the example of the role of social relations when using new media for the transfer of knowledge. Senior citizens, for example, often prefer to learn from another senior citizen how the newest cell phone works, women would often rather learn such things from other women than from men, and migrants often prefer to be informed by other migrants instead of by non-migrants. A third example that illustrates the importance of integrating a Smart City project into the social context relates to the preexisting daily lives of those living in Friedrichshafen. An urban society and its citizens, their organizations and societies, their administration and policies are already running their largely satisfactory daily course. Thus, a new project idea competes with this daily life and has to offer an obvious added benefit to persuade the people, who have limited resources, to become involved. People have to be made aware of the new benefits a project can offer.

About trust in the system and concerns—are the technologies harmless?

This chapter not only deals with the risk of a Smart City project like T-City in Friedrichshafen crashing and how this can be avoided, it also takes a look at how the inhabitants handled the new media in their everyday lives. The long-term success of a Smart City can only be ensured if as many residents as possible try out and use the new ICT and its wealth of new applications, and even develop them further. From the outset in T-City Friedrichshafen, however, residents were somewhat reluctant to participate in the project actively and wholeheartedly. This reluctance was caused partly by generalized concerns and fears, and also partly by a significant amount of distrust regarding the new technologies. This included concerns about radiation in the area of mobile communications, worries about data protection and data security, as well as general reservations about the prospect of being increasingly dependent on and determined by ICT.

Radiation
Data protection
Data loss

For developers of new applications, it is essential to be aware of the reasons why some users are reluctant to participate in what is offered by a Smart City. This awareness enables them to learn lessons for the future. They can improve their products or overcome reluctance in other ways, so that applications that are essentially perceived as helpful can be put to use.

Suppliers of new applications are faced with two distinct problems. Firstly: the cautiousness towards new technologies is often not clearly substantiated. The suppliers can only make guesses as to the reasons their offers are not taken up. Therefore, it is necessary to seek dialogue with the users and non-users who are the intended addressees of the available offers. In T-City Friedrichshafen, such dialogues took place over the course of the project, with specific focus on various target groups. There was an array of initiatives for approaching target groups designed to determine their wishes and requirements. Accompanying research with a well-thought-out structure can support such initiatives. In order to get to know the reasons behind the reservations toward the project ideas and to understand the concerns and fears, it is important for the suppliers to listen carefully and be willing to learn.

Concerns are often latent.

The ability and willingness to listen is important for improving ideas.

Secondly, the concerns and fears that the suppliers get to know by listening are often difficult to counteract. *"Maybe it really is dangerous…"* can be heard from discussion partners in Friedrichshafen, too. It simply isn't possible to know and foresee all the consequences of putting the technologies into practice, even if a lot of effort and money is spent on researching its effects and offering solutions for dealing with them. The high degree of complexity of modern technological and organizational applications is often difficult to figure out for laypeople, sometimes even for the experts. Terrible crashes, such as the nuclear power plant catastrophe in Fukushima in Japan, show the public that the risks of large-scale technologies aren't fully controllable (Beck 1986). Concerns and fears of users of the new information and communication technologies are not directly related to such large and spectacular events, but nevertheless a level of skepticism about the use of apparently harmless technological solutions remains.

Risks of large-scale technologies

So even among the users who navigate the Internet self-confidently there is a latent distrust of the system (DIVSI 2012). There are even risks associated with the straightforward and everyday applications, engraved into society's cultural memory at the beginning of the nineteen-sixties because of the Thalidomide scandal. To be able to continue to use the Internet at ease, despite personal experiences of system failures or those portrayed in the media, the continual fostering of significant trust in the system is required—this means trust in a depersonalized system that functions autonomously.

More information on the topic of trust: Luhmann (2000)

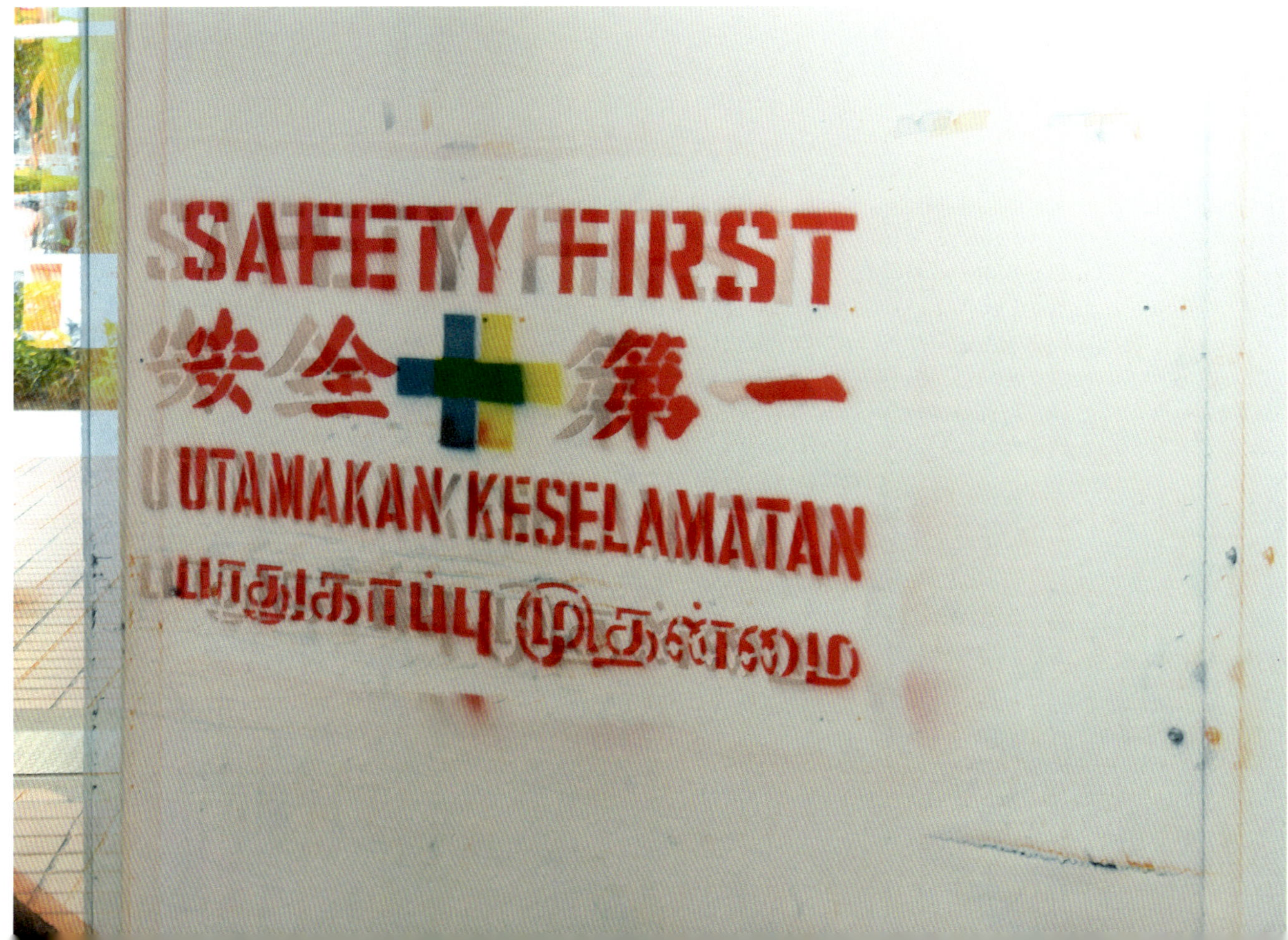

Mobile communications and WLAN— "They are bringing radiation directly into the home …"

Users of mobile communications are concerned about the issue of electromagnetic radiation. One Friedrichshafen resident stated: *"Of course I don't know whether the radiation is harmful or not. I am unable to judge this. I also don't know yet whether it will kill me one day. Maybe I will die because I used to smoke, or maybe I will be run over by a car. I have no idea."* Invisible radiation is an unavoidable aspect of the operation of mobile communications and wireless Internet via WLAN at home or in public spaces. The effects of radiation have been examined by many research analyses (BfS 2012). They indicate a high probability of harmlessness, but are unable to completely sweep aside many concerns.

The many analyses of electromagnetic radiation are so complex that they are virtually incomprehensible to laypeople and there is reluctance to take them on board, Even experts argue occasionally about the interpretation of the results (Schrader 2012). At the same time, people often have a resigned attitude and decide in the end to accept the risks. Some, however, remain skeptical because it can take a while before the first negative effects are apparent, and it is feasible that some causes and effects of damage have not yet been recognized. There could be a harmful impact that has not yet been connected to radiation. However, these concerns about possible harmful effects can contribute to increasing measures to reduce the potential dangers of transmissions as far as possible. The following opinion of one woman in Friedrichshafen on the subject of cell phone radiation reflects a similar standpoint: *"Well, I rarely hear that someone has done research and then says: ›Okay, there are ways to reduce the radiation.‹ It is only ever about packing even more technology in. So that it can do more and not so it can be safer. The opposite would be great."*

Users always make decisions about the application of the new technologies based on weighing their costs and usefulness. However, they often lack sufficient information. Furthermore, users have very differing attitudes and preferences. For example, some people use mobile access to the Internet but would never entrust their data to cloud hosts such as Google or Facebook. Others are willing to put all sorts of data online, but limit their use of mobile transmissions as far as possible to avoid its potentially harmful effects. These contradictions and individual preferences also came up in our interviews in Friedrichshafen: *"How many people already have wireless Internet in their homes nowadays? Or wireless telephones and the like? In doing so they are bringing radiation directly into the home, but then they turn around and say that the masts bother them."*

Uncertainties remain despite numerous studies

Ideally, a Smart City should pick up on all of these varying attitudes and turn them into assets for the decision-makers in the T-City project, as well as for the inhabitants. In order to achieve this, it is helpful to be aware of the concerns and fears that cause people to be skeptical towards new applications because of ICT. If the decision-makers in a Smart City, who are investing time and money into developing new solutions, know the concerns, they can take them into account, adjust to them, and improve their offers accordingly.

Data protection—"Where did they get my address?"

Data protection is another area where concerns and fears are frequently expressed regarding the use of the new ICT. *"Concerns about data abuse rank the highest in Germany with above-average frequency"* (Münchner Kreis 2011). The results of the representative survey, which was carried out annually from 2008 as part of T-City's accompanying research and in which inhabitants evaluated the application of and attitudes towards the ICT, confirm these concerns and fears also in relation to the city of Friedrichshafen.

Data protection is present

The inhabitants were asked to evaluate the two statements:
"I am concerned that the protection of my personal data is not sufficiently
taken into consideration in the implementation of new ICT."
"I perceive ICT as an invasion of my private space."
The result shows that around half of those questioned shared the general concern about the protection of personal data. In 2012 around 20 percent perceived ICT as an invasion of their personal space. Such concerns regarding data protection within ICT, which are evidently shared by a significant number of people, have to be taken into account and used constructively in order to create a networked Smart City that the inhabitants are also actively involved in.

Therefore, discussions about data protection are ongoing among the inhabitants when introducing a Smart City project, and play an important role in the success or failure of such a project. It is not the actual number of overt critics in the public debate that is pivotal. Instead, what is more decisive is the often latent concern that personal data could be misused. This lingering suspicion is a possible explanation for why the inhabitants tend to have reservations about the new Smart City projects.

Despite the occasionally critical perception of data protection, there is evidence of a widespread resigned attitude towards this issue, reflected in some of the comments made in interviews. *"I'm under no illusion. I think that anyone who wants to can already get at a whole bunch of data now."*

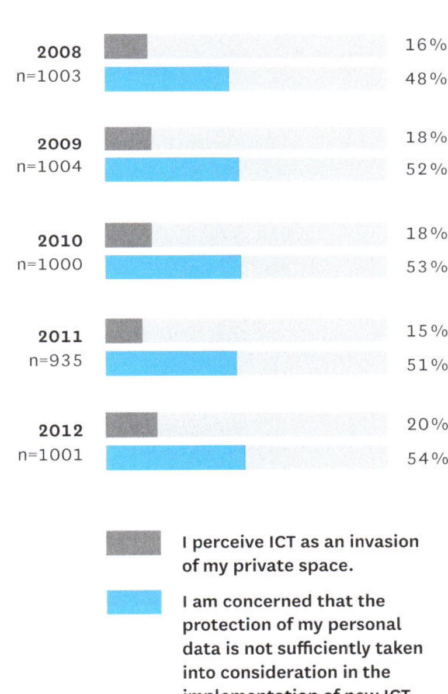

Data protection has various facets

Taking into account not only the results of the survey, but also the statements made in the interviews held as part of the accompanying research in Friedrichshafen, it becomes clear that the issue of data protection has many different facets. On the one hand, it is about the question of how the personal data is handled, which the user himself makes available on the web. The comments on this in our interviews range from convictions such as, *"I know that the data is sold for advertising purposes,"* to general concerns such as, *"In the end, it can't be ruled out that this information is perhaps also used for criminal purposes."* The fact that a telecommunications service provider has access to information that gives him the location of the user and could use this to his own advantage is perceived as alarming by some people. This issue was the subject of public debate in Germany in spring 2011.

Furthermore, it is speculated that personal information in cyberspace is visible to others who should not be seeing it. During a group discussion, seventh-grade students from a secondary school in Friedrichshafen were very aware that it was advisable to upload their photos onto social networks with the *"friends only"* setting, which limits who would be able to view them. However, the students were largely unaware of the possibility that their personal data might be used by network providers. This is also a source of subliminal unease among adult users. Users have no retrospective control over the possibility of uploaded data such as photos later being analyzed in detail using new technologies, such as face recognition, and being automatically linked to other arbitrary data.

Students are aware of some of the dangers.

The concerns and fears with regard to the handling of personal data are also leading to protests in areas of daily life that up until now have had nothing to do with the issue of data protection. A concerned Canadian citizen secured his traditional electricity meter in such a way that the electricity provider couldn't exchange it for a Smart Meter (Calanego 2012). The increasing implementation of communicating technologies opens up new issues. For instance, the use of Smart Meters—the intelligent meters for measuring electricity consumption, which enable the direct reading of values by the electricity supplier—makes it possible to draw conclusions about the personal behavior of the electricity customer. Researchers from the University of Applied Sciences Münster carried out a practical experiment, which showed that the data transmitted by a Smart Meter even enables deductions about which television programs are being watched (Greveler et al. 2011).

chat.cityandict.de

"Intelligent electricity meters give everything away"

Andreas Bentz, T-Systems (Wummer 2011)

A study carried out by IBM on Smart Metering shows that better knowledge about new technologies doesn't necessarily lead to a greater sense of ease about using them. Among those questioned in a survey, the group with the best knowledge of energy issues had the largest proportion (38 percent) of those who were of the opinion that Smart Metering opens up new risks regarding data protection. The groups who knew less about energy issues were less concerned about data protection: with an average knowledge of energy issues it was 25 percent, with little or no knowledge 21 percent (IBM 2012b, 5f.). These percentages correspond to the responses in the survey of Smart Meter customers in the T-City project in Friedrichshafen, in which 36 percent of the trial customers agreed with the statement that they are concerned that the protection of their personal data is not sufficiently taken into consideration when implementing the new technology.

In some cases though, the sharing of data can be a positive experience. For example the heart disease patients in the "Mobile Clinic" project, who benefit from close monitoring of their illness enabled by independent access to various vital statistics and their transfer to those in charge at the hospital, speak of a *"positive surveillance."*

Data protection within the T-City

In the T-City project, the issue of data protection is mentioned in the public relations work but doesn't play a significant role. Looking through all the publicly available documents in which information about T-City or the individual projects was provided by Deutsche Telekom, the city of Friedrichshafen, or other project partners over the course of the project, it can be seen that the issue of data protection was mentioned in only around 15 percent of them. In most cases—especially regarding the compact project flyers—it is limited to one or two sentences about *"safe data transfer"* or *"safe data access."* The exception is the project magazine "T-City Spiegel", with two issues reporting extensively about this topic. There is a double-page interview with the data protection officer at Deutsche Telekom, in which he discusses aspects of security with regard to data transfer, data security on the web, and the corresponding guidelines (T-City Friedrichshafen 2009). In a second article, the Smart Metering project manager from the municipal utility Stadtwerke Friedrichshafen talks about the issues of data protection and data abuse. Furthermore, the procedures for data acquisition and the data encryption measures are presented in relation to the Smart City project in Friedrichshafen (T-City Friedrichshafen 2010).

"(…) the more knowledge consumers had about energy, the more concerned they were with privacy issues with home energy usage data."

IBM (2012b)

166
For more information about the "Mobile Clinic" project, see the chapter "Open".

Data protection is taken into account, but not communicated adequately.

In the local press coverage of the project T-City Friedrichshafen, there is only sporadic mention of the data protection issue. During the period from June 2007 to December 2011, only sixteen articles about the T-City project were published in the two local daily newspapers in Friedrichshafen in which the data protection issue was mentioned. Most of the articles about data protection only mention it in passing; during this period, there were more than 1,000 articles about T-City.

According to the motto "Do good and talk about it," there are two ways of dealing with the problem of data protection regarding the use of the new ICT in Smart Cities. First of all, *good must be done.*" This means that the measures taken for effective data protection have to be thought of and resources allocated to them right from the start of the development of the new applications. Here, special emphasis should be placed from the outset on a *"principle of data economy,"* as has been requested for a long time by the national and regional data protection officers (National and Regional Data Protection Officers 1997). To do so, it can be helpful to involve the users who have major reservations and concerns. Secondly, it has to be talked about, in other words it is necessary to communicate the data protection solutions actively and positively.

"39 percent of the German population feel overwhelmed by the topic of data security and data protection on the Internet, and thus feel a sense of insecurity."
DIVSI 2012

Data reduction is the best form of data protection.

datasecurity.cityandict.de

202

Data security—"Oops! Your data could not be uploaded"

There is also great insecurity among many citizens concerning the security of stored personal data. Google's rather trite error message—"Oops! Your calendar cannot be accessed at the moment, please try again later"—to inform users of its electronic calendar about temporary malfunctions, doesn't inspire trust in the system. Several recent, temporary data losses within the cloud fuel the concern that one's personal data is not secure.

At the same time, there is evidence of a certain resigned attitude towards the issue of data security. One interviewee remarked on this: *"I am of the opinion that the web is to a certain extent secure, but nevertheless anything can happen. So I am fairly open-minded and say what can happen, will happen and I'm not too concerned about it."*

The inherent possibility of a malfunction of technical systems is a matter of concern for the citizens who were interviewed and it is borne out by their own experiences. This goes far beyond security when storing data, and ranges from a lack of mobile signal availability, to PC crashes and false alarms by smoke detectors integrated into a home network. Many computer users have experienced a hard drive crash or a computer invaded by viruses. Technical systems, whose operative readiness is unquestioningly taken for granted by many, to our surprise don't function flawlessly anymore. A sudden loss of data and the ensuing resetting and recovery cost a great deal of time and sometimes money. The developers and operators of ICT products and offers are relatively powerless in the face of the resulting discontent when using the new media. This is similar to the situation regarding the concerns and fears on the subject of cell phone radiation levels. Even if there were no reports about data losses, the concerns about a potential future malfunction can't be swept aside with positive statistics from the past.

There is little faith in the promise of work simplification through the use of new technologies, among other reasons, because of these bad experiences with malfunctions and crashes. While most users perceive technology as a facilitator, there are frequent reports of the hidden costs and undue effort involved in keeping systems functioning. This includes the many necessary updates of computer systems and programs.

Amazon Cloud Service: *"Many customers even have to come to terms with the fact that their data have been lost."*
Heise Online, 10.08.2011

Google-Mail: *"According to Google sources, it was not several hundred thousand as originally estimated, but only around 40,000 users who were affected by the loss of e-mails."*
Heise Online, 01.03.2011

Evernote: *"When questioned, a German spokesperson from Evernote revealed to Heise Online that the loss of notes reported by users was probably caused by the synchronization problems too."*
Heise Online, 07.01.2011

SideKick USA: *"Roz Ho, the Vice President at Microsoft responsible for 'Premium Mobile Experiences', reported that most, if not all of the data were restored."*
Heise Online, 15.10.2009

Apart from these unwanted side effects, which are related to the processing of information as the actual core application, there are concerns about the social consequences of the use of ICT. The changes in our use of time, the possible alienation from other people through the intensive preoccupation with technical systems, and the risks of a new dependence on ICT are issues to which other concerns and fears about the use of technology can be attributed.

204

Attitudes towards information and communication technology— taking concerns seriously

Among users, one can identify a wide range of attitudes to dealing with ICT on a daily basis. This applies to all areas of the new ICT, from handling a cell phone to the use of social networks, to name just two examples. These attitudes are typified by

- On the one hand, users who view technology as a mere tool for achieving certain objectives, and therefore often welcome innovations as a facilitator in their daily lives
- On the other hand, users who effectively perceive technology as an opponent, and struggle with the basics of using it, which keeps them from appreciating the actual purpose of usage

For example, the first type considers an E-mail simply as a means of making contact with someone. The second type, on the other hand, perceives this E-mail as something he has to deal with, instead of as communicating with someone as actually intended. If one doesn't succeed in presenting technology as a simple tool that can easily be of use, it is readily viewed as an interference and therefore rejected—except maybe by users who are technology enthusiasts.

There is another area that affects the relationship between the use of ICT and other activities in daily life. In the interviews with people living in Friedrichshafen, the topic of the organization of daily life frequently came up. The use of ICT applications has a wider scope nowadays and is perceived to be competing with other activities to a certain degree. The concern is frequently expressed that the new ICT leads to less physical exercise or to fewer social and cultural activities. In the surveys from 2009 to 2012, as many as a quarter of the inhabitants were of the opinion that the information and communication technologies tend to reduce *"activities, such as those of a sporting, cultural, or social nature."*

Other fears expressed by discussion partners, which can lead to a reluctance to use ICT, are of a clearly normative nature. This includes the concerns that spending time on the new technologies is *"a waste of time,"* that the web contains *"false information",* and that the use of the Internet has a tendency to be *"addictive."* One woman formulated her concern that technology might come to dominate her life as, *"people are becoming slaves to technology."*

Some users complain that the cost of Internet and mobile usage is too high. In particular, the interviewed students do not have enough money at their disposal to use the technology as widely as they would like. All age groups complain about the cost of mobile communications and data usage when abroad. In addition, there are complaints not only about the high direct costs, but also about too much advertising in various media. In this case, spam and pop-ups are mentioned exclusively, so it can be concluded that the form of the advertising plays an important role in its acceptance.

The concerns and fears presented in this chapter, which are harbored by a number of the people living in the city, make it seem plausible that the Smart City offers are only used in small measures. The organizers responsible for Smart Cities would be well advised to take the expressed concerns and fears seriously. In doing so, they can both increase the scope and acceptance of the Smart City solutions, and improve the offers themselves. If these aspects are not taken into consideration sufficiently, then in the worst-case scenario it could lead to the *"crash"* of the entire project.

A long step-by-step process

by Stephan Althoff, Director of Corporate Sponsoring and Events at Deutsche Telekom AG, Bonn

It all started with an idea. We simply wanted to show how modern information and communication technology (ICT) can change lives. Not just the lives of individual people, but also of businesses and administration—basically the life of a whole city. This is why we launched the T-City project in 2006. This new, modern city was to demonstrate the opportunities and potential that new technologies offer and how they can raise the quality of life.

Of course, creating T-City was a long step-by-step process. First of all, we laid state-of-the-art fiber optic cables throughout the city and determined locations for transmitter masts. It was at this point that the questions really started: "What does T-City have to do with me?" and "What is going on here?"

Throughout the project, we worked tirelessly to gain the support of the local population and companies for the project. We distributed information and encouraged participation with magazines, information events, a radio and TV broadcast, an online presence, and also later the relevant social media activities via Twitter, Facebook, YouTube, etc. We were also supported in this by the involvement of the ambassadors, a "citizens inform citizens" initiative designed to overcome barriers.

Of course, a city like Friedrichshafen is multilayered. People engage with technologies to different extents, are interested in different topic areas, and have very different requirements. In addition, some people have concerns about the protection of personal data, justifiably so. A wide range of target group initiatives aimed at businesses, school pupils, senior citizens, or families with children helped to convey our vision, projects, and ideas. The people welcomed these initiatives and were always curious to know what T-City was all about. We also benefitted from these initiatives, as this was the only way for us to gain a better understanding of what people really want or in what respects we had not taken their interests into consideration.

In 2009, we accelerated the T-City project further and embarked on a search for "Futurists." State-of-the-art devices could be actually used and tested in daily life in initially nine households—from single people to apartment-sharing communities, families with children, and senior citizens. It attracted great interest and was all set up on a voluntary basis, free of charge. It was sheer curiosity that motivated their participation. The Futurists were an important part of the project for us, as we always received honest and quite critical feedback from them. Furthermore, the Futurists personalized the T-City project—which perhaps seemed rather abstract—by putting it into practice with concrete examples and projects relating to people's everyday life, thereby making the project very tangible. The Futurists were always in demand as discussion partners, whether by the media, or even by many national and international groups of visitors. These visitors gathered information not only from us, but especially from the Futurists themselves, becoming infected by their enthusiasm for new technologies.

Not only did visitors come to T-City, however, but the T-City project was also widely presented outside of the Lake Constance region with a strong presence at CeBIT (the largest information technology trade fair in the world), nationwide road shows, media workshops, and participation in international contests in the context of urban development and ICT.

The extension of the cooperation between the city of Friedrichshafen and Deutsche Telekom for an additional three years from December 2011 created the basis for the continuation of this globally unique flagship project. We have many more ideas, and citizens and businesses in Friedrichshafen will continue to benefit from the opportunity of remaining pioneers in the field of networked living and working.

E-government in Germany: progress, naivety, and déjà vus

*by Tino Schuppan, Professor of Public Managment
at the Institute of the Federal Employment Agency and
Director of Science at the Institute for E-government (IfG.CC), Potsdam*

For more than a decade, e-government has been driven forward in Germany on all state levels. The start of this process was closely linked to the development of the Internet, although it is often disregarded that the use of information and communication technology (ICT) in administration already has a long history. The administrative information systems that emerged in the nineteen-seventies were already tasked with linking ICT to the modernization of administration. Whether intentionally or not, the use of ICT brought about organizational changes that were probably greater than many of the widely proclaimed management reforms.

The start of e-government in Germany can be traced back to the end of the nineteen-nineties, when large cities began to develop their web pages. At that time, city governments were primarily concerned with the portrayal of their cities, with some information about municipal services. E-government was limited to a showcase function, featuring the mayor's "famous" short welcoming address. Therefore, organizationally, it was then in the remit of the municipal public relations offices.

The project Media@komm, with which the Federal Ministry of Economics aimed to achieve a breakthrough for the electronic signature, is regarded as a milestone in e-government. Although at the end of the nineties Germany had the first electronic signature law in the world, there were hardly any applications for it. The first phase of e-government was characterized by technical naivety, experimentation, and errors—although large cities in particular, such as Mannheim or Stuttgart, were quick to recognize that e-government also necessitated changes to administrative processes.

The initiative BundOnline 2005 was set up in the year 2000 with the aim of making all web-enabled federal services available online. This concept is problematic because: 1) the state actually offers very few services directly to citizens; 2) not every "web-enabled" service is necessarily suitable for the Internet; and 3) the objective of "putting everything possible online" limits the project to a large extent just to online services, while not dealing with matters such as the reorganization of administration and its processes on the basis of ICT.

A new phase of e-government began in 2005 with the initiative Deutschland Online. Representatives of all administrative levels participated in this program because it finally acknowledged that an approach that spanned all administrative levels was necessary. It pushed for numerous standardizations, however the strategic objective was not always quite clear. In some areas of practice and e-government research in the field of information technology, the notion still persists that an overarching form of cooperation can only succeed by means of standardization, disregarding all too often that administration also has to be capable of cooperation on a cultural, organizational, and individual action level.

The experience of Deutschland Online led to focusing on projects that were a special priority for all government departments, such as vehicle registration, notification systems, or civil status registrations. The emphasis was therefore on the further development of the infrastructure and the improvement of registration processes. Over time, the range of schemes was extended through further new projects, such as the EU services directive and the standard public services hotline number D115. This number is unprecedented, because the state took over the supervision of the scheme and parts of the management. It is surprising that, despite the predominance of federal structures, the state managed to take control to a certain extent of the core municipal business of public services.

This development shows that there is significant willingness at all state levels to implement e-government. However, the projects are still primarily driven by technology. Organizational restructuring and change management clearly play a more minor part. Pilot schemes are often discontinued before the end of a project, so that new solutions are not incorporated into daily administrative life. The administrative policy and strategy are still lacking direction and clarity about their objectives. What could and should the state provide and how can it operate in future? These are the principal questions raised by e-government.

It can thus be concluded that the e-government projects in Germany that have failed so far have not done so because of a lack of ICT support, but because they do not take sufficient account of the administrative context. In many cases, consultancy firms determine the agenda, which has led to a degree of privatization of the objectives of administrative policies. In any case, this development clearly demonstrates that greater competence has to be established within governing authorities in terms of knowledge, skills, and abilities.

Electronic participation— a new participation channel

by Oliver Märker, Managing Director of Zebralog Ltd, Berlin

The idea of involving citizens in public planning and decision-making processes using the Internet emerged in Germany at the end of the nineteen-nineties, with the first attempts on a municipal level (cf. Märker/Wehner 2011a). About fifteen years later, the Internet has become an important basic hub of information and interactivity with regard to civic participation, especially when planning the municipal budget (cf. www.buergerhaushalt.org) and in urban development. Later on, this development was also applied on a regional and national level, opening up decision-making processes—previously largely shielded from the public—to ideas and suggestions from the residents, especially regarding policies and the drafting of laws (cf. www.besser-studieren.nrw.de; www.ich-will-deinen-kopf.de; www.mitreden-u.de; or www.e-konsultation.de).

This development reflects an increasing public willingness to participate, demonstrated and also driven by Web 2.0: citizens no longer want to be merely the addressees of information and decisions, they want to contribute to the formulation of solutions. This development also proves that electronic participation processes in administration and politics are gaining popularity, not least because of the decreasing faith in the political and administrative institutions' competence in providing solutions. Politics and administration are the initiators as well as the sponsors of electronic procedures, through which the civic population is informed about relevant issues and pending plans in politics, and at the same time administration and politics are also informed about the prioritization of relevant measures or planning schemes and about alternative ideas on the part of the citizens. Generally speaking, online participation enables residents to comment on and evaluate suggestions and schemes within administration and politics. In addition, they provide citizens with the opportunity to make their own suggestions and add their knowledge and experience to the

pool of possible plans and strategic goals. For example by providing ratings for planned cuts, which should be taken into consideration in the budget planning policies.

Apart from these opportunities for the exchange of information between residents, local administration, and politics, online processes also lead to increased legitimization: actions can generally be better justified if the affected citizens were consulted beforehand. This is especially the case for those decisions that are unpopular but necessary. This shows the nature of these online consultations: indirectly they are democratic processes that do not question the decision-making authority of politics. Suggestions from citizens serve the purpose of additional consulting input, with the elected representatives ultimately deciding to what extent it can contribute to solving problems. Paradoxically, it is precisely their inherent non-binding nature that makes online consultations acceptable to political institutions. This form of participation provides the participants with a new opportunity to make their concerns and suggestions the subject of parliamentary debates. In any case, there is a shifting of boundaries: the political-administrative process becomes more accessible through e-participation, increasing the pressure on politics. For instance, not only does all basic information about decisions have to be disclosed, ideally as machine-readable Open Data, but why and to what extent e-participation output is (not) incorporated into decisions also has to be justified publicly.

Critics of electronic participation processes point out the low participation rate compared to elections or their lack of representativeness, therefore doubting the usefulness of the participation output (cf. Märker/Wehner 2011b). The first point disregards the fact that e-participation processes constitute means of participation that take place in the interim period in between elections and achieve high participation rates compared to the earlier participation model (e.g., municipal budget www.bonn-packts-an.de). The second point neglects the fact that these processes do not claim to be representative, as not all individual residents contribute their opinion—which would be the case for truly representative processes. Instead, information should be accessible to everyone. Therefore, a basis has to be created for an open exchange of ideas and opinions. This doesn't preclude improving the existing procedures so that the hitherto only poorly represented sections of the population—especially young people and children—can be included as
participants. A new challenge that existed even before the Internet was used as a participation channel has become even more evident and greater as a consequence of its use. It shows, hardly surprisingly: e-participation is also participation.

Social media—driver of the mediatization of society

by Caja Thimm, Professor of Media Studies and Intermedia at the University of Bonn

For a long time people have been taking it for granted that they can communicate with others who are separated from them by space or time. Nowadays, however, it is especially the social networks or "social media"—such as Facebook, Twitter, XING, or the VZ networks (SchülerVZ or StudiVZ, for pupils and students respectively), as well as extensive reference resources like Wikipedia and blogs—that have evolved on Web 2.0 and constitute the new means of communication of our everyday media. These Web 2.0 applications organize and support social contacts, they enable new work relationships, friendships and close relationships, they provide people with information from all spheres of life, society and politics, they organize and promote citizens' movements and social revolutions (for example in Myanmar, Tunisia, and Egypt), they create new economic systems and types of market, and they make the technology of the media infrastructure available to counter-public movements (e. g., WikiLeaks).

Thus, on the one hand, social networks are a marketplace, a communication platform, and an entertainment medium; on the other hand, they are also a knowledge and information resource. They form a new interactive (living) space, in which the consumer becomes the producer—today everyone is an author and the strict regulations of the production and publication controls of mass media are no longer applicable.

The social relevance of Web 2.0 is now undisputed and since the start of the Internet's expansion through participatory online offers, various forms of social media—blogs, social communities, Wikis, etc.—have become one of its mainsprings, with regard to both private and institutional communication.

Opinions on this development are clearly divided. On the one hand, there are those who are overtly enthusiastic about media, who embrace new participatory options, or are already talking about a global café. For them, social networks are a medium that technically recreates the oral cultures of the past. According to this idea, electronic communities are viewed as emulating the real public places that no longer exist, where people met with others and communicated. They are considered as public forms of communication in the tradition of the nineteenth-century salons and cafés and described as an "electronic agora." This is based on the premise that a communicative culture, like the traditional oral cultures that existed before the advent of writing, is capable of being technically reproduced. Here, the web is viewed as the hub for the technical realization of modernity, as a forum for idealized communicative cultures in which the "wisdom of the masses" produces the best ideas for society.

The critical perspective, on the other hand, is characterized by fundamental skepticism regarding inflated expectations of digital social communities and views computer-mediated communication as the cause for a decrease in sociability, intimacy, and intellectual competence. Owing to the filter functions of the large social media corporations, for example, manipulative perception and relationship frameworks can be constructed among users. Furthermore, it is claimed that the Internet in itself is a medium of inequality and is divisive. Criticism is also directed towards aspects of digital socialization. Although the participation culture of the social networks may contribute towards group formation, identity, and community, at the same time web technology is deemed as limiting interpersonal relationships.

Whatever view one shares, the social networks can be considered one of the most significant drivers of the complete mediatization of society, which will continue to present us with new challenges for a long time.

Interpersonal skills in relation to local competitiveness

by Stephan A. Jansen, Founding President and managing Director of Zeppelin University, and Member of the Advisory Board of T-City Friedrichshafen

The German sociologist Georg Simmel was aware of the fact already in 1903: *"It must be reiterated that major cities are the real breeding grounds for this culture that has grown away from everything personal … with such an overwhelming mass of crystalized and impersonalized minds that personality can't survive it. [Cities are] constructs of the highest degree of impersonality."* (Simmel 1903, p. 185f.)

Major cities and major corporations would be wise to view their personal culture of interpersonal skills and relationship building as the key to their competitiveness, both local and commercial. In this respect, the trialing of electronic and especially personal networks within T-City Friedrichshafen, as a relationship between the large corporation Deutsche Telekom and the medium-sized city of Friedrichshafen, was a good idea from start to finish.

Converting a good idea into an innovation, apart from developing good "governance" of the project, requires precisely these interpersonal skills in two ways:

1. The interpersonal skills of the governance:

As regards the possibly largest municipal cooperation project in the area of "E-government" up until now, the project "d-NRW" involving municipalities in North Rhine-Westphalia, I was not particularly aware of any special committees, ambassadors, "Futurists," etc. That project had an experimental culture of failure and recovery. Initially, T-City was very bold in the face of organized and disorganized resistance. However, the Advisory Board itself should have had less of a role at times in favor of wider civic participation, as our importance was only secondary. Owing to the necessarily selective information we provided and our infrequent meetings, our input and our constructive criticism was certainly not considered too significant.

2. *The interpersonal skills of the municipal partners:*
The T-City paradox is that the particular individual interpersonal skills
(i.e., "working together locally") proved to be more important than
the technology; they breathed life into the electronic networking opportunities. The ambassadors, the workshops, the Futurists, and
various other media activities were ultimately more important for the
development than the formal governance structure. Nevertheless,
throughout the project, many applications remained unavailable to
the citizens and herein lies the paradox of the "invisible supporting
technology": appreciating the complexity of simplification.

Recommendations
The future of cities lies in the stronger orientation towards personalization, while professionalizing the procedures—especially those concerning "compulsory communication" between citizens and the state.

In the face of globalization, we are experiencing a remunicipalization of concrete plans for reform and of processes of change. And this is the right way to go, because our neighbors are what is important and spatial co-presence is key to the formation of new virtual spaces. We are familiar with what it takes to succeed from the so-called cluster research, at least in an abstract way and, as always in science, only retrospectively!

1.

Cooperative applications: the application that Zeppelin University was also supposedly part of could have been made more representative, as a product of the wishes of all the participants. The appetite for a project is fueled by a good menu.

2.

Cooperative management team: a full-time, strongly connected, and regionally interlinked team is essential for the success of a cluster. The governance should be inclusive and motivational, rather than exclusive and controlling.

3.

Emotionalizing communication: technology can be a sensory experience, for example, in the way we can enjoy the look or feel of certain gadgets. Communication for the purpose of forwarding relationships—whether between the town hall and citizens, doctor and patient, student and teacher, etc.—needs a story. We only remember few facts and technical details, but we remember extraordinary stories.

4.

Focus on added value and business models and not on technology: technology corporations have enough test labs and market research. An entire city is about more than that and it comes down to what analyses and researches can't achieve: local exchanges and added value through the innovation of commercial business models and through service innovations for citizens, patients, pupils, and students. If one succeeds in this, then mid-sized cities can become the next attractive metropolises, but without the impersonality factor.

Urbanity 2.0—about the development of the urban in the age of increasing virtuality

by Stefan Schmitz, Head of Division, Federal Ministry for Economic Cooperation and Development (BMZ), Bonn/Berlin

Technical progress and social change have always transformed the city and life within it. Modern information and communication technology is also making its mark on the physiognomy of the city and the urban make-up. However, on closer inspection, the relationship between urbanity and virtuality proves to be more complex and multifaceted than one would at first assume.

On the one hand, urbanity is something very concrete. One can find urbanity where people enter into contact with each other and meet face to face, where the density of buildings and diversity of functions create vitality, where a juxtaposition of public and private spaces gives each individual the choice of whether to be in the public lime-light, to withdraw into the anonymity of the masses, or to retreat within one's own four walls. This freedom of choice also makes urbani-ty a state of mind that goes beyond the concrete framework. It reflects an attitude towards life that is characterized by open-mindedness and tolerance. Urbanity is a combination of the specific and the gener-al: the particular historical, cultural, and architectural features of the location alongside the blueprint of a universally applicable notion of how the "city" is perceived beyond the specific location. Urbanity has an architectural, spatial, political, and social dimension, but it is also a mental imag. **Urbanity is not only a real reality, but also a virtual reality.**

Virtual reality has existed for mankind since the emergence of cave painting and script. Virtuality is our world of pictures and symbols, of vision and imagination. The emergence of technical media such as the radio, TV, cell phone, and finally the Internet has greatly increased the significance of virtual reality. It seems that to an ever-increasing extent we are turning away from direct human interaction in favor of media-based relationships. These media-based relationships, along with the acceleration of means of transport, form the basic precondition for the spatial unbundling of formerly closely connected functions and the widening of social and economic interaction at all levels—from the suburbanization of cities to world-economic integration. Even if the virtuality created by computer technology is only one of many explanatory factors in this "despatialization" and its negative effects in themselves are fewer than might be feared, one can nevertheless conclude: ***virtual reality is a threat to the traditional bases of urbanity.***

New media open up fascinating possibilities. For each individual, they can bring a broadening of one's horizons and a greater freedom of choice, between real and the most wide-ranging virtual offers. For communities, they provide the opportunity for new forms of communication and collective intelligence. This also creates a parallel urbanity in virtual space. This Internet-based, virtual urbanity displays a surprising number of similarities to the conventional type of urbanity. The dialectic that is so typical of the real city, between the conscious self-expression of the individual on the one hand, and the withdrawal into anonymity on the other, is also reflected in all the current social networks provided nowadays by the Internet. Furthermore, it appears that surfing and chatting in virtual public space don't preclude strolling around in real public space and that virtual urbanity and real urbanity can really exist in parallel. Even if many high-flying expectations regarding the virtual presence of cities on the web are perhaps not fulfilled, one can nevertheless observe: ***virtual reality itself is becoming a new, complementary urbanity.***

06

Update

Deutsche Telekom and the city of Friedrichshafen put
a Smart City into practice over the course of five years,
by means of the "T-City" project. A wide range of
ideas and concepts that apply new information and
communication technologies (ICT) to everyday life in
a city were tested as a trial for the future. Apart from a
summary of the challenges faced and the conditions
for success in such a project, this chapter contains four
general conclusions. First, a Smart City project needs
to be integrated into the particular local circumstances
and has to create relevant and widely applicable solutions. Second, in order to do so, it requires a framework
that enables the benefits of a Smart City to be experienced by users on a practical level through concrete and
tangible individual projects. Third, it is only this that
will lead to a widespread identification with such an
idea, which is essential for the long-term integration of
the project. Fourth, in order to be able to cooperate successfully over a long period of time, the many participating partners who carry out a Smart City project have
to formulate and regularly review their roles, objectives,
and mutual expectations. All of this can contribute to
converting a vision into a project that can comprehensively improve the quality of life of the inhabitants.

Taking chances— learning from experience

"Those who don't make mistakes are not innovative enough."
Hamid Akhavan, former Chief Technology Officer, Deutsche Telekom

Every program in the digital world needs to be updated regularly. The practical use of the programs reveals their operational problems; furthermore, weaknesses in their development and installation become apparent retrospectively. Repeatedly opening and using programs on a daily basis reveals that small improvements are necessary and that certain optimizations would be helpful. Mistakes that were made at the development and installation stages can be corrected and eliminated by means of an update.

This concluding chapter will provide a further comprehensive summary of the current significance of Smart City concepts. Some twenty years after the term was first used in expert circles and about five years after a profusion of Smart City concepts started cropping up all over the world, it is time to take stock of these new initiatives. This is the first aim of this book.

The second aim of this book is not to present Smart Cities in an abstract and generalized way, but instead to provide a more in-depth analysis of a concrete Smart City project by using specific examples and to relate it to the context of urban development concepts. The T-City in Friedrichshafen at Lake Constance presented itself for this purpose. Around five years after this project was launched, the time has come to present a summary introducing the unusual Public-Private Partnership (PPP) between Deutsche Telekom and the city of Friedrichshafen. The presentation of this Smart City project shows how the inhabitants react to the new information and communication technologies and to what extent they take up the concrete offers.

After the summary, we conclude with four questions, the answers to which we consider to be the central messages of this book: In what ways are the new Smart City concepts integrated into spatial structures? How do the integrative Smart City concepts relate to the urban development debate in Germany?

How should a partnership between private and public sector partners be structured in the future when putting such concepts into practice? How can Smart City concepts foster the enthusiasm of the users too?

228

In a nutshell—summary

A wide array of Smart City concepts has emerged in recent years. Whether it is in Singapore, in Songdo in South Korea, in Luxembourg or in Paredes in Portugal—ideas for Smart Cities can be found in nearly all parts of the world. A common feature of all the initiatives is that they use the new information and communication technologies to meet the current and global challenges faced by the people there and attempt to contribute to solving them. The new technologies are intended to support a higher level of efficiency within cities in a wide range of spheres, thereby ideally improving the living conditions of the people.

Many Smart City concepts all around the world

Integrative approach

The analyses carried out by current technology studies and the ideas behind selected Smart City projects show in the second chapter of this book that a lot of what is grandiosely promised is still only on paper and to a large extent has not yet been put into practice. This applies both to the large-scale "Greenfield" projects—which are planned especially in the Asian growth regions and are not a realistic proposition in densely populated Germany—and to the concepts that seek to adapt and optimize preexisting city structures.

But often merely visions and …

The Smart Cities concept often includes integrative initiatives, but upon closer inspection these turn out to be merely trendy labels for a whole host of activities in individual sectors. The majority of the projects that are labeled as Smart Cities only focus on isolated areas of daily life. In particular, they involve the conscious and efficient management of increasingly depleted energy resources or the regulation of the increasing volume of traffic all over the world, which is an ever-increasing challenge for our cities and in some cases leads to chaotic conditions. With regard to these, Smart Metering and Smart Traffic promise intelligent monitoring solutions through new information and communication technologies.

… often just a label

In the light of this, it is remarkable that Deutsche Telekom—as the largest telecommunications enterprise in Europe—set itself the goal six years ago of developing a concrete Smart City over a long period of time. The corporation held a nationwide city contest for all mid-sized German cities in order to find the best partner for this goal. Deutsche Telekom pledged to finance the installation of state-of-the-art broadband technology, which isn't a matter of course in cities of this size. Furthermore, the corporation gave a five-year commitment to develop new projects based on the fast broadband connections together with the winner of the contest. The city of Friedrichshafen at Lake Constance was selected. Comparable city contests by other large private-sector enterprises—such as IBM, Google, and Philips—are either more conceptual or more short-term.

City contest held by Deutsche Telekom led to the T-City in Friedrichshafen.

The T-City, as the chosen Smart City at Lake Constance was called, was launched in spring 2007. It took less than a year for Deutsche Telekom to install the fastest available broadband connection across the whole urban area. During this time, the two unequal project partners laid down the ground rules for their further cooperation and set out the content of the project areas that they wanted to engage in. Shortly afterwards, they developed the first individual projects together, in which the inhabitants were offered new applications on the basis of the broadband technology. However, it took a long time for the inhabitants to muster any enthusiasm for the T-City. The third chapter presents, among other things, why this was the case.

The T-City project had to be integrated into the urban society and also into the corporation. The city, which already enjoyed an exceptional quality of life, lacked a creative milieu for a Smart City project, despite the local technology enterprises. Friedrichshafen is characterized by a high level of economic prosperity and excellent recreational value in an unusual symbiosis, with a high degree of satisfaction regarding the living conditions. Deutsche Telekom and the city of Friedrichshafen found it difficult, despite an imaginative public relations campaign, to convince the inhabitants of the benefits of the project. At the same time, the municipal government was hesitant to support the project as its highest priority, while T-City also had to be integrated into Deutsche Telekom as a cross-over project, which wasn't always easy either and which affected the project in certain areas. Despite the difficulties, numerous individual projects were implemented during the course of the project, with varying degrees of success. Some individual projects went into production, while others had to be abandoned for various reasons. In this respect, the city served as a testing ground for the future, in which the applications were tried out, and in some cases shelved.

As shown in the fourth chapter, through the many interviews with the inhabitants about the concrete use of new media, the citizens of Friedrichshafen generally perceived the new information and communication technologies as giving them further options in their daily lives. They use a wide range of mobile or stationary media, depending on the situation, to interconnect worldwide or communicate locally with friends or family. It is also apparent that not all of the inhabitants have access to these options and that not everyone is capable of using them. Thus, in Friedrichshafen there is also a Digital Divide with regard to demographic aspects—such as age and sex.

The spatiotemporal changes experienced by the inhabitants through the use of ICT are perceived ambivalently. While the new forms of communication, the new ways of using media, or even the increasing blurring of spheres of daily life that used to be clearly delineated are on the one hand perceived as enhancing daily life and bringing a new level of freedom, on the other hand these aspects are also seen as competing with the "real" city and its qualities, as an additional burden, or as social pressure.

The T-City of Friedrichshafen—which is based on the application of new ICT to the various aspects of life within the city, with the purpose of enhancing the quality of life and of creating locational advantages—remains largely "invisible" in the perception of many inhabitants. The non-visible technology solutions are regarded by many people as too abstract and intangible. The inhabitants do not seem to understand their purpose and would like further explanations. Ultimately, the project is not really perceived as being developed in conjunction with the urban society. It is viewed as having limited local relevance, despite imaginative public relations campaigns by the corporation. The individual projects that were evaluated show that the users who are directly involved have positive experiences, but this "visibility" remains elusive for the majority of inhabitants. And so the "Tumor Conference" only facilitates the daily working lives of the participating doctors at the hospitals, the "Mobile Clinic" gives heart disease patients a sense of security in their daily lives and in dealing with their illness, the platform "Kindergarten Online" will simplify the planning of requirements and organizational matters in the future for child care workers, the "Smart Meter" helps the residents to identify the power guzzlers in their household. The positive effects are mostly limited to the direct addressees of the application. These individual projects show clearly that the opportunity to try them out fosters enthusiasm and can make the T-City tangible.

The project in Friedrichshafen was carried out over five years as a PPP between Deutsche Telekom and the city of Friedrichshafen. The fifth chapter shows that if there are conflicting objectives within the project, then it is a threat to the smooth cooperation between the two partners. If fundamentally different orientations are seen as being complementary rather than as competing, then such a project can succeed. The orientation towards corporate profit and the orientation towards public welfare don't have to be mutually exclusive. One can create win-win situations that benefit both partners. However, to do so it is necessary to communicate extensively to clarify different points of view and expectations.

Apart from the risk factors affecting the execution of the project, the concerns and fears of users relating to the new information and communication technologies are another important issue in Smart Cities. While many citizens and businesses welcome the development and the application of new technologies, there are also many people who have reservations towards them. These include the electromagnetic radiation of wireless connections, the misuse of personal data stored in virtual space, and the potential loss of data through technical malfunctions.

These concerns cause considerable difficulties for the suppliers who are developing the Smart City solutions. As the concerns are often latent, they are generally not expressed explicitly and therefore dampen the demand for Smart City offers somewhat indirectly. These concerns can often be difficult to counteract, because they are in relation to a potential future problem that is still uncertain. Therefore, skeptics are difficult to convince. However, these concerns and fears expressed by the inhabitants and businesses also open up an opportunity for the Smart City suppliers to take these critical points on board at an early stage and use them to improve the Smart City "product" for everyone.

232

Finding balance—considering the local context and adapting to the world

As the example of the T-City in Friedrichshafen clearly demonstrated, a Smart City is affected by a wide range of local, regional, national, and global circumstances, which have to be taken into consideration during its development and implementation. The ICT-based solutions that are developed and applied in a Smart City should be transferable to other cities. This first aspect is based on the objectives of the private sector businesses that are involved in Smart City projects. After all, a Smart City is not a *"goodwill project"* for these companies, but a new business sector that has to ensure long-term profitability.

At the same time, the example of the T-City in Friedrichshafen showed that a Smart City has to take the respective local sociocultural and specific historical contexts into account. These aspects are interwoven with the respective city and make up its idiosyncrasies (Löw 2008). This second aspect affects the integration of a Smart City project into the city and its level of acceptance by the urban society. After all, every city "ticks" in its own particular way and therefore requires individual solutions. The chapter "Install" shows that this aspect plays an important role not only with regard to the cities, but also with regard to the participating businesses. A certain historical background and individual company cultures have to be taken into account.

Ultimately, cities are not isolated units that function and act completely independently. They are not only regionally and nationally, but also increasingly globally linked to a network of cities characterized by hierarchies and specialized functions (Blotevogel 2002). This results in fierce competition, which plays an important role in the development of Smart City concepts. Therefore, a Smart City cannot become "smart" by itself. Many fields of action within a city, for which Smart City projects are developing solutions, are affected by regional, national, and even global circumstances, and they are shaped by them. For example, technical solutions that have been introduced into the educational sector in Germany have to conform not only to municipal guidelines but also, and in particular, to the respective regional directives. A second example of such dependencies is in the area of telemedicine. It emerged here that applications can only offer an added value if they are compatible with other systems and can be used not just locally, but also nationally, or even worldwide. Smart City concepts that offer locally limited "insular solutions" are therefore no longer viable.

Hence, a Smart City is faced with the challenge of implementing solutions that are both transferable and tailored to local requirements, which furthermore have to be compatible with both local and transregional structures. The Smart City concepts cannot apply only to the particular urban area, but nevertheless they must take the historical background and the city's idiosyncrasies into account and make the most of them to be able to implement the project successfully.

Visions and individual projects—both are needed

The Smart City concepts that form part of recent debates about urban development policies have very wide-ranging ambitions on many levels. They seek to contribute to improving the living conditions of the inhabitants of a city in as many areas as possible. This is reminiscent of the urban development plans in Germany, where public planning authorities have been striving for an integrative procedure for more than forty years. The late nineteen-sixties and early nineteen-seventies, in particular, were shaped by the ambition to combine all aspects of life together in the most comprehensive and integrated way possible and to pursue urban development objectives in the form of temporally, spatially and financially delineated schemes. This type of urban policy had a high and wide appeal.

However, this policy referred to as the *"God-Father Model"* of planning by the urban sociologist Walter Siebel (1989) was doomed to failure to a large extent, because the cities and municipalities rarely managed to bring the individual departmental policies together integratively, let alone get private investors to commit to such comprehensive initiatives. The consequence was a rather pragmatic procedure within urban development policy from the end of the nineteen-eighties, in which the municipal objectives were pursued in individual manageable projects. Furthermore, this was more compatible with the interests of the private sector, whose investment is essential for converting the objectives into reality. Thereafter, urban policies continued to be oriented towards overall concepts, so as to give the schemes some direction, but the ideals behind the overall concepts of spatial development were decided on quite pragmatically. The individual projects were not necessarily derived from these ideal overall objectives, but were measured against them when they were carried out. Karl Ganser, who directed the International Building Exhibition Emscher Park in the Ruhr district for ten years and coordinated more than one hundred individual projects for the ecological, economical, and social modernization of the Emscher zone, referred to this procedure as *"perspective incrementalism"* (Ganser 1991).

In contrast to the urban development concepts of the last forty years in Germany, it is the private sector that has initiated some of the Smart City concepts. It was Deutsche Telekom that invited the participants in the T-City contest to submit a comprehensive and integrative concept for a city in which the new information and communication technologies were to play a significant role. While it sought the German Association of Towns and Municipalities as a partner, the initiator and the driving force was the private corporation. The objectives of the project were very wide-ranging and highly ambitious. The T-City project was to significantly improve the quality of life for the people, and the locational advantages for the businesses in the city of Friedrichshafen. Therefore, the idea was to incorporate the daily life of an urban society in its entirety and with all its facets in a very integrative way. All of the inhabitants and municipal institutions were invited to play an active part.

However, during the concrete implementation of T-City it emerged that the individual projects could not fulfill the ambition of enhancing the quality of life as a whole. Instead, each individual project had very specific addressees, such as students and teachers with the educational platform "Edunex," elderly people and care workers with the telemonitoring project "Mobile Clinic," or passengers and suppliers of transport services with the E-ticketing project "KatCard," to name just three examples from the extensive portfolio of individual projects. However, the sum of all the individual solutions didn't really succeed in sparking the intended synergies between the participating partners and didn't lead to a new general urban character beyond the respective impact of the individual projects. Interconnection of the whole urban area was only partially achieved by the T-City project.

Innovations through PPP—
using what is familiar
and making changes possible

The example of the T-City project as a cooperation between Deutsche Tele-kom and the city of Friedrichshafen represents a special form of PPP. In most cases, it has been the cities and municipalities that have sought a private sector business to participate in a PPP, which would support them in the financing, the building, or the management of real estate project or infrastructural development. In the case of the T-City project, it was the other way round. It was a private-sector business that sought a city, with which it could demonstrate how an improvement of the quality of life and of the location could be achieved through broadband networking. Deutsche Telekom wanted to show what it was capable of as a telecommunications enterprise and how the modern information and communication technologies can engender widespread usage.

The T-City project differs in two ways from many other Smart City projects. Firstly, the project isn't only restricted to the development of visions or to merely providing consulting for the city of Friedrichshafen. Instead, it is about concretely implementing the numerous ideas for applications based on the new information and communication technologies over a period of five years. Secondly, contrary to other Smart Cities, the T-City follows a participatory approach. The joint development of projects between a large corporation and an urban society was the ambitious objective that couldn't be fulfilled in all respects, but which was very instructive for both partners and led to interesting insights.

The ambitious plan to develop, plan, execute, and operate long-term projects together with the managers of a global corporation and the various partners within a mid-sized city required a fundamental change of the previous roles of all those involved. This was a big difficulty that couldn't always be satisfactorily overcome. If all those involved suddenly find themselves playing a different role, then the old ground rules no longer apply. Modes of behavior that have been established for many years provide a mutual feeling of reassurance and enable trust, although it also creates a certain "path dependency" on decisions made in an earlier era. "Paths" that were embarked on in the past can't be sidestepped easily: *"one's self-image is bound up with a web of norms which one has contributed to creating, from which it is difficult to extricate oneself without leaving parts of the self behind"* (Luhmann 2000). This leads among other things to resistance within groups and organizations. It seems that this not only threatens the individuals involved, but also leads to conflict with regard to mutual expectations.

In Friedrichshafen, Deutsche Telekom wasn't—as with its other projects—a product developer or a marketer of standard services for a market consisting of millions of customers. It also wasn't a supplier of software system solutions submitting a tender to a public or private organization. Instead, it set out to develop and implement projects together with a wide array of partners from urban society in a creative and open-ended process, which were to be as marketable as possible in the future and could also be applied to other cities and municipalities.

In the T-City project, the city administration of Friedrichshafen also hadn't called for bids and wasn't a commissioner of services or other products. It didn't have the authority to instruct contractors what to do and what not to do. It didn't act sovereignly towards its inhabitants and didn't provide any customary services, as it would do normally. Instead, it set out to be creative in partnership with the citizens, associations, and businesses on an equal footing.

The municipal policy was suddenly no longer dedicated to the wishes of the citizens and to issuing directives for the administration on the basis of these, nor was its sole purpose just to guide the administration. Now with T-City it was expected of those involved and the honorary council politicians that they develop their own positions and ideas, beyond a party political profile and the usual reading and processing of draft resolutions from the administration.

The heterogeneous business world in Friedrichshafen—consisting of freelancers, the self-employed, small and medium-sized businesses, and global corporations—was also called upon to depart from the usual way of doing things. Participation in the project didn't involve the winning of contracts or the advertising or selling of products, instead it sought the contribution of the businesses' expertise to the development of the Smart City projects; although nobody could know at the beginning whether they would really be implemented or would yield any returns.

The citizens, their associations, the schools, and the small university were also faced with new challenges. The citizens were suddenly supposed to do more than just complain about their council politicians or top municipal officials while reading the newspaper. They were supposed to put forward ideas for projects and for all the great things that can be done with ICT to improve the quality of life and locational advantages for businesses. The societies were supposed to think outside the box of Carnival celebrations and volleyball events and consider which new applications on PCs or mobile devices would bring new opportunities and developments for themselves and their members.

The individual participants found it difficult to adapt to their respective new roles in this process. In retrospect, it would be easy to say that it was doomed to failure. And it did in fact fail to a certain extent, but on a number of occasions it worked. So perhaps the really remarkable aspect of this project is that there were some people, companies, and organizations that succeeded in doing things somewhat differently than normal and in being open to new ideas. This enabled small innovations and the city did receive a bit of a new "operating system," a key element within a Smart City.

Recommendations for Smart Cities

The following tasks can be identified as recommendations for the development of a
vibrant Smart City based on a Public Private Partnership:

— **Clarify the defined objectives**
The common and differing objectives of those involved
have to be identified and communicated.

— **Clarify the role expectations**
Furthermore, it is necessary to formulate clearly
the respective mutual expectations regarding services
and performance.

— **Set up a project structure**
It is essential to set up a joint project structure with
responsibilities and decision-making processes that
are transparent both internally and externally.

— **"Open Culture"**
Resources and processes for an "Open Culture" have
to be provided, if a Smart City project is striving for the
ambitious objective of incorporating a whole urban
society. All partners involved have to be supported in
adapting existing processes and cultures in relation
to the project cooperation.

— **Communication**
It is necessary to communicate the objectives, structures,
processes, and operative procedures continuously. One
has to choose suitable information channels for the
respective addressees (press, radio, events, testimonials,
newsletter, database, web, blog, wiki, social networks).
This communication has to be directed both internally
in relation to the project and externally to all the relevant
target groups.

Regular reviews

It is necessary to review the objectives, structures and processes regularly. In long-term projects, fluctuating external circumstances, technical and organizational innovations, and changes in the attitudes of individual partners are to be expected. Therefore, regular assurance with regard to the agreement is required.

Willingness to listen

It is essential for all the involved partners to be willing to listen to each other and to all the relevant target groups, especially when critical or skeptical comments are expected.

External evaluation

An external accompaniment of the procedures in the form of continuous evaluation, as well as of presentations and consulting during the review phases, offers the advantage of an external point of view, which helps to identify one's own blind spots and wrong turnings.

Suitable partners

Ideally partnerships are "complementary." One has to choose partners who have differing competences in relation to the problems that have to be solved. The partners should extend and complement each other and not compete within a project. Furthermore, for the success of complex projects that require a high level of cooperation, it is important that both parties are equally interested in achieving success.

240

Focusing on concrete applications— necessary for fostering enthusiasm

Smart Cities are talked about a lot, but relatively little is said about the people who live there. The use of the new information and communication technologies can open up new possibilities for people in their daily lives. Their means of communication, access to information, and sharing of information are facilitated and enhanced. On the other hand, concerns and fears can arise among inhabitants at the prospect of certain areas of life in a city being infiltrated by and potentially controlled by technology. In the ubiquitously networked Greenfield projects in Asia, the switch point of these new cities—where all the data merges centrally—is owned by a single enterprise. This is undoubtedly disconcerting not only for the lesser technophiles among us.

In the T-City of Friedrichshafen, clear objectives were articulated, which—as also highlighted in the city contest application documents—were intended to increase the interconnection of the urban society by means of broadband technology and the solutions based on it, as well as to raise the quality of life and of the location. Apart from these objectives, the application submitted by Friedrichshafen formulated real-life scenarios. However, during the concrete implementation of T-City it emerged that many individual projects were lacking innovative strength and the acceptance and involvement of the inhabitants.

In order to integrate a Smart City into an urban society, it is important that it offers useful applications that benefit the majority of the population. Moreover, there should be clarity of purpose, and also participation by inhabitants, in order to make an "invisible" Smart City "visible" and tangible for them.

Information about the overall concept, the status of development, planned initiatives and the concrete content of individual projects has to be clear from the outset, in order to achieve the widest possible acceptance. During the development of the infrastructure in "HotCity Luxembourg," for example, there was an information container where the development process was presented and interested citizens could learn more about it.

It is advantageous for the communication initiatives to focus on different target groups, in order to respond to the interests and concerns of as wide a range of people as possible. However, the communication should focus more on listening to than on "handling" the target groups. A positive example of this is T-City's cooperation with senior citizens in Friedrichshafen. A society was founded in which senior citizens explain the use of the new technologies to other senior citizens, taking their particular requirements into account.

This example shows that the active participation and inclusion of the civic population and partners in the generation of ideas and the drafting of Smart City projects is of fundamental importance. However, care must be taken that the people's ideas don't just lead to nothing. The ideas and the participation should consequently be brought together within a framework that regulates the communal generation, drafting, and implementation of project ideas, which everyone involved is aware of. Even if the implementation of a Smart City isn't possible without external

Clarity and the participation of the inhabitants …

… can make identification easier.

competences, the incorporation of local knowledge is also important because it strengthens the local connection of a Smart City project. It enables those involved to feel as if they are part of the Smart City and to identify with it. Furthermore, it enables the development of relevant solutions for local problems and it anchors the project more firmly within the city. This is one of the reasons why the T-City "Tumor Conference" is welcomed enthusiastically by the people involved, as it is a project that was developed by local partners in cooperation with Deutsche Telekom, and tackles the obvious inconvenience of having to cross Lake Constance for conferences.

In addition, it is important for individual projects to "reach" the city, in order to create a "tangible" Smart City for the inhabitants, and to integrate the project in the urban society. First, this means that the inhabitants have to be informed about the individual projects and made aware of particular issues, and second, that they also have to have the opportunity to try out and use the solutions actively. Hence, there should be some projects with wide coverage, such as "Smart Metering" in Friedrichshafen, and others with a high impact, such as "Mobile Clinic." Furthermore, the projects should have a tangible purpose in relation to the everyday lives of the inhabitants and in relation to the city. The precondition for this is that the applications can be incorporated into daily life without a high entry barrier, can be used intuitively, and are perceived as beneficial solutions for dealing with certain aspects of life. In order to establish what might be beneficial to people or what local challenges or problems the city needs solutions for, one skill in particular is key when realizing a Smart City: the ability and willingness to listen. If a Smart City is to succeed, then it has to be about the people in the cities and not just about implementing technological solutions.

A tangible purpose

242

In conclusion

The T-City project in Friedrichshafen differs from other Smart City projects around the world in one significant way. While in Friedrichshafen—as in most other initiatives—there was also a vision of a better world, the project did not stop at formulating future ideals. Instead, T-City was put into practice concretely over five years, and many projects were in fact implemented by the partnership between the city and the corporation. The inhabitants were also able to experience some initial benefits by participating in the individual projects. Even though some projects had to be abandoned for various reasons, this was very instructive for Deutsche Telekom and the city of Friedrichshafen. T-City Friedrichshafen wasn't just about high-flying general principles, instead the individual project areas sought applications pragmatically and then they were also carried out.

Maybe the T-City project asked too much of some partners with its expectation that everyone would go about things differently than before. Maybe five years wasn't long enough either. Those partners, who were willing to, learned a lot. Perhaps such a project needs even more structure and clarity. In any case, what is needed are more concrete attempts to test how a Smart City can be developed.

PLYMETAL
DOOR

Appendix

Authors

Stephan Althoff
*Director of Corporate Sponsoring and
Events at Deutsche Telekom AG, Bonn*
Stephan Althoff has been responsible for
the areas of Corporate Sponsoring and
Events in the Corporate Communications
division of Deutsche Telekom AG since
2008. He started out in 1993 as Press Officer
at Deutsche Telekom. After several years
heading up Corporate Communications
and Advertising at the Telekom subsidiary
T-Mobile, Althoff switched to the landline
division, where he was the Director of
Communications and Sponsoring until
2005. Stephan Althoff also oversaw the
T-City project for five years.
Further information: www.telekom.de

Hans-Joachim Bachmann and family
Futurist, Friedrichshafen
The Bachmann family has been living
in Friedrichshafen for thirteen years.
Mr. Bachmann is a teacher and Head of
Department at the Vocational Business
School and the Technical School of Frie-
drichshafen. Mrs. Elke Bachmann is a
French and German teacher at the Montfort
Secondary School and the Tettnang Elec-
tronics School. Their daughter Maren is
a student at Dualen College in Villingen-
Schwenningen; the twins Arnd and Nina
are pupils at the Claude-Dornier School
and the Karl-Maybach Secondary School
in Friedrichshafen.

Jörg Bollow
*T-City Project Director at Deutsche Telekom
AG from 2006 to 2009*
Business economist; Jörg Bollow has held
positions as Marketing Manager at Nokia,
Hutchison/Orange, T-Mobile, and T-Online.
He was Vice President Marketing, Product
& Consumer Sales 2006 FIFA World Cup
at Deutsche Telekom AG, BMC Bollow
Management & Consulting since 2009.
His areas of expertise include consulting,
marketing, strategies, and innovations.
Further information: www.bollow.co.uk

Andreas Brand
Mayor of the city of Friedrichshafen since 2009
Andreas Brand held an apprenticeship within
the higher levels of non-technical administration in the major district town of Ostfildern.
Brand studied at the College for Public Administration in Ludwigsburg, where he earned
a degree as qualified public administration
specialist. From 2004 to 2009, Brand was the
First Mayor of the major district town of
Böblingen. As the mayor of Friedrichshafen,
he is Chairman of the Zeppelin Foundation.
Further information: www.friedrichshafen.de/
verwaltung-politik/oberbuergermeister

Josef Büchelmeier
*Mayor of the city of Friedrichshafen from
2001 to 2009*
Josef Büchelmeier studied Latin and theology.
He worked as a teacher and journalist for
many years. SPD deputy in the Lake Constance
county council. He is now Managing
Director of the Lake Constance International
Association of Cities.
Further information: www.buechelmeier.de/
Website/Josef_Buchelmeier.html

Jaqueline Egger-Buck
*Business Development/Assistant to the
Managing Board, Fränkel AG Friedrichshafen*
MBA; Jaqueline Egger-Buck received her
bachelor's degree in business management
Zeppelin University in Friedrichshafen and
went on to earn an MBA at Donau University
in Krems. She held earlier positions at the
Friedrichshafen Trade Fair in the area of busi-
ness development and market research.
E-Mail: jaqueline.egger-buck@fraenkel-fn.de

Sebastian Gölz

Fraunhofer Institute for Solar Energy Systems ISE, Freiburg

Certified psychologist; The certified psychologist Sebastian Gölz has been working at Fraunhofer ISE since 1998, initially in the area of off-grid power supplies, later as the team leader for user behavior and field tests in the Intelligent Energy Systems division. Professional competences: psychology, socio-empirical research in the area of Smart Metering and innovative tariff systems, intelligent monitoring systems in households and industry.
E-Mail: sebastian.goelz@ise.fraunhofer.de

Franz-Reinhard Habbel

Press Officer and Policy Director at the German Association of Towns and Municipalities (DStGB), Berlin

Franz-Reinhard Habbel is the Director of the DStGB Innovators' Club, a think tank for municipalities in Germany. He is a member of the IT planning council, a member of the board in the European Society for E-government, and co-founder of the Quadriga network in Berlin. Since 2009, he has been a lecturer at the University of Osnabrück, Department of Social Sciences. In his capacity as an E-government expert, he lectures at home and abroad on the subject of globalization, the Internet, and the modernization of politics and administration. Habbel regularly writes features on the topic of modernization, published on his blog (www.habbel.de). Core research areas: ICT, media, Web 2.0, E-democracy, Open Government, and the modernization of administration.
E-Mail, further information: franz-reinhard.habbel@dstgb.de, www.habbel.de

Lena Hatzelhoffer

T-City accompanying research, University of Bonn

M. A.; Lena Hatzelhoffer studied geography, Sinology, and economics at the University of Bonn, and at Huazhong Normal University in Wuhan. She spent time in China to complete research for her Master's thesis. Since 2009 she has been a research associate in the T-City project study by the Department of Geography at the University of Bonn, in the work group Urbanism and Regional Science. She also undertook a research project in Singapore, to promote the use of ICT in the daily activities of German expatriates there. Core research areas: social science urban studies, cultural and social geography, spatial perception in everyday life, ICT, and urban spaces.
E-Mail: lenahatzelhoffer@geographie.uni-bonn.de

Prof. Dr. Dietrich Henckel

Professor for Urban and Regional Economics at the Institute for Urban and Regional Planning at the Technical University of Berlin

Dr. Dietrich Henckel studied national economics, social sciences, and law at Konstanz University. He previously worked as a research associate at the Institute for Construction Economics at Stuttgart University, and until 2004 at the German Institute for Urban Studies, in the area of economics and finance. Core research areas: structural changes in the economy and its spatial consequences, site selection and land use for businesses, the future of work, changes in time structure and municipal working hours policies, and urban security.
E-Mail, further information: d.henckel@isr.tu-berlin.de, http://www.isr.tu-berlin.de/index.php?id=193

Stefan Höffken

Research associate at the Technical University of Kaiserslautern (CAD)

Stefan Höffken studied urban and regional planning at the Technical University of Berlin and architecture in Madrid. He worked as a lecturer at the Technical University of Berlin and is the founder and member of Urbanophil. Core research areas: Computer-Aided Design methods (mobile participation, GeoWeb, and social media).
E-Mail, further information: s.hoeffken@rhrk.uni-kl.de, http://cpe.arubi.uni-kl.de/mitarbeiter/stefan-hoffken, www.urbanophil.net

Kathrin Humboldt

T-City accompanying research, University of Bonn

Certified economic geographer; Kathrin Humboldt studied economic geography, business administration, and economics at the Ludwig Maximilian University of Munich. During her studies, she undertook work and research stays in China. She previously worked as a research associate at Heinritz, Salm & Segen, Munich. Since 2011, she has been a research associate in the T-City project study by the Department of Geography at the University of Bonn, in the work group Urbanism and Regional Science. Core research areas: the economic areas of China and Latin America, site selection by companies, regional economics, and urban development.
E-Mail: kathrin.humboldt@geographie.uni-bonn.de

Prof. Dr. Stephan A. Jansen

Founding President and managing director of Zeppelin University, and Member of the Advisory Board of T-City

After a banking apprenticeship, Dr. Stephan A. Jansen studied economics at Witten/Herdecke, at New York University, and at Tokyo Keizai University, graduating with distinction. He held further economics-related positions at Stanford University and Harvard Business School. Since 2003, he is the Founding President and Managing Director of Zeppelin University in Friedrichshafen, Professor of Stragetic Organization and Founding. Core research areas: management, leadership and organizational theory of social enterprises, analysis of networks according to communication and organizational theory, comparative civil society research, interdisciplinary innovation theory, merging of enterprises, analysis of educational systems.
E-Mail: praesident@zeppelin-university.de

Jens-Rainer Jänig

External consultant for the T-City project, Berlin

Jens-Rainer Jänig is a certified economist. He lectures on branding at HTW Berlin (Institute of Technology and Economics), the Technical University of Berlin, and UMC Potsdam. Managing partner of the branding agency and public relations consultancy mc-quadrat. He is a consultant for the T-City project and has made significant contributions to its development. Key areas of work: branding, strategic communication of innovations, and internal corporate communications.
Further information: www.mc-quadrat.com

Dr. Jürgen Kaack

Managing Director of the municipal project association of T-City Friedrichshafen from 2007 to 2009

Dr. Jürgen Kaack studied physics at Cologne University. He has held positions in the telecommunications and high-tech market, including at SEL/Alcatel and AEG, as the Sales and Marketing Director at debitel AG, as Managing Director of MCN Management Consulting Group, and as Chief Executive and founder of the network provider mcm tele.com AG. Founder and Managing Director of STZ-Consulting Group, Erftstadt. Key areas of work: projects for extending broadband in residential and commercial areas for municipalities and counties, development and execution of new business models, identification of cooperation partners, partner management, drafting of long-term broadband initiatives with fiber optic cable networks and broadband applications, development and optimization of sales organizations, and interim management.
Further information:
www.stz-consulting.de

Prof. Dr. Rainer Kazig

Professor of social geography with a focus on sustainability at the Geography Department at the Ludwig Maximilian University of Munich (temporary), associate scientist of the CNRS research group CRESSON in Grenoble

Dr. Rainer Kazig studied geography, economics, and sociology in Munich. He held earlier positions as a research associate at the Geographical Institute at the Technical University of Munich, and at the Geographical Institute at the University of Bonn. Core research areas: everyday and environmental aesthetics, urban atmospheres, public spaces, research on poverty.
E-Mail, further information:
rainer.kazig@geographie.uni-muenchen.de,
www.geographie.uni-muenchen.de/
department/fiona/personen/index.
php?personen_details=1&user_id=151

Michael Lobeck

Director of the T-City accompanying research, University of Bonn

Certified geographer; Michael Lobeck studied geography, political science, and developmental sociology at the University of Bonn. He held earlier positions at empirica city research in Bonn, and as an independent consultant in the area of urban development. From 1996 to 2004, he was the project manager at LEG Location and Project Development Ltd Düsseldorf. Mr. Lobeck is currently an independent advisor and business mediator (IHK) and a research associate in the T-City project study at the Department of Geography of the University of Bonn. Core research areas: governance of political (urban development) procedures, correlation between ICT usage and society
E-Mail, further information: lobeck@
geographie.uni-bonn.de, www.xing.com/
profile/Michael_Lobeck

Dr. Oliver Märker

Managing Director of Zebralog Ltd, Berlin

Dr. Oliver Märker studied geography, psychology, and sociology at the University of Bonn. He earned his PhD at Oldenburg University on the subject of E-participation. Until 2006, he was a research associate at Fraunhofer Institute for Intelligent Analysis and Information Systems (IAIS). Key areas of work: E-participation; E-governance; development of procedural concepts; planning, operation, and moderation of participation platforms for urban and regional planning; municipal budget planning; consulting on a regional and national level.
E-Mail, further information: maerker@
zebralog.de, http://www.zebralog.de/
node/49

René Obermann
*Chairman of the Board of Management,
Deutsche Telekom AG, Bonn*
René Obermann has been Chairman of
the Board of Management of Deutsche
Telekom AG since November 2006. Since
January 1, 2012, he is also responsible
for the area of products and innovations.
Obermann joined Deutsche Telekom
in 1998 as Sales Director of T-Mobile
Deutschland Ltd. In April 2000, he became
Chairman of the Management Board.
One year later, as Chairman of European
Operations and Group Synergies, he also
took over responsibility for the European business sector of T-Mobile International. From 2002 until December 2006,
Obermann was both Chairman of the
Executive Board of T-Mobile International
and Chairman for the corporate area of
mobile communications. During this time,
Deutsche Telekom continued its growth
course as one of the leading mobile communications providers in the world with
more than 100 million customers and successfully launched the brand in eleven
countries.
Further information: www.telekom.de

Dr. Stefan Schmitz
*Head of Division, Federal Ministry for
Economic Cooperation and Development
(BMZ), Bonn/Berlin*
Dr. Stefan Schmitz studied geography and
mathematics at the Universities of Bonn
and St. Andrews (Scotland). He earned a
PhD in Applied Geography at the FU Berlin.
Before joining BMZ in 2001, he held posi-
tions as research associate at the Federal
Office for Building and Regional Planning
(BBR) in Bonn, and advisor to the Federal
Ministry for Regional Planning, Building
and Urban Development. From 2007 to
2009, Dr. Schmitz was Director of the area
"outcome management and effectiveness
of development aid initiatives" at the
OECD secretariat in Paris. Since 2009, he is
Head of Division for "rural development;
feeding the world." Key areas of work:
spatial structure, transport and environment, global urban development and urban
policy issues, rural development, co-operation development, and the effectiveness
of development aid.
E-Mail: stefan.schmitz@bmz.bund.dee

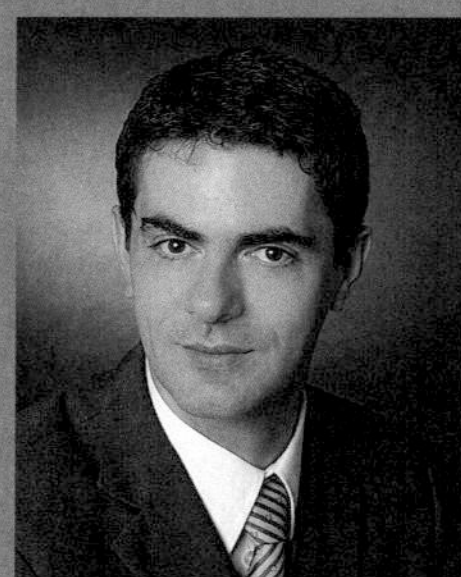

Prof. Dr. Tino Schuppan
*Professor of Public Management at the
Institute of the Federal Employment Agency
and Director of Science at the Institute for
E-government (IfG.CC) in Potsdam*
Dr. Tino Schuppan holds a PhD in public administration sciences from Potsdam
University. He is the editor of the journal
Verwaltung und Management and the
German editor for the Swiss E-government
journal eGovPräsenz. As the Director of
Science at IfG.CC, he is responsible for carrying out and managing numerous national
and international research and consultancy
projects. Core research areas: E-government, public management, organizational
change, cooperation in development.
E-Mail, further information: schuppan@
ifg.cc, www.ifg.cc

Stefan Söchtig
*Managing Director of the municipal project
association of T-City Friedrichshafen*
Until 2007, Stefan Söchtig held various
positions and management roles within
subsidiary companies of WVV (Würzburger
Versorgungs- und Verkehrs-GmbH) in
the areas of energy, local public transport,
telecommunications, and IT, latterly as
Business Unit Manager in the areas of law,
real estate, ports. From 2007 to 2011, he
was Commercial Director at Technische
Werke Friedrichshafen. Since October 2011,
Söchtig has been a Member of the Board
in the business development division at
Wilken Ltd in Ulm, a software and services
company for around 400 energy providers,
among others.
E-Mail, further information:
soechtig@fn-dienste.de, www.t-city.de,
www.friedrichshafen.de

Ferdinand Tempel

Since 2007 Director of the T-City representative office in Friedrichshafen
Certified engineer; Ferdinand Tempel held an apprenticeship as a radio and TV technician. He studied communications engineering in Siegen. He joined Deutsche Telekom in 1984, initially in the areas of planning and development of landline and mobile networks. From 1989 to 1991, he developed sales and marketing structures in a branch of the former Federal Post Office. From 1991 to 1993, he was advisor to the Department for Corporate Policy, Corporate Strategy, and Governance at the head office of Deutsche Telekom. From 1993 to 2005, Tempel was part of the General Management as Regional Director for sales and customer services and from 2005 to 2007, Business Unit Manager for Sales Structures at the head office of T-Com Bonn. Key areas of work: project development, all coordination and control tasks and communications within the T-City project in Friedrichshafen.
E-Mail, further information:
Ferdinand.Tempel@telekom.de,
www.t-city.de

Prof. Dr. Caja Thimm

Professor of Media Science and Intermedia at the University of Bonn
Dr. Caja Thimm studied German philology, American studies, and political science in Munich, Heidelberg, San Francisco, and Berkeley, USA and was a postdoctoral scholarship recipient of the Baden-Württemberg region. She has held guest professorships in Cardiff (GB) and Santa Barbara (USA). Dr. Thimm is a member of the jury of the INA (an initiative for the reconnaissance of communications), federal government commissioner for the Sixth Elderly Report, member of the commission of inquiry "Responsibility in the Digital World," and the inquiry "Citizen Participation."
Core research areas: mobile Internet, social media, political communication, corporate communication, E-learning.
E-Mail, further information: thimm@uni-bonn.de, http://caja-thimm.de

Dr. Matthias Wefer

External consultant for the T-City project
Dr. Matthias Wefer studied political science, history, and German philology and holds a PhD in social systems theory. Independent communications and strategy consultant in Berlin. Key areas of work: positioning, relationship management, communication of change, reputation management, and Corporate-Citizenship projects.
Further information: www.die-denkbank.de

Prof. Dr. Claus-Christian Wiegandt

Professor of Urban and Regional Geography at the University of Bonn, Director of the T-City accompanying research
Dr. Claus-Christian Wiegandt studied geography and law in Münster and Freiburg. He was a research associate at the Department of Geography of Münster University and at the Federal Institute for Building, Urban Affairs and Spatial Management (formerly the Federal Research Office for Regional Studies and Planning) in Bonn. Before the professorship in Bonn, he was professor of Applied Geography at Ludwig Maximilian University (formerly the Geographical Institute at the Technical University of Munich). Key research areas: social-scientific urbanism, demographic change, regional differentiation in building culture, effects of new information and communication technologies on urban society, perception of the urban environment.
Further information:
www.wiegandt-stadtforschung.de

Glossary

AAL (Ambient Assisted Living) Encompasses concepts, products, and services that enable new technologies and social circumstances to complement and enhance each other, in order to improve the quality of life for people in a wide range of situations. For example, fall sensors built into the floors of senior citizens' homes can enable faster reaction times for care workers, or interactive displays can facilitate contact with the outside world.

App (Application) An application program that can be installed quickly and easily on smartphones or tablet PCs via an integrated online shop, thereby extending their functionality.

Augmented Reality Signifies the computer-based enhancement of reality by means of the superimposition of additional text-based information or graphics. This leads to a blending of real and virtual worlds. For example, when using digital cameras, information about the shot can be added on the display in real time.

Bit, Byte, Kilo-Byte (kB), Mega-Byte (MB), Giga-Byte (GB) A bit is the smallest information unit. It can take the form of 0 or 1. A byte refers to 8 bits, which in many computer character sets can represent exactly one character (for example a letter). The prefixes kilo-, mega- or giga- in front of byte mean a thousand, one million, or one billion bytes respectively.

Broadband (connection) Internet access with a high data transfer rate. The rate from which the term broadband can be applied is debatable, and ranges from 128kB/s to 1 GB/s.

Cloud Computing The metaphorically used term describes the on-demand supply of technical infrastructures (for example hard drive space or computational power) and services (for example software), which are accessible to the user via a network (Internet). These services that are provided to the user from a distance are difficult to delineate and are therefore referred to as a "cloud."

Digital Divide The term refers to the differing levels of access to, use of, and knowledge of modern information and communication technologies (see ICT). It often involves comparing groups with similar social or demographic characteristics with regard to their Internet usage (old vs. young, men vs. women, high vs. low levels of education).

(V)DSL (Very High Speed Digital Subscriber Line) DSL is a transmission standard in which data can be received and sent via simple copper wires, such as the telephone connection. DSL refers to download rates of up to 25 MBit/s. VDSL is an enhancement of the DSL standard, providing significantly higher transmission rates of effectively up to 100MBit/s upstream and downstream.

Greenfield project Originally meant a construction project on a "green field," meaning outside of the built-up area of a municipality. The term is also used figuratively for projects in which no preceding constructional elements or existing buildings have to be taken into consideration.

Hotspots (Semi) public Internet access points using WLAN technology, and available either free of charge or against payment of a fee.

HSDPA (High Speed Downlink Packet Access) Also called 3.5G, 3G+, or UMTS Broadband. It refers to a mobile communications standard that uses UMTS. This process enables transmission rates in the range of DSL speeds. LTE is currently being introduced in Germany as a successor technology with higher transmission rates.

ICT (Information and Communication Technology) Refers to technologies that are used to store and process information and communication. It applies to the organization and use, as well as to the technological bases.

LTE (Long Term Evolution) The newest mobile communications standard (also 4G), intended to exceed the UMTS standard with transmission rates that are ten times higher. This standard should primarily provide rural areas with broadband connections.

Open Source This is a license from the Open Source Initiative, which is issued for software whose source text is freely available and has permission to be copied, distributed, used, modified, and developed further.

Public Private Partnership (PPP) A long-term, contracted co-operation between the private and public sectors in order to achieve a specific purpose.

Regulatory authority In Germany, this is the Federal Network Agency whose responsibilities include monitoring competition in the telecommunications market. Its purpose is to control and support competition in markets that tend towards monopolies.

Retrofitting Originally meant the addition of new technology or features to older systems. The term is also used figuratively for projects in which innovative ICT solutions will be integrated into existing structures.

Smart Grid The optimization of the energy supply network through the communicative interconnection of the individual components (provider, storage, consumer, etc.). Its purpose is to increase the efficiency and reliability of the energy supply network.

Smart Metering An initiative to equip households with electronic "intelligent" meters that enable functions extending beyond conventional consumption measurements. Information about consumption can be transmitted to the customer and to the provider (see Smart Grid).

Smartphone Compared to a conventional cell phone, it is a multifunctional device. Smartphones are optimized not only for telephoning, but also for apps, mobile Internet, multimedia services (music, videos, etc.), and Office applications, among others.

Social Media Comprise the whole spectrum of web-based applications and services that enable communication and the sharing of information, experiences, and opinions.

Tablet(-PC) A portable computer that is used without a keyboard, via a touch-sensitive monitor.

Ubiquitous Means omnipresent or available everywhere—objects, commercial goods, or technologies.

URL (Uniform Resource Locator) Enables the identification and localization of resources in computer networks via network protocols. In general terms, URL is also used as a synonym for "web address."

VoIP (Voice over IP) Refers to telephoning via computer networks, also Internet telephony.

WLAN (Wireless Local Area Network) Refers to a local wireless networks, in which data is transferred via a communication standard.

Literature

A

Abdoullaev, A. (2011): A Smart World: A Development Model for Intelligent Cities. 11th IEEE International Conference on Computer and Information Technology, 01. 09. 2011. www.cs.ucy.ac.cy/CIT2011/files/SMARTWORLD.pdf (last accessed 13. 02. 2012).

ABIresearch (2011): Smart Cities. Municipal Networking, Communications, Traffic/Transportation, and Energy. www.abiresearch.com/research/1007213 (last accessed 13. 02. 2012).

Acatech (ed.) (2011): Smart Cities. Deutsche Hochtechnologie für die Stadt der Zukunft. Aufgaben und Chancen. acatech bezieht Position – no. 10. Munich.

Alusi, A., Eccles, R. G., Edmondson, A. C. and T. Zuzul (2011): Sustainable Cities: Oxymoron or the Shape of the Future? Working Paper 11-062. Harvard.

B

Banavar, G. (2011): Building a Smarter Planet, City by City. www.infocommindustryforum.com/downloads/Dr%20Guruduth%20Banavar.pdf (last accessed 12. 02. 202).

BCG, The Boston Consulting Group GmbH (2009): SMART 2020 Addendum Deutschland: Die IKT-Industrie als treibende Kraft auf dem Weg zu nachhaltigem Klimaschutz. www.gesi.org/LinkClick.aspx?fileticket=X7m82qhz%2F60%3D&tabid=60 (last accessed 03. 02. 2012).

Beck, U. (1986): Risikogesellschaft. Auf dem Weg in eine andere Moderne. Suhrkamp Verlag, Frankfurt.

Beniger, J. R. (1986): The Control Revolution. Technological and Economic Origins of the Information Society. Harvard University Press, Cambridge.

Benjamin, W. (1982): Der Flaneur. In: Benjamin, W.: Gesammelte Schriften V.1. Das Passagenwerk. vol. 5.1, published by R. Tiedemann. Frankfurt. p. 524–569.

BeWITEC, Berliner Wireless Transfer- und Entwicklungs-Center (2012): Aktuelles. www.bewitec.htw-berlinde/index.html (last accessed 14. 02. 2012).

BfS, Federal Office for Radiation Protection (2012): Zusammenstellung der Studien, die öffentliches Interesse erweckt haben, und deren Bewertung durch das BfS. www.bfs.de/de/elektro/hff/papiere.html/Synopse_EMF.pdf (last accessed 10. 02. 2012).

BITKOM (ed.) (2011): «Smart Cities» – Grüne ITK zur Zukunftssicherung moderner Städte. Diskussionspapier zur 5. Jahreskonferenz BMU/UBA/BITKOM. Berlin.

BITKOM (2011): Tablet-PCs boomen. www.bitkom.org/de/themen/54894_67058.aspx (last accessed 09. 02. 2012).

BITKOM (2011): Zahl der App-Downloads explodiert. www.bitkom.org/de/themen/54894_66877.aspx (last accessed 09. 02. 2012).

BITKOM (2011): Computernutzung nimmt weiter zu. www.bitkom.org/de/presse/64050_67616.aspx (last accessed 09. 02. 2012).

BITKOM (2010): 61 Prozent aller Berufstätigen arbeiten mit dem Computer. www.bitkom.org/64775_64770.aspx (last accessed 09. 02. 2012).

BITKOM (2007): Zahl der Mobilfunk-Anschlüsse steigt weiter in Deutschland. www.bitkom.org/de/presse/49919_44673.aspx (last accessed 09. 02. 2012).

Blotevogel, H. H. (2002): Städtesystem und Metropolregionen. In: Nationalatlas Bundesrepublik Deutschland, Dörfer und Städte, vol. 5. p. 40–43.

BMWi, Federal Ministry of Economics and Technologies (2012a): E-Energy – Smart Grids made in Germany. www.e-energy.de/958.php (last accessed 14. 02. 2012).

BMWi, Federal Ministry of Economics and Technologies (2012b): IKT für Elektromobilität. www.ikt-em.de (last accessed 14. 02. 2012).

BMWi, Federal Ministry of Economics and Technologies (2011): Rösler: Digitalisierung ist große Chance für Deutschland. press release, 06. 12. 2011. www.bmwi.de/BMWi/Navigation/Presse/pressemitteilungen,did=460560.html (last accessed 14. 02. 2012).

Boden, D. and H. Molotch (2004): Cyberspace meets the compulsion of proximity. In: Graham, S. (ed.): Cybercities Reader. Routledge, London. p. 101–105.

Bruhn, M., Hadwich, K. and J. Büttner (2009): Qualität von E-Health-Services in der Beziehung zwischen Leistungserbringer und -empfänger. In: Bruhn, M. and B. Stauss (ed.): Kundenintegration. Forum Dienstleistungsmanagement. Wiesbaden. p. 492–524.

Burdett, R. and D. Sudjic (2011): Living in the Endless City. Phaidon, Berlin.

C

Calanego, B. (2012): Der Feind in meiner Steckdose. In: Süddeutsche Zeitung, 16. 01. 2012.

Caragliu, A., Del Bo, C. and P. Nijkamp (2009): Smart cities in Europe. Serie Research Memorande 0048, VU University Amsterdam. ftp://zappa.ubvu.vu.nl/20090048.pdf (last accessed 14. 02. 2012).

Castells, M. (1996): The Rise of the Network Society. Blackwell Publishers, Oxford.

City Administration Sant Cugat (2011): Sant Cugat Smart City. Strategic Plan. Document summary. http://smartcity.cugat.cat/docs/en/SantCugat_Plan%20 Estratégico_110209%20_EN.ppt (last accessed 12. 02. 2012).

City of Cologne (2012): Erste Schritte auf dem Weg zur SmartCity Cologne. Pressemitteilung, 4. 01. 2012. www.stadt-koeln.de/1/presseservice/mitteilungen/2012/06530/ (last accessed 14. 02. 2012).

City of Friedrichshafen (2007): T-City Wettbewerbs-beitrag der Stadt Friedrichshafen. Unpublished document.

Clark, G. and T. Moonen (2011): The Business of Cities. City Indexes in 2011. www.thebusinessofcities.com/PDFs/The%20 Business%20of%20Cities%20City%20Indexes%20Greg%20Clark%20 Tim%20Moonen%20July%202011.pdf (last accessed 13. 02. 2012).

Coe, A., Paquet, G. and J. Roy (2001): E-Governance and Smart Communities: A Social Learning Challenge. In: Social Science Computer Review, vol. 19, no. 1. p. 80–93.

Crang, M., Crosbie, T. and S. Graham (2007): Techno-logy, time – space, and the remediation of neighbourhood life. In: Environment and Planning A, vol. 39, no. 10. p. 2405–2422.

Crang, M., Crosbie, T. and S. Graham (2006): Variable geometries of connection: Urban digital divides and the uses of Information Technology. In: Urban Studies, no. 43. p. 2551–2570.

D

Deutsche Telekom (2012): Das Geschäftsjahr 2011. www.telekom.com/static/-/102686/7/120223-gb11-pdf-si (last accessed am 04. 04. 2012).

Deutsche Telekom (2011): Das Geschäftsjahr 2010. www.telekom.com/static/-/8806/1/gb-2010-si (last accessed am 29. 01. 2012).

Deutsche Telekom (2010): Das Geschäftsjahr 2009. www.telekom.com/static/-/8698/1/gb-2009-si (last accessed 29. 01. 2012).

Deutsche Telekom (2009): Connected life and work. Mitten in der Zukunft. Das Geschäftsjahr 2008. www.telekom.com/static/-/8558/1/2008-gb-pdf-download-si (last accessed 29. 01. 2012).

Deutsche Telekom (2008): Connected life and work. Vernetzt denken. Vernetzt handeln. Vernetzt leben. Das Geschäftsjahr 2007. www.telekom.com/static/-/8436/1/ 2007-gb-pdf-download-si (last accessed 29. 01. 2012).

Deutsche Telekom (2007): Service. Mehr als ein Versprechen! Das Geschäftsjahr 2006. www.telekom.com/static/-/8306/1/2006-gb-pdf-download-si (last accessed 29. 01. 2012).

Deutsche Telekom (2006): T-City-Wettbewerb. Teilnahmeunterlagen. Unpublished Document.

DIVSI, Deutsches Institut für Vertrauen und Sicherheit im Internet (2012): DIVSI Milieu-Studie zu Vertrauen und Sicherheit im Internet. https://www.divsi.de/sites/default/files/ presse/docs/DIVSI-Milieu-Studie_Gesamtfassung.pdf (last accessed : 01. 03. 2012).

Dueck, G. (2011): Das Internet als Gesellschafts-betriebssystem. www.youtube.com/watch?v=woA4R3KrACg&feature =related (last accessed 09. 02. 2012).

E

Energy Agency NRW (2011): EU-Programm für Smart Cities und Communities Initiative. www.energieagentur.nrw.de/_infopool/page.asp?InfoID=10440 (last accessed 13. 02. 2012).

European Commission (2012a): Europa 2020. Leitinitiativen. http://ec.europa.eu/europe2020/tools/flagship-initiatives/index_de.htm (last accessed 13. 02. 2012).

European Commission (2012b): European Initiative on Smart Cities. http://setis.ec.europa.eu/about-setis/technology-road-map/european-initiative-on-smart-cities (last accessed 13. 02. 2012).

F

Federal Network Agency (2011): Tätigkeitsbericht 2010/2011. Bonn. www.bundesnetzagentur.de/SharedDocs/Downloads/DE/BNetzA/Presse/Berichte/2011/Taetigkeitsbericht TK20102011pdf.pdf?__blob=publicationFile (last accessed 12. 02. 2012).

Federal Statistical Office (2010): 40% der Haushalte besitzen ein Notebook. www.destatis.de/jetspeed/portal/cms/Sites/destatis/Internet/DE/Presse/pm/2010/07/PD10__245__631 (last accessed 09. 02. 2012).

Florida, R. (2001): The Rise of the Creative Class. Basic Books, New York.

Florida, R. and G. Gates (2001): Gates, Technology and Tolerance. The Importance of Diversity to High-Technology Growth. In: Survey Series, no. 6. p. 1–12.

G

Ganser, K. (1991): Instrumente von gestern für die Städte von morgen? In: Ganser, K. und C. Zöpel (Hrsg.): Die Zukunft der Städte. Forum Zukunft, vol. 6. Baden-Baden. p. 54–66.

Gibson, D. V., Kozmetsky, G. and R. W. Smilor (1992): The Technopolis phenomenon: smart cities, fast systems, global networks. Rowman & Littlefield, Lanham.

Giffinger, R., Fertner, C., Kramar, H., Kalasek, R., Pichler-Milanovic, N. and E. Meijers (2007): Smart cities. Ranking of European medium-sized cities. Wien. www.smart-cities.eu/download/smart_cities_final_report.pdf (last accessed 07. 03. 2012).

Gordon, Wendy (2010): American Cities Get Smart about Energy. In: Smarter Cities. A Project of the Natural Recources Defense Council. smartercities.nrdc.org/articles/american-cities-get-smart-about-energy (last accessed 14. 02. 2012).

Gödderz, K. (2011): Möglichkeiten von e-Health-Technologien zur Unterstützung der Gesundheitsversorgung im ländlichen Raum. Diploma thesis at the Department of Geography, University Bonn (unpublished).

Green, Z. (2011): Through trial and error, »smart cities« are slowly getting smarter. http://globalurbanist.com/2011/12/14/smart-cities (last accessed 12. 02. 2012).

Greenbang (2011): Who's the leading smart-city brand?. www.greenbang.com/whos-the-leading-smart-city-brand_17172.html (last accessed 13. 02. 2012).

Greveler, U., Justus, B. and D. Löhr (2011): Hintergrund und experimentelle Ergebnisse zum Thema »Smart Meter und Datenschutz«. Arbeitspapier – Technischer Report. www.its.fh-muenster.de/greveler/pubs/smartmeter_sep11_v06.pdf (last accessed 03. 02. 2012).

H

Hampton, K. and B. Wellman (2003): Neighboring in Netville: How the Internet Supports Community and Social Capital in a Wired Suburb. In: City and Community, no. 2. p. 277–311.

Handelsblatt (2008): T-Systems kann umbauen. 05. 11. 2008. www.handelsblatt.com/unternehmen/it-medien/telekommunikation-t-systems-kann-umbauen/3048970.html (last accessed 13. 02. 2012).

Hanna, N. K. (2010): Transforming Government and Building the Information Society: Challenges and Opportunities for the Developing Countries. Springer, New York.

Hanson, J. (2007): 24/7: how cell phones and the Internet change the way we live, work and play. Praeger Publishers, Westport.

Hatzelhoffer, L. (2011a): Die smart vernetzte Stadt? www.architekten24.de/news/umweltschutz_energie/14495-smart-vernetzte-stadt/index.html (last accessed 08. 02. 2012).

Hatzelhoffer, L. (2011b): Die ubiquitäre Stadt – Hype oder Blick in eine smarte Zukunft? In: Bauwelt, vol. 102, no. 24/2011. p. 52–57.

Hatzelhoffer, L. (2011c): Friedrichshafen auf dem Weg zur »Smart City«? In: Euractiv (ed.): Yellow Paper – Stadt der Zukunft. p. 16–17. www.euractiv.de/fileadmin/images/EurActiv_YellowPaper_Stadt_der_Zukunft_2011.pdf (last accessed 10. 02. 2012).

Hatzelhoffer, L. (2010): Friedrichshafen auf dem Weg zur Smart City – Erkenntnisse der Begleitforschung zur Steigerung der Lebensqualität durch den Einsatz von IKT. In: Eberspächer, J. und J. Lorenz (ed.): Smart Cities. Lebensqualität und Geschäfts-möglichkeiten in der Stadt der Zukunft. Munich. p. 20–26.

Hatzelhoffer, L., Lobeck, M. and C.-C. Wiegandt (2011a): Einführung in das Themenheft Räumliche Aspekte von Informations- und Kommunikationstechnologien. In: Informationen zur Raumentwicklung, no. 10/11. p. I–III.

Hatzelhoffer, L., Lobeck, M., Müller, W. and C.-C. Wiegandt (2011b): Verändern die neuen Informations- und Kommunikationstechnologien die europäische Stadt? In: Informationen zur Raumentwicklung, no. 10/11. p. 579–588.

Hatzelhoffer, L., Lobeck, M., Müller, W. and C.-C. Wiegandt (2010a): E-Government und Stadtentwicklung. Schriftenreihe Stadtzukünfte, vol. 8. LIT Verlag, Muenster.

Hatzelhoffer, L., Lobeck, M., Müller, W. and C.-C. Wiegandt (2010b): Wandel in Friedrichshafen – von der Stadt des Zeppelin zur T-City. In: Die alte Stadt, vol. 37, no. 2. p. 147–162.

Heise Online (2011): Amazons Europa-Cloud weiterhin gestört, 10. 08. 2011. www.heise.de/ix/meldung/ Amazons-Europa-Cloud-weiterhin-gestoert-1321111.html (last accessed 07. 02. 2012).

Heise Online (2011): Evernote in Servernot [Update], 07. 01. 2011. www.heise.de/newsticker/meldung/ Evernote-in-Servernot-Update-1165258.html (last accessed 07. 02. 2012).

Heise Online (2011): Verschwundene Google-Mails werden wiederhergestellt, 01. 03. 2011. www.heise.de/ newsticker/meldung/Verschwundene-Google-Mails-werden-wiederhergestellt-1200083.html (last accessed 07. 02. 2012).

Heise Online (2009): Microsoft stellt Daten von Sidekick-Kunden wieder her, 15. 10. 2009. www.heise.de/ newsticker/meldung/Microsoft-stellt-Daten-von-Sidekick-Kunden-wieder-her-829724.html (last accessed 07. 02. 2012).

Helminger, P. (2010): »Luxembourg goes smart«. http://summit2010.uni.lu/publish/100602%20VdL%20Future%20 Internet%20def.pdf (last accessed 29. 01. 2012).

Henckel, D. (2011): Beschleunigung – Effizienzsteigerung oder Zeitverlust?. In: Informationen zur Raumentwicklung, no. 10/11. p. 599–607.

Hennemann, M. and C.-C. Wiegandt (2010): E-Partizipation in der Stadtplanung. Chancen und Grenzen der Bürgerbeteiligung im Informationszeitalter. In: Hatzelhoffer, L., Lobeck, M., Müller, W. und C.-C. Wiegandt (ed.): E-Government und Stadtentwicklung. Muenster. p. 99–114.

Heumann, P. (2008): Großprojekt Masdar-City. Grüne Öko-Stadt in der Wüste. In: Spiegel Online, 09. 02. 2008. www.spiegel.de/wirtschaft/0,1518,534205,00.html (last accessed 06. 02. 2012).

Hilbert, M. and P. López (2011): The World's Technological Capacity to Store, Communicate, and Compute Information. In: Science, vol. 332, no. 6025. p. 60–65.

Hischke, S. and J.-R. Jänig (2010): Die Realität als Labor – Eine Stadt als Zukunftswerkstatt. In: Hischke, S., Mühlner, J., Salwiczek, C., Wolf, M. und B. Engel (ed.): Erst fragen, dann machen – Mit Marktwissen zum Erfolg digitaler Innovationen. Berlin. p. 185–196.

Hodgkinson, S. (2011): Is Your City Smart Enough? www.cisco.com/web/strategy/docs/Is_your_city_smart_enough-Ovum_Analyst_Insights.pdf (last accessed 13. 02. 2012).

Hoornweg, D. (2011): Masdar: Mirage or Green-City? http://blogs.worldbank.org/sustainablecities/ masdar-mirage-or-green-city-mecca-0 (last accessed 28. 01. 2012).

Höffken, S. (2011): Die Kartierungs-Revolution. In: StadtBauwelt, no. 24/2011. p. 14–21.

I

Ibert, O., Mayer, H.-N. and W. Siebel (1999): Projekt-orientierte Planung – ein neues Paradigma? In: Informationen zur Raumentwicklung, no. 3/4. p. 163–172.

IBM (2012a): About the Smarter Cities Challenge. http://smartercitieschallenge.org/about.html (last accessed 05. 02. 2012).

IBM (2012b): Knowledge is power. Driving smarter energy usage through consumer education. www.ibm.com/common/ssi/ cgi-bin/ssialias?subtype=XB&infotype=PM&appname=GBSE_GB_TI_ USEN&htmlfid=GBE03475USEN&attachment=GBE03475USEN.PDF (last accessed 02. 02. 2012).

IBM (2010): Smarter Cities: die Herausforderung – Programmübersicht. http://smartercitieschallenge.org/files/ Smarter_Cities_Challenge_Program_Overview_German.pdf (last accessed 07. 02. 2012).

IDA (2006): Innovation. Integration. Internationalisation. Report by the iN2015 Steering Commitee. Singapore.

IDA Singapore (2012a): iN2015 Masterplan. www.ida.gov.sg/About%20Us/20070903145526.aspx (last accessed 05. 02. 2012).

IDA Singapore (2012b): Wireless@SG Registration and Operators. www.ida.gov.sg/Infrastructure/20061027163310.aspx (last accessed 05. 02. 2012).

Initiative D21 (2011): (N)Onliner Atlas 2011. www.nonliner-atlas.de/ (last accessed 09. 02. 2012).

J

Jendrischik, M. (2012): RheinEnergie installiert 30.000 Smart Meter in Cologne. In: CleanThinking, 10. 01. 2012. www.cleanthinking.de/rheinenergie-installiert-30-000-smart-meter-in-koeln/23356/ (last accessed 14. 02. 2012).

Just, T. and C. Thater (2008): Megacitys: Wachstum ohne Grenzen? In: Deutsche Bank Research, Aktuelle Themen 412. p. 1–18.

K

Kim, C.-H. (2009): U-City Infrastructure and Applications in Korea. www.iccsaudi.com/eng/contents/presentation/DrKimChoon.ppsx (last accessed 12.02.2012).

KOOPTECH (2008): »Social Media«, »Social Computing«, »Web 2.0«, »Social Web« oder »Kooperative Technologien«? http://blog.kooptech.de/2008/11/social-media-social-computing-web-20-social-web-oder-kooperative-technologien/ (last accessed 15.02.2012).

Köster, R. (2008): Zwang zur Neuausrichtung des Konzerns: Zeppelin 1928 bis 1929. In: Stadt Friedrichshafen (ed.): Zeppelin 1908 bis 2008. Stiftung und Unternehmen. Piper, Munich. p. 81–112.

Kubicek, H. and S. Welling (2000): Vor einer digitalen Spaltung in Deutschland? Annäherung an ein verdecktes Problem von wirtschafts- und gesellschaftspolitischer Brisanz. In: Medien- & Kommunikationswissenschaft, vol. 48, no. 4. p. 497–517.

L

Landry, C. (2000): The Creative City. A Toolkit for Urban Innovators. Earthscan Publications, London.

Linder, S. B. (1970): The harried leisure class. Columbia University Press, New York.

Lindsay, G. (2011): Stadt in der Tüte. In: Baumeister, vol. 9/2011. p. 70–73.

Lindsay, G. (2010): The New New Urbanism: New Songdo & Creating Cities From Scratch. In: Fast Company, 01.02.2010. www.fastcompany.com/magazine/142/the-new-new-urbanism.html (last accessed 13.02.2012).

Living PlanIT (2012): PlanIT Valley – the benchmark for future cities and sustainable urban communities. http://planitvalley.org (last accessed 13.02.2012).

Lobeck, M. (2010): Die Zukunft der Telekommunikation als PPP. Ein Werkstattbericht zur Evaluation des Innovationsprojektes T-City Friedrichshafen. In: Gräf, P. (ed.): Regionale Komponenten der Informationsgesellschaft. Geographie der Kommunikation, vol. 9. LIT Verlag, Muenster. p. 85–98.

Lobeck, M., Müller, W. and C.-C. Wiegandt (2009a): Auf dem Weg zur vernetzten Stadt. Erfahrungen aus Friedrichshafen. In: Planerin, no. 5. p. 31–32.

Lobeck, M., Müller, W. and C.-C. Wiegandt (2009b): Die neuen Informations- und Kommunikationstechnologien – Veränderungen im Alltagsleben. In: Standort – Zeitschrift für Angewandte Geographie, vol. 33, no. 1. p. 6–12.

Lobeck, M., Müller, W. and C.-C. Wiegandt (2009c): Neue Medien verändern Städte. Auswirkungen der neuen Informations- und Kommunikationstechnologien. In: Stadt und Gemeinde, no. 4. p. 139–141.

Lobeck, M., Müller, W. and C.-C. Wiegandt (2009d): Stadtentwicklung durch Auszeichnung – der Städtewettbewerb T-City. In: Raumforschung und Raumordnung, no. 3/2009. p. 261–271.

Lobeck, M., Müller, W. and C.-C. Wiegandt (2008): Gedanken zum Zusammenhang von Stadtentwicklung und Informations- und Kommunikationstechnologien. In: PNDonline IV|2008. www.planung-neu-denken.de/images/stories/pnd/dokumente/2008-4_lo_m_wi.pdf (last accessed 10.02.2012).

Louis, C. K. (2009): Everything's amazing right now and nobody's happy. www.youtube.com/watch?v=8r1CZTLk-Gk&feature=related (last accessed 31.01.2012).

Löw, M. (2008): Soziologie der Städte. Suhrkamp Verlag, Frankfurt.

Luhmann, Niklas (2000): Vertrauen. Lucius & Lucius, Stuttgart.

M

Mahizhnan, A. (1999): Smart cities. The Singapore case. In: Cities, vol. 16, no. 1. p. 13–18.

Märker, O. and J. Wehner (2011a): Online-Bürgerbeteiligung in Kommunen. Anfänge – Aktuelle Verfahren – Weiterführende Fragen. In: Forum Wohnen und Stadtentwicklung, no. 4/2011. p. 201–206.

Märker, O. and J. Wehner (2011b): Online-Bürgerhaushalte. Elektronische Partizipation in der kommunalen Haushaltsplanung. In: Planerin, no. 4/2011. p. 21–23.

Mayntz, R. (2008): The Changing Governance of Large Technical Infrastructure Systems. In: Mayntz, R. (2009): Über Governance. Institutionen und Prozesse politischer Regelung. Campus, Frankfurt. p. 121–150.

Meckel, M. (2008): Wie Web 2.0 unsere Kommunikation verändert. In: Aus Politik und Zeitgeschichte, no. 39. p. 17–23.

Medin, M. (2011): Ultra high-speed broadband is coming to Kansas City, Kansas. http://googleblog.blogspot.com/2011/03/ultra-high-speed-broadband-is-coming-to.html (last accessed 06.02.2012).

Morley, D. (2000): Home Territories: Media, Mobility and Identity. Routledge, London.

Münchner Kreis (ed.) (2011): Zukunftsbilder der digitalen Welt. Nutzerperspektiven im internationalen Vergleich. Eigenverlag, Berlin.

N

National and Regional Data Protection Officers (1997): Entschließung: Erforderlichkeit datenschutzfreundlicher Technologien. www.bfdi.bund.de/SharedDocs/Publikationen/Entschliessungssammlung/DSBundLaender/54DSK-ErforderlichkeitDatenschutzfreundlicherTechnologien.pdf?__blob=publicationFile (last accessed 12.02.2012).

Negroponte (1998): Beyond Digital. In: Wired, issue 6.12. www.wired.com/wired/archive/6.12/negroponte.html (last accessed 31.01.2012).

Ng, P. T. (2010): Embracing Emerging Technologies: The case of Singapore Intelligent Nation 2015 Vision. In: De Pablos, P. O., Lee, W. B. und J. Zhao (ed.): Regional Innovation Systems and Sustainable Development: Emerging Technologies. Hershey. p. 115–123.

Novak, J. and B. Voigt (2007): Mashups: Strukturelle Eigenschaften und Herausforderungen von End-User Development im Web 2.0. In: I-COM, vol. 10, no. 3. p. 19–24.

O

Osorio, C. (2011): PlanIT Valley começa a ser construída em 2012. http://noticias.sapo.pt/tec_ciencia/artigo/planit-valley-comeca-a-ser-construida-em-2012_1486.html (last accessed 13.02.2012).

P

PHILIPS (2011): Philips awards € 125,000 to help make cities more livable. www.newscenter.philips.com/wpd.aspx?p=/main/standard/news/press/2011/20110428_livable_cities_award.wpd (last accessed 07.02.2012).

Plamper, J. (2008): Danke, danke, danke. In: ZEIT Online, 27.08.2008. www.zeit.de/2008/31/PS-Danksagung (last accessed 15.02.2012).

Poggenpohl, J., Müller, M. and S. Köhler (2012): Die bewegliche Stadt. Auf der Suche nach Friedrichshafens Gesicht. Gessler, Friedrichshafen.

Pulakkat, H. (2011): How smart tech is drawing city of tomorrow. In: The Times of India, 03.11.2011. http://timesofindia.indiatimes.com/articleshow/10593075.cms (last accessed 13.02.2012).

R

Rauterberg, H. (2001): Drinnen ist draußen, draußen ist drinnen. Hat der öffentliche Raum noch eine Zukunft? In: Deutsches Architektenblatt, no. 2. p. 6–10.

Renz, P. (2008): Friedrichshafen. Eine deutsche Stadt am See. Klöpfer & Meyer, Tubingen.

Rieger-Benkel, B. (2008): Das Brouillon von 1824 – ein wichtiges Dokument zur frühen Stadtgeschichte Friedrichshafens. In: Oellers, J. (ed.): Friedrichshafener Jahrbuch für Geschichte und Kultur, vol. 2. Aichhalden. p. 8–39.

Rooney, B. (2011): Microsoft Powers Portuguese Smart City. In: The Wall Street Journal, 24.03.2011. http://blogs.wsj.com/tech-europe/2011/03/24/microsoft-powers-portuguese-smart-city (last accessed 14.02.2011).

Rosa, H. (2005): Beschleunigung. Die Veränderung der Zeitstrukturen in der Moderne. Suhrkamp Verlag, Frankfurt.

S

Sack, D. (2009): Governance und Politics. Die Institutionalisierung öffentlich-privater Partnerschaften in Deutschland. Nomos Verlagsgesellschaft, Baden-Baden.

Schmitz, S. (2010): Urbanität 2.0 – Zur Entwicklung des Städtischen im Zeitalter zunehmender Virtualität. In: Wiegandt, C.-C. (ed.): Neue Informations- und Kommunikationstechnologien. Die alte Stadt, vol. 37, no. 2. Remshalden. p. 111–122.

Schrader, C. (2012): Die umstrittene Wirkung. Ob Strahlung krank macht, ist längst nicht gut genug erforscht. In: Süddeutsche Zeitung, 11./12.02.2012.

S+CC, Smart Connected Communities Institute (2012): IBM's Smarter Planet & Cisco´s Smart Connected Communities. www.smartconnectedcommunities.org/message/1670#1670 (last accessed 14.02.2012).

Schwäbische Zeitung (2011): Der Stadtrand bleibt erhalten. Gemeinderat stimmt Fortführung zu. 08. 11. 2011.

Semmler, H. (2008): Die Zeppelin-Stiftung nach dem Zweiten Weltkrieg. In: Stadt Friedrichshafen (ed.): Zeppelin 1908 bis 2008. Stiftung und Unternehmen. Piper, Munich. p. 249–296.

Siebel, W. (1989): Zukünftige Perspektiven der Stadtentwicklung. In: Deutsche Akademie für Städtebau und Landesplanung/Landesgruppe Niedersachsen-Bremen (ed.): Planung oder Anpassung? Fragen an künftige Stadt- und Regionalplanung. Bericht Nr. 11 der Landesgruppe Niedersachsen-Bremen. Bremen. p. 83–93.

Siebel, W. and J. Wehrheim (2003): Öffentlichkeit und Privatheit in der überwachten Stadt. In: DISP 153. p. 4–12.

Siemens AG Corporate Communication (ed.) (2007): Megacities und ihre Herausforderungen. Die Perspektive der Städte. Munich.

Simmel, G. (1903): Die Großstädte und das Geistesleben. In: Petermann, T. (ed.): Die Großstadt. Vorträge und Aufsätze zur Städteausstellung. Jahrbuch der Gehe-Stiftung zu Dresden, vol. 9. Dresden. p. 185–206.

Spaus, J.-M. (2010): Die vernetzte Stadt. Ein ganzheitlicher Ansatz für die Stadt der Zukunft – Beispiel Stadt Luxemburg. In: Eberspächer, J. und J. Lorenz (ed.): Smart Cities. Lebensqualität und Geschäftsmöglichkeiten in der Stadt der Zukunft. Munich. p. 70–76.

Stegbauer, C. (2008): Raumzeitliche Struktur im Internet. In: Aus Politik und Zeitgeschichte, no. 39. p. 3–9.

Steinbach, M. (2011): Unterstützes Wohnen im Alter: Das Innovationshaus in der T-City Friedrichshafen. Bachelor thesis at the Department of Geography, University Bonn (unpublished).

Stiftung Weltbevölkerung (2012): Die Weltbevölkerungsuhr. www.weltbevoelkerung.de/ oberes-menue/publikationen-downloads/zu-unseren-themen/ weltbevoelkerungsuhr.html (last accessed 01. 02. 2012).

Streich, B. (2011): Stadtplanung in der Wissensgesellschaft – Ein Handbuch. VS Verlag, Wiesbaden.

Streich, B. and P. Zeile (2011): Stadtplanung im GeoWeb. Ein Methodenaufriss im neuen Modus der Wissensgesellschaft. Document in preparation; estimated date of publication 2012. Preliminary results retrievable at: http://geoweb.arubi.uni-kl.de.

Süddeutsche Zeitung (2011): Deutschland wird zum Smartphone-Land. 14. 08. 2011. www.sueddeutsche.de/digital/ mobile-internetnutzung-deutschland-wird-zum-smartphone-land-1.1130888 (last accessed 09. 02. 1012).

T

Tan, M. (2007): From Wired to Wireless: Singapore's Ubiquitous Digital Hub. In: Qureshi, S. und D. Vogel (ed.): Information Technology Application in Emerging Economies: A Monograph of a Symposium at HICSS-40. p. 34–51. www.hicss.hawaii.edu/Reports/40ITApplication.pdf (last accessed 08. 02. 2012).

T-City Friedrichshafen (ed.) (2010): T-City Spiegel Ausgabe 1/10. Schwerpunkt: Smart Metering. Friedrichshafen. www.telekom2.de/006/ecard/tcs_2010_1/index.html (last accessed 14. 02. 2012).

T-City Friedrichshafen (ed.) (2009): T-City Spiegel Ausgabe 4/09. Schwerpunkt: Bürger und Staat. Friedrichshafen. www.telekom2.de/006/ecard/tcs_2009_4/index.html (last accessed 14. 02. 2012).

Trischler, H. (2002): Innovationskulturen im Deutschen Luftschiffbau: Zeppelin und Schütte im Vergleich. In: Meighörner, W. (ed.): Wissenschaftliches Jahrbuch 2002. Friedrichshafen. p. 68–79.

U

UNFPA (2011): Weltbevölkerungsbericht 2011. New York. www.weltbevoelkerung.de/ oberes-menue/publikationen-downloads/zu-unseren-themen/ unfpa-weltbevoelkerungsbericht.html (last accessed 28. 01. 2012).

UN-HABITAT (2010): State of the World's Cities 2010/2011. Bridging The Urban Divide. Earthscan, London.

United Nations (2010): World Urbanization Prospects: The 2009 Revision. New York.

V

Vaggione, P. (2011): Urban planning challenges and "smartness". Smart City Expo Barcelona, 30. 11. 2011. Unpublished document.

Virilio, P. (1993): Open Sky. Verso, London.

W

Washburn, D. and U. Sindhu (2010): Helping CIOs Understand »Smart City« Initiatives. Defining The Smart City, Its Drivers, And The Role Of The CIO. Forrester Research, Cambridge.

Welt Online (2007): T-Systems soll verkauft und zerteilt werden. 02. 06. 2007. www.welt.de/wirtschaft/article914956/T_Systems_soll_verkauft_und_zerteilt_werden.html (last accessed 13. 02. 2012).

Wiener Stadtwerke Holding AG (2011): Smart City: Begriff, Charakteristika und Beispiele. Materialien der Wiener Stadtwerke zur nachhaltigen Entwicklung, no 7. Vienna.

Wimmer, B. (2011): Intelligente Stromzähler plaudern alles aus. http://futurezone.at/future/5321-intelligente-stromzaehler-plaudern-alles-aus.php (last accessed 03. 02. 2012).

Winkler, T. J., Schöndienst, V. and G. Tamm (2009): Wireless City Berlin – Solutions for a Smarter City. Berlin.

Wüst, T. (2004): Urbanität. Ein Mythos und sein Potential. VS Verlag, Wiesbaden.

Y

Yeoh, B. S. A. and T. C. Chang (2001): Globalising Singapore: Debating Transnational Flows in the City. In: Urban Studies, vol. 38, no. 7. p. 1025–1044.

Yeoh, B. S. A. and S. Huang (2004): "Foreign Talent" in Our Midst – New Challenges to Sense of Community and Ethic Relations in Singapore. In: Eng, L. A. (ed.): Beyond Rituals and Riots – Ethic Pluralism and Social cohesion in Singapore. Singapore. p. 316–338.

Picture Credits

01
Enter

02
Develop

[A]

03
Install

[B]

05
Avoid crash

188	*Reflecting facade*, Buenos Aires, 2005, © Stefan Schmitz
190 t.	*Three way conversation*, no place, 2006, © codswollop, photocase.com
190 b.	*Top-level domain*, no place, 2010, @ suze, photocase.com
191	*Streamlined*, no place, 2010, © ohneski, photocase.com
194	*Safety first*, Singapore, 2010, © Lena Hatzelhoffer
196	*Babel*, no place, 2010, © ts-grafik.de, photocase.com
198 l.	*Multiple video security cameras*, no place, 2010, © enviromatic, istockphoto.com
198 r.	*Modern Stalking*, Vienna, 2009, © Michael Lobeck
199	*Satellite dish*, Vienna, 2009, © Fontom, photocase.com
201	*Security Camera with shades*, no place, 2005, © Stefan Schmitz
203	*Indernett III*, no place, 2008, © hannesleitlein, photocase.com
205	*Market scene*, Otavalo, 2011, © Kathrin Humboldt

[D]

207	*Zeppelin*, Friedrichshafen, 2007, © Deutsche Telekom
209	*Cebit*, Hannover, 2010, © Deutsche Telekom
210	*Facade*, Berlin, 2008, © Felix Guntermann
211	*Facade*, Los Angeles, 2010, © Claus-C. Wiegandt
214	*Internet-graffiti*, Paris, 2012, © Claus-C. Wiegandt
216	*Mobile*, Los Angeles, 2011, © Claus-C. Wiegandt
217 t.	*Winter Café*, Paris, 2010, © Stefan Schmitz
217 b.	*Public space*, New York City, 2010, © Claus-C. Wiegandt
218	*Sonnenkönigin*, Lake Constance, 2008, © Deutsche Telekom
219	*Aerial view of square*, Friedrichshafen, 2008, © Deutsche Telekom
220	*ATM*, Paris, 2009, © Stefan Schmitz
222 t.	*Facing reality no 3*, Vienna, 2008, © Stefan Schmitz
222 b.	*Facing reality no 4*, Vienna, 2008, © Stefan Schmitz

06
Update

226	*Facade*, Seoul, 2009, © Thomas Wucherpfennig
231	*Waiting and thinking*, Seoul, 2009, © Thomas Wucherpfennig
234	*La Defense*, Paris, 2008, © Stefan Schmitz
237	*Lake Constance*, Friedrichshafen, 2008, © Deutsche Telekom
241	*Street*, Paris, 2008, © Stefan Schmitz
243	*Road marking*, Seoul, 2009, © Thomas Wucherpfennig

Acknowledgements

"Research into gratitude has only just begun. Sociologists do agree on this though: acknowledgements prove that books are not created in isolation, but as the result of a multitude of contacts."

(Plamper 2008)

The creation of this book also wouldn't have been possible without the help of many contacts and the contributions by a wide range of people:

Interview partners

First of all, we are grateful for the special contributions made by our interview partners, who are so numerous that we are unable to name all of them here individually. There were not only experts, business people, and users who patiently answered all of our questions, but also inhabitants, the T-City Futurists, and other participants in the project. We thank them for the informative interviews and their willingness to support our accompanying research so dynamically.

The Deutsche Telekom employees

We would also like to offer a big thank you for the good cooperation to all of the Deutsche Telekom employees who are or were involved in the project. In particular, we would like to mention: Stephan Althoff, Jörg Bollow, Meinhard Köpperschmidt, Oliver Kramer, Thilo Mosch, Lutz Pinkert, Melanie Schmitt, and Ferdinand Tempel, as well as the team at the project headquarters in Friedrichshafen.

Dr. Matthias Wefer and Jens-Rainer Jänig are not employees, but independent advisors to Deutsche Telekom. They have been closely involved with the T-City project from the beginning. We are very grateful to them for all the highly stimulating discussions over the course of the project.

The city of Friedrichshafen

Furthermore, we owe thanks to the city of Friedrichshafen for their support. This applies to the senior mayors Josef Büchelmeier and Andreas Brand and other politicians from the city council, who took time for interviews. This also applies to those working for the municipal administration, who supported us in many ways. Special thanks goes to the staff of FN-Dienste Ltd, especially the former team of Dr. Jürgen Kaack, Andreas Roth, Kathrin Lanz and Dorothee Rütschle, and their successors Stefan Söchtig and his colleagues.

The research network and guest authors

Also behind the scenes, many researchers worked together on different levels for this book.

As can be seen when leafing through the book, we received extensive support by a number of guest authors. We would like to present our special thanks to them for their contributions, pointers, and helpfulness:

Stephan Althoff, Hans-Joachim Bachmann, Jörg Bollow, Andreas Brand, Josef Büchelmeier, Jacqueline Egger-Buck, Sebastian Gölz, Franz-Reinhard Habbel, Prof. Dr. Dietrich Henckel, Stefan Höffken, Prof. Dr. Stephan A. Jansen, Jens-Rainer Jänig, Dr. Jürgen Kaack, Prof. Dr. Rainer Kazig, Dr. Oliver Märker, René Obermann, Dr. Stefan Schmitz, Prof. Dr. Tino Schuppan, Stefan Söchtig, Ferdinand Tempel, Prof. Dr. Caja Thimm, and Dr. Matthias Wefer.

Furthermore, we would like to thank our colleagues in the interdisciplinary research network for their time, the valuable discussions, and the partnerships gained. Their extensive specialist knowledge provided us with many ideas for our social-scientific work. Without their knowledge, ideas and criticism the research project would never have come so far. Actively involved were: Dr. Jan Becker, Dr. Romeo Bertolini, Prof. Dr. Rainer Danielzyk, Dr. Manfred Fuhrich, Christian Geiger, Prof. Dr. Gernot Grabher, Prof. Dr. Markus Hesse, Prof. Dr. Oliver Ibert, Andrea Dittrich-Wesbuer, Dr. Herbert Kemming, Dr. Dorothea Kleine, Prof. Dr. Marion Klemme, Prof. Dr. Andreas Koch, Prof. Dr. Theo Kötter, Prof. Dr. Jörn von Lucke, Dr. Oliver Märker, Heidrun Müller, Prof. Dr. Jürgen Rauh, Prof. Dr. Gebhard Rusch, Dr. Stefan Schmitz, Prof. Dr. Erhard Schüttpelz and Prof. Dr. Tino Schuppan

Scientific support at the Department of Geography of the University of Bonn

We also owe great thanks to all of those at the Department of Geography of the University of Bonn, who were always on hand with help and advice, not to mention a great deal of patience. Competent support from and constructive lunch breaks with Katharina Hackenberg, Prof. Dr. Rainer Kazig, Dr. Stefanie Föbker and Felix Guntermann were very valuable. Thank you. Furthermore, we offer our special thanks to Elke Hedke for the smooth organization of, among other things, our conference series "e-motion" and the cheerfulness she exuded at all times during the project.

We are also especially grateful to the supporting staff of students, some of whom accompanied our research over a number of years: Reza Bijaleh, Sascha Fabri, Elke Geratz, Thomas Kannen, Vera Klein, Emanuel Klimschak, Anna-Maria Müther, Dirk Pfeil, Helena Schmidt, Nadine Schuster, Malte Steinbach, Michaela Stich, Alice Thomas, Dennis Tomfort, and Ira Viehmann. You were a great team! Thank you for your commitment, the constructive co-operation and your perspective as digital natives.

Photographers and cartographers

We thank our photographers, Dr. Volkmar Kroesch and Dr. Stefan Schmitz, for their excellent work regarding the compilation of the pictorial material. This also applies to Martin Gref and Gerd Storbeck from the cartography department at Bonn University for designing the maps and graphics. In addition, we are grateful to all others who contributed their photos to this book.

Publisher and agency

We would like to thank jovis Publishers and the agency labor b for the enjoyable and professional cooperation.

Friends and family of the research team

Last but not least we owe heartfelt thanks to our families and friends for their understanding and their "open ears."

P.S. In the middle of 2006, Deutsche Telekom agreed to assign an independent accompanying research team to their T-City project. As the work group Urbanity and Regional Studies at the Department of Geography of Bonn University, we took on this task. Our request for independence was granted. The accompanying research and this book were financed by Deutsche Telekom. This did not have any influence on the content or the design, for which we thank Deutsche Telekom.

From the research team
Lena Hatzelhoffer, Kathrin Humboldt, Michael Lobeck and Prof. Dr. Claus-Christian Wiegandt

Imprint

Smart City in Practice

Editors
Lena Hatzelhoffer, Kathrin Humboldt, Michael Lobeck
and Claus-Christian Wiegandt

Photographic editor
Felix Guntermann, University of Bonn

Proofreading
Reza Bijaleh, University of Bonn
Rachel Hill, London

Translation
Lynne Kolar-Thompson, Feld am See

Design, Lithography
labor b designbüro, Dortmund

Cover Design
labor b designbüro, Dortmund

Typography
National (Klim)
Tiempos (Klim)

Paper
LuxoArt Samt New, 135 g/sqm

Printing and binding
Grafisches Centrum Cuno
GmbH & Co. KG
Gewerbering West 27
39240 Calbe

Also available in German:
Smart City konkret

Bibliographic information published
by the Deutsche Nationalbibliothek
The Deutsche Nationalbibliothek lists this publication in
the Deutsche Nationalbibliografie; detailed bibliographic
data are available on the Internet at http://dnb.d-nb.de

jovis Verlag GmbH
Kurfürstenstraße 15/16
10785 Berlin
www.jovis.de

ISBN: 978-3-86859-151-4